BUDD

◆ 法 源 译 丛 ◆

中国佛学院英文教材（初级）

THE WORD OF THE BUDDHA

佛 言

园 慈 主编

社会科学文献出版社

SOCIAL SCIENCES ACADEMIC PRESS (CHINA)

《佛言》顾问及编委会名单

中国佛学院版《佛言》出版说明

《佛言》是德国人三界智尊者（Nyāṇatiloka, 1878—1957）编写的一本佛学入门读物，其内容译自巴利文原典。在《佛言》中，三界智尊者对部分经文内容进行了归纳、提要，并根据南传义疏，做了些诠释。《佛言》系统阐述了佛教的基本思想，已流传百余年，受到好评。

《佛言》英文版 *The Word of the Buddha* 译文整体准确、生动。通过这本书，既可学习佛法，亦可学习英语，一举两得。因此，自 2007 年至 2011 年此书被选为中国佛学院研究生教材、中级居士英语佛学班教材。为更好地发挥《佛言》英文版的作用，在中国佛学院研究部园慈法师指导下，经过一年多的努力，《佛言》被改编为佛学英语教材。

佛学院版《佛言》以 *The Word of the Buddha* 第十四版为蓝本，同时，为了适应教学需要，对原著进行了一些调整或补充，主要有以下几个方面。

1. 将全书分为 15 个教学单元，每单元基本上由相对完整的原著独立章节组成，为了平衡各教学单元，也适当合并或拆分了部分章节。

2. 在每个单元后增加了以下内容：

   （1）英中对照词汇表。词汇表中给出的释义和词性主要限于课文中的用法。

   （2）语法要点。对《佛言》英文的特点和难点进行了必要的提示。

   （3）思考题。对内容要点进行归纳，引导读者进一步思考。

3. 附录中附加了巴利语词汇索引（巴利、英、中词汇对照表）。

4. 附加了中文参考译文，以便于读者理解英文课文。中译文以园慈法师讲课录音整理的译稿为基础，由英语佛学读书班部分学员集体校对、修改。也参考了网上其他译本，以及叶均、庄春江等大德的相关翻译，但未在文中一一标示。译文力求平易、质朴、达意，适当使用传统经典译文，不刻意追求"古雅"风格。

编写佛学英文读物是一项非常重要的工作。校对、修改者自身佛学功底和英文能力都十分欠缺，原本难堪此任。但出于对三宝事业及英语佛学的热忱，还是不揣浅陋，尝试对 *The Word of the Buddha* 的译文进行了校改，这主要是学习的过程，仅为引玉，供读者参考、批评和指正。

佛学院版《佛言》从无到有，是众缘和合的产物。离不开中国佛学院领导以及北京释迦翻译有限公司同仁等诸位大德的关心和支持；离不开英语佛学班同学们的用心校对；离不开园慈法师的悉心指导；离不开前出版商斯里兰卡康提城佛教出版社（Buddhist Publication Society）的善意授权。谨致以衷心的感谢！

中国佛学院外语教材编校组

2014 年 8 月 16 日

THE WORD OF THE BUDDHA

CONTENTS

Abbreviations

The source of each quotation is shown by a marginal note at the head of the quotation. The citations use the following abbreviations:

Abbreviation	Document referred to
D.	Dīgha Nikāya. The number refers to the Sutta.
M.	Majjhima-Nikāya. The number refers to the Sutta.
A.	Aṅguttara-Nikāya. The Roman number refers to the main division into Parts or Nipaatas; the second number refers to the Sutta.
S.	Saṃyutta-Nikāya. The Roman number refers to the division into 'Kindred Groups' (Saṃyutta), e.g. Devat-Saṃyutta = I, etc.; the second number refers to the Sutta.
Dhp.	Dhammapada. The number refers to the verse.
Ud.	Udāna. The Roman number refers to the Chapters, the second number refers to the Sutta.
Snp.	Sutta-Nipāta. The number refers to the verse.
VisM.	Visuddhi-Magga ('The Path of Purification').
B.Dict	Buddhist Dictionary, by Nyanatiloka Mahāthera.
Fund.	Fundamentals of Buddhism, by Nyanatiloka Mahāthera.

The Pronunciation of Pali

Adapted from the American edition

Except for a few proper names, non-English words are italicized. Most such words are in Pali, the written language of the source documents. Pali words are pronounced as follows.

Vowels

Letter	Should be sounded
a	As *u* in the English word *shut*; never as in *cat*, and never as in *take*.
ā	As in *father*; never as in *take*.
e	Long, as *a* in *stake*.
i	As in *pin*.
ī	As in machine; never as in *fine*.
o	Long as in *hope*.
u	As in *put* or *oo* in *foot*.
ū	As *oo* in *boot*; never as in *refuse*.

Consonants

Letter	Should be sounded
c	As *ch* in *chair*; never as *k*, never as *s*, nor as *c* in *centre*, *city*.
g	As in *get*, never as in *general*.
h	Always, even in positions immediately following consonants or doubled consonants; e.g. *bh* as in *cab-horse*; *ch* as *chh* in *ranch-house*: *dh* as in *handhold*; *gh* as in *bag-handle*; *jh* as *dgh* in *sledge-hammer*, etc.
j	As in *joy*.
ṃ	As the 'nazalizer' is in Ceylon, usually pronounced as *ng* in *sung*, *sing*, etc.
s	Always as in *this*; never as in *these*.
ñ	As *ny* in *canyon* (Spanish: cañon) or as *gn* in *Mignon*.
ph	As in *haphazard*; never as in *photograph*.
ṭh	As in *hot-house*; never as in *thin* nor as in *than*.
y	As in *yes*.

ṭ, ṭh, ḍ, ḍh, ḷ are lingual sounds; in pronouncing, the tongue is to be pressed against the palate.

Double consonants: each of them is to be pronounced; e.g., *bb* as in scrub-board: *tt* as in *cat-tail*.

Unit One

Introduction

The Buddha

Buddha or Enlightened One—lit. Knower or Awakened One—is the honorific name given to the Indian Sage, Gotama, who discovered and proclaimed to the world the Law of Deliverance, known to the West by the name of Buddhism.

He was born in the 6th century B.C., at Kapilavatthu, as the son of the king who ruled the Sakya country, a principality situated in the border area of modern Nepal. His personal name was Siddhattha, and his clan name Gotama (Sanskrit: Gautama). In his 29th year he renounced the splendor of his princely life and his royal career, and became a homeless ascetic in order to find a way out of what he had early recognized as a world of suffering. After a six-year's quest, spent under various religious teachers and in a period of fruitless self-mortification, he finally attained to Perfect Enlightenment (sammā-sambodhi), under the Bodhi tree at Gayā (today Buddh-Gayā). Five and forty years of tireless preaching and teaching followed and at last, in his 80th year, there passed away at Kusinārā that 'undeluded being that appeared for the blessing and happiness of the world.'

The Buddha is neither a god nor a prophet or incarnation of a god, but a supreme human being who, through his own effort, attained to Final Deliverance and Perfect Wisdom, and became 'the peerless teacher of gods and men.' He is a 'Saviour' only in the sense that he shows men how to save themselves, by actually following to the end the Path trodden and shown by him. In the consummate harmony of Wisdom and Compassion attained by the Buddha, he embodies the universal and timeless ideal of Man Perfected.

The Dhamma

The Dhamma is the Teaching of Deliverance in its entirety, as discovered, realized and proclaimed by the Buddha. It has been handed down in the ancient Pali language, and preserved in three great collections of books, called Ti-Piṭaka, the "Three Baskets," namely: (I) the Vinaya-Piṭaka, or Collection of Discipline, containing the rules of the monastic order; (II) the Sutta-Piṭaka, or Collection of Discourses, consisting of various books of discourses, dialogues, verses, stories, etc. and dealings with the doctrine proper as summarized in the Four Noble Truths; (III) the Abhidhamma-Piṭnaka, or Philosophical Collection; presenting the teachings of the Sutta- Piṭaka in strictly systematic and philosophical form.

The Dhamma is not a doctrine of revelation, but the teaching of Enlightenment based on the clear comprehension of actuality. It is the teaching of the Fourfold Truth dealing with the fundamental facts of life and with liberation attainable through man's own effort towards purification and insight. The Dhamma offers a lofty, but realistic, system of ethics, a penetrative analysis of life, a profound philosophy, practical methods of mind training-in brief, an all-comprehensive and perfect guidance on the Path to Deliverance. By answering the claims of both heart and reason, and by pointing out the liberating Middle Path that leads beyond all futile and destructive extremes in thought and conduct, the Dhamma has, and will always have, a timeless and universal appeal wherever there are hearts and minds mature enough to appreciate its message.

The Sangha

The Sangha—lit. the Assembly, or community—is the Order of Bhikkhus or Mendicant Monks, founded by the Buddha and still existing in its original form in Burma, Siam, Ceylon, Cambodia, Laos and Chittagong (Bengal). It is, together with the Order of the Jain monks, the oldest monastic order in the world. Amongst the most famous disciples in the time of the Buddha were: Sāriputta who, after the Master himself, possessed the profoundest insight into the Dhamma; Moggallāna, who had the greatest supernatural powers: Ananda, the devoted disciple and constant companion of the Buddha; Mahā-Kassapa, the President of the Council held at Rājagaha immediately after the Buddha's death; Anuruddha, of divine vision, and master of Right Mindfulness; Rāhula, the Buddha's own son.

The Sangha provides the outer framework and the favorable conditions for all those who earnestly desire to devote their life entirely to the realization of the highest goal of deliverance, unhindered by worldly distractions. Thus the Sangha, too, is of universal and timeless significance wherever religious development reaches maturity.

The Threefold Refuge

The Buddha, the Dhamma, and the Sangha, are called 'The Three Jewels' (ti-ratana) on account of their matchless purity, and as being to the Buddhist the most precious objects in the world. These 'Three Jewels' form also the 'Threefold Refuge' (ti-sarana) of the Buddhist, in the words by which he professes, or re-affirms, his acceptance of them as the guides of his life and thought.

The Pali formula of Refuge is still the same as in the Buddha's time:

Buddhaṃ saraṇaṃ gacchāmi
Dhammaṃ saraṇaṃ gacchāmi
Saṅghaṃ saraṇaṃ gacchāmi.

It is through the simple act of reciting this formula three times that one declares oneself a Buddhist. (At the second and third repetition the word Dutiyampi or Tatiyampi, 'for the second/third time,' are added before each sentence.)

The Five Precepts

After the formula of the Threefold Refuge follows usually the acceptance of the Five Moral Precepts (pañca-sila). Their observance is the minimum standard needed to form the basis of a decent life and of further progress towards Deliverance.

1. *Pāṇātipātā veramaṇī-sikkhāpadaṃ samādiyāmi.*

   I undertake to observe the precept to abstain from killing living beings.

2. *Adinnādāna veramaṇī-sikkhāpadaṃ samādiyāmi.*

   I undertake to observe the precept to abstain from taking things not given.

3. *Kāmesu micchācārā veramaṇī-sikkhāpadaṃ samādiyāmi.*

   I undertake to observe the precept to abstain from sexual misconduct.

4. *Musāvādā veramaṇī-sikkhāpadaṃ samādiyāmi.*

   I undertake to observe the precept to abstain from false speech.

5. *Surāmeraya-majja-pamādaṭṭhā veramaṇī-sikkhāpadaṃ samādiyāmi.*

   I undertake to observe the precept to abstain from intoxicating drinks and drugs causing heedlessness.

New Words and Expressions

abstain (from) / əb'steɪn/ *vi.*	戒绝；戒除
actuality / ˌæktʃu'æləti / *n.*	现实；事实
Ananda / *n.*	阿难陀
Anuruddha / *n.*	阿那律
ascetic / ə'setɪk / *n.*	苦行者；禁欲者
adj.	苦行的；禁欲主义的
assembly / ə'semblɪ / *n.*	集会；集合
attain (to) / ə'teɪn / *vt. / vi.*	证得
Awakened One	觉者；佛陀
Bengal / ben'gɔːl, beŋ–,'bengəl, 'beŋ– / *n.*	孟加拉
Bhikkhu / *n.*	比丘
bodhi tree / *n.*	菩提树
Buddha / 'bʊdə / *n.*	佛陀；佛像
Buddhism / 'bʊdɪzəm / *n.*	佛教
Buddhist / 'bʊdɪst / *n.*	佛弟子；佛教徒
adj.	佛教的；佛陀的
Burma / 'bəːmə / *n.*	缅甸
Cambodia / kæm'bəʊdɪə / *n.*	柬埔寨
Ceylon / si'lɔn / *n.*	锡兰（斯里兰卡 Srilanka）
Chittagong / 'tʃitəgɔŋ / *n.*	吉大港
clan / klæn / *n.*	宗族；部落；集团
Collection of Discipline	律藏
Collection of Discourses	经藏
community / kə'mjuːnətɪ / *n.*	团体
companion / kəm'pænɪən / *n.*	侍者；同伴
compassion / kəm'pæʃn / *n.*	悲；悯
deliverance / dɪ'lɪvərəns / *n.*	解脱
disciple / dɪ'saɪpl / *n.*	弟子；佛弟子
discipline / 'dɪsəplɪn / *n.*	戒律；律仪
discourses, dialogues, verses, stories / *n.*	论述，对话，偈颂，故事
doctrine / 'dɒktrɪn / *n.*	教义
Enlightened One	觉者

enlightenment / ɪnˈlaɪtnmənt / *n.*	觉；悟
extreme / ɪkˈstriːm / *n.*	边；极端
false speech	妄语
Final Deliverance	最终的解脱
Four Noble Truths	四圣谛
Gotama / *n.*	乔达摩（释迦牟尼的俗姓）
harmony / ˈhaːmənɪ / *n.*	圆融；和谐
heedlessness / hiːdlisnis / *n.*	放逸
incarnation / ˌɪnkaːˈneɪʃn / *n.*	化身
intoxicating / ɪnˈtɒksɪkeɪtɪŋ / *adj.*	醉人的
Kapilavatthu / *n.*	迦毗罗卫城
killing living beings	杀生
Kusinara / *n.*	拘尸那罗
Laos / laʊs / *n.*	老挝
Law of Deliverance	解脱道（法）
liberation / ˌlɪbəˈreɪʃn / *n.*	解脱
Mahā-Kassapa / *n.*	大迦叶
mendicant / ˈmendɪkənt / *adj.*	乞讨的；托钵僧的
n.	托钵者；出家人
mind / maɪnd / *n.*	心；意
mindfulness / ˈmaɪndfulnɪs / *n.*	念；留心；专注
misconduct / ˌmɪsˈkɒndʌkt / *n.*	不善行；不当行为
Moggallana / *n.*	目犍连
monastic / məˈnæstɪk / *adj.*	寺院的；修道院的
Monastic Order	僧伽；僧团
mortification / ˌmɔːtɪfɪˈkeɪʃn / *n.*	苦行
Nepal / nəˈpɔːl / *n.*	尼泊尔
observe the precept	守戒
perception / pəˈsepʃn / *n.*	想
Perfect Enlightenment	正觉
Perfect Wisdom	无上智；圆满的智慧
Philosophical Collection	论藏
purification / ˌpjʊərɪfɪˈkeɪʃn / *n.*	清净；止
purity / ˈpjʊərətɪ / *n.*	清净；寂静
Rahula / *n.*	罗睺罗

Rajagaha / *n.*		王舍城
realization / ˌriːəlaɪˈzeɪʃn / *n.*		证悟；悟道
renounce / rɪˈnaʊns / *vt.*		出离；放弃
Right Mindfulness		正念
sage / seɪdʒ / *n.*		圣者
Sakya / ˈsaːkjə / *n.*		释迦族
Sangha / ˈsæŋgə / *n.*		僧伽
Sanskrit / ˈsænskrɪt / *n.*		梵文
adj.		梵文的
saviour / ˈseɪvjə(r) / *n.*		救世主
self-mortification		自我苦修
sexual misconduct		邪淫
Siam / ˈsaiæm,saiˈæm / *n.*		暹罗（泰国）
Siddhattha / *n.*		悉达多
suffering / ˈsʌfərɪŋ / *n.*		苦
supernatural powers		神通
taking things not given		不与取
the Dhamma / *n.*		佛法
the Five (Moral) Precepts		五戒
the Knower		觉者
Three Baskets		三藏
Three Jewels		三宝
Threefold Refuge		三皈依
wisdom / ˈwɪzdəm / *n.*		智慧；慧

Grammar

1. 名词：

A. 需要大写的名词：佛陀的尊号，佛教特有的基本概念，专有术语。如：Buddhism（佛教），Noble Truth（圣谛），Dhamma（法），Sangha（僧伽）等都要大写。

B. 不必大写的名词：一般名词（略）

2. 冠词：

A. 定冠词：

表示唯一，或特指：The Buddha，The Four Noble Truths。

由普通名词构成的佛教基本概念词组一般要加定冠词：

The Five Groups of Existence（五蕴）

The Perfect One（如来）

The Four Absorptions（四禅定）

The Path to Deliverance（解脱之道）

B. 不定冠词：这些词一般不是佛教特有的概念。

Everything is without a" Self".

All dhammas lack an Ego.（诸法无我）

C. 零冠词：Man Perfected

佛教特有的概念（类似专有名词）：

Nibbana（涅槃），Vipassana（观），Absorptions（禅定），Suffering（苦）

注意：这种用法一般要大写。

另外，当名词前有其他限定词时，如 "some, any, every, each, such, either" 等，冠词的使用往往受到限制，如：

All Buddhas of the three periods of time.（三世诸佛）

可以说 "all the Buddhas"，不可以说 "every the Buddha"，或 "each the Buddha"。另一方面，却可以说 "such a Buddha"。

限定词的组合，排列顺序也是有规律的。可参考以下网页：

http://baike.baidu.com/link?url=XItqKz-l9JJuB8XbyzjMhm5kx7OO1HyIx74eGNKZ5OXJ-xtUZrklKKs9dKpVqbWp

佛教名词及其冠词（包括零冠词）的用法，虽有规律可循，但语言是约定俗成的，文无定法，一切规则皆有例外，一切皆取决于具体语境。这些都需要在学习和翻译实践中自己留意，总结。

Exercises

1. Outline the major events in the Buddha's life. (In a chronological order)
2. Which of the following words best describe(s) the Buddha? Why?

   A. god   B. prophet   C. savior   D. man perfected

3. Is dhamma "a doctrine of revelation"? If yes, why? If no, why not?
4. Explain the words "mature" and "maturity" in the text.

   Is the maturity of mind related to the maturity in religious development?
   If yes, how?

Unit Two

The Four Noble Truths

Thus has it been said by the Buddha, the Enlightened One:

D.16.

It is through not understanding, not realizing four things, that I, Disciples, as well as you, had to wander so long through this round of rebirths. And what are these four things? They are:

The Noble Truth of Suffering (dukkha);

The Noble Truth of the Origin of Suffering (dukkha-samudaya);

The Noble Truth of the Extinction of Suffering (dukkha-nirodha);

The Noble Truth of the Path that leads to the Extinction of Suffering (dukkha-nirodha-gāmini-paṭipadā).

S. LVI. 11

As long as the absolutely true knowledge and insight as regards these Four Noble Truths was not quite clear in me, so long was I not sure that I had won that supreme Enlightenment which is unsurpassed in all the world with its heavenly beings, evil spirits and gods, amongst all the hosts of ascetics and priests, heavenly beings and men. But as soon as the absolute true knowledge and insight as regards these Four Noble Truths had become perfectly clear in me, there arose in me the assurance that I had won that supreme Enlightenment unsurpassed.

M. 26

And I discovered that profound truth, so difficult to perceive, difficult to understand, tranquilizing and sublime, which is not to be gained by mere reasoning, and is visible only to the wise.

The world, however, is given to pleasure, delighted with pleasure, enchanted with pleasure. Truly, such beings will hardly understand the law of conditionality, the Dependent Origination (paticca-samuppāda) of everything; incomprehensible to them will also be the end of all formations, the forsaking of every substratum of rebirth, the fading away of craving, detachment, extinction, Nibbāna.

Yet there are beings whose eyes are only a little covered with dust: they will understand the truth.

The Noble Truth of Suffering

D.22

What, now, is the Noble Truth of Suffering?

Birth is suffering; Decay is suffering; Death is suffering; Sorrow, Lamentation, Pain, Grief, and Despair are suffering; not to get what one desires, is suffering; in short: the Five Groups of Existence are suffering.

What, now, is Birth? The birth of beings belonging to this or that order of beings, their being born, their conception and springing into existence, the manifestation of the Groups of Existence, the arising of sense activity: this is called birth.

And what is Decay? The decay of beings belonging to this or that order of beings; their becoming aged, frail, grey, and wrinkled; the failing of their vital force, the wearing out of the senses: this is called decay.

And what is Death? The departing and vanishing of beings out of this or that order of beings, their destruction, disappearance, death, the completion of their life-period, dissolution of the Groups of Existence, the discarding of the body: this is called death.

And what is Sorrow? The sorrow arising through this or that loss or misfortune which one encounters, the worrying oneself, the state of being alarmed, inward sorrow, inward woe: this is called sorrow.

And what is Lamentation? Whatsoever, through this or that loss or misfortune which befalls one, is wail and lament, wailing and lamenting, the state of woe and lamentation: this is called lamentation.

And what is Pain? The bodily pain and unpleasantness, the painful and unpleasant feeling produced by bodily impression: this is called pain.

And what is Grief? The mental pain and unpleasantness, the painful and unpleasant feeling produced by mental impression: this is called grief.

And what is Despair? Distress and despair arising through this or that loss or misfortune which one encounters, distressfulness, and desperation: this is called despair.

And what is the 'Suffering of not getting what one desires'? To beings subject to birth there comes the desire: 'O, that we were not subject to birth! O, that no new birth was before us!' Subject to decay, disease, death, sorrow, lamentation, pain, grief, and despair, the desire comes to them: 'O, that we were not subject to these things! O, that these things were not before us!' But this cannot be got by mere desiring; and not to get what one desires, is suffering.

The Five Khandhas, or Groups of Existence

M. 28

And what, in brief, are the Five Groups of Existence? They are corporeality, feeling, perception, (mental) formations, and consciousness.

M. 109

All corporeal phenomena, whether past, present or future, one's own or external, gross or subtle, lofty or low, far or near, all belong to the Group of Corporeality; all feelings belong to the Group of Feeling; all perceptions belong to the Group of Perception; all mental formations belong to the Group of Formations; all consciousness belongs to the Group of Consciousness.

These Groups are a fivefold classification in which the Buddha has summed up all the physical and mental phenomena of existence, and in particular, those which appear to the ignorant man as his ego or personality. Hence birth, decay, death, etc. are also included in these five Groups which actually comprise the whole world.

The Group of Corporeality (rūpa-khandha)

M. 28

What, now, is the 'Group of Corporeality?' It is the four primary elements, and corporeality derived from them.

The Four Elements

And what are the four Primary Elements? They are the Solid Element, the Fluid Element, the Heating Element, the Vibrating (Windy) Element.

The four Elements (dhātu or mahā-bhūta), popularly called Earth, Water, Fire and Wind, are to be understood as the elementary qualities of matter. They are named in Pali, paṭhavī-dhātu, āpo-dhātu, tejo-dhātu, vāyo-dhātu, and may be rendered as Inertia, Cohesion, Radiation, and Vibration. All four are present in every material object, though in varying degrees of strength. If, e.g., the Earth Element predominates, the material object is called 'solid', etc.

The 'Corporeality derived from the four primary elements' (upādāya rūpa or upādā rūpa) consists, according to the Abhidhamma, of the following twenty-four material phenomena and qualities: eye, ear, nose, tongue, body, visible form, sound, odour, taste, masculinity, femininity, vitality, physical basis of mind (hadaya-vatthu; see B. Dict.), gesture, speech, space (cavities of ear, nose, etc.), decay, change, and nutriment.

Bodily impressions (phoṭṭhabba, the tactile) are not especially mentioned among these twenty-four, as they are identical with the Solid, the Heating and the Vibrating Elements which are cognizable through the sensations of pressure, cold, heat, pain etc.

1. What, now, is the 'Solid Element' (paṭhavī-dhātu)? The solid element may be one's own, or it may be external. And what is one's own solid element? Whatever in one's own person or body there exists of karmically acquired hardness, firmness, such as the hairs of head and body, nails, teeth, skin, flesh, sinews, bones, marrow, kidneys, heart, liver, diaphragm, spleen, lungs, stomach, bowels, mesentery, excrement and so on-this is called one's own solid element. Now, whether it be one's own solid element, or whether it be the external solid element, they are both merely the solid element.

And one should understand, according to reality and true wisdom, 'This does not belong to me; this am I not; this is not my Ego'.

2. What, now, is the 'Fluid Element' (āpo-dhātu)? The fluid element may be one's own, or it may be external. And what is one's own fluid element? Whatever in one's own person or body there exists of karmically acquired liquidity or fluidity, such as bile, phlegm, pus, blood, sweat, fat, tears, skin-grease, saliva, nasal mucus, oil of the joints, urine, and so on-this is called one's own fluid element. Now, whether it be one's own fluid element, or whether it be the external fluid element, they are both merely the fluid element.

And one should understand, according to reality and true wisdom, 'This does not belong to me; this am I not; this is not my Ego'.

3. What, now, is the 'Heating Element' (tejo-dhātu)? The heating element may be one's own, or it may be external. And what is one's own heating element? Whatever in one's own person or body there exists of karmically acquired heat or hotness, such as that whereby one is heated, consumed, scorched, whereby that which has been eaten, drunk, chewed, or tasted, is fully digested, and so on—this is called one's own heating element. Now, whether it be one's own heating element, or whether it be the external

heating element, they are both merely the heating element.

And one should understand, according to reality and true wisdom, 'This does not belong to me; this am I not; this is not my Ego'.

4. What, now, is the 'Vibrating (Windy) Element' (vāyo-dhātu)? The vibrating element may be one's own, or it may be external. And what is one's own vibrating element? What in one's own person or body there exists of karmically acquired wind or windiness, such as the upward-going and downward-going winds, the winds of stomach and intestines, the wind permeating all the limbs, in-breathing and out-breathing, and so on—this is called one's own vibrating element. Now, whether it be one's own vibrating element or whether it be the external vibrating element, they are both merely the vibrating element.

And one should understand, according to reality and true wisdom, 'This does not belong to me; this am I not; this is not my Ego.'

Just as one calls 'hut' the circumscribed space which comes to be by means of wood and rushes, reeds, and clay, even so we call 'body' the circumscribed space that comes to be by means of bones and sinews, flesh and skin.

New Words and Expressions

absolutely / 'æbsəluːtli / *adv.*   绝对地；完全地

arise / ə'raɪz / *vi.*   生起；出现

being / 'biːɪŋ / *n.*   有情；存在；生命

Birth / bɜːθ / *n.*   生

bodily impressions   身触

body / 'bɒdɪ / *n.*   身净色；身体

comprise / kəm'praɪz / *vt.*   包含；构成

corporeality / kɔː,pɔːrɪ'ælɪtɪ / *n.*   色；物质性；肉体的存在

corporeality derived from the four primary elements   四大所造色

corporeality, feeling, perception, (mental) formations, and consciousness / *n.*   色，受，想，（心）行，识

Decay / dɪˈkeɪ / *n.*		老
Dependent Origination		缘起
diaphragm / ˈdaɪəfræm / *n.*		隔膜
dissolution / ˌdɪsəˈluːʃn / *n.*		衰败；死亡；消亡
distress / dɪˈstres / *n.*		焦虑
ear / ɪə(r) / *n.*		耳净色；耳
encounter / ɪnˈkaʊntə(r) / *vi.*		遇到（困难或不利的事）
evil spirits		魔
excrement / ˈekskrɪmənt / *n.*		排泄物；粪便
extinction / ɪkˈstɪŋkʃn / *n.*		灭；消亡；消失
eye / aɪ / *n.*		眼净色；眼
femininity / ˌfeməˈnɪnəti / *n.*		女性根色
Five Groups of Existence		五蕴；五蕴有；五取蕴
fivefold / ˈfaɪvfəʊld / *adj.*		五重的
Fluid Element		水大
Four Elements		四界；四大
gesture / ˈdʒestʃə(r) / *n.*		身表；姿态
gods / ˈgɒdz / *n.*		梵天；神
grease / griːs / *n.*		油膏；油脂
Group of Consciousness		识蕴
Group of Corporeality		色蕴
Group of Feeling		受蕴
Group of Formations		行蕴
Group of Perception		想蕴
Groups of Existence		诸蕴
Heating Element		火大
heavenly beings		天；天人
ignorant / ˈɪgnərənt / *adj.*		无知的
karmically / *adv.*		依业地
Law of Conditionality		缘起法
life-period		一期生命
manifestation (of) / ˌmænɪfeˈsteɪʃn / *n.*		……的显现；表现形式
masculinity / ˌmæskjuˈlɪnəti / *n.*		男性根色
mental formations		行

mental impression	意触
mesentery / ˈmesəntərɪ / *n.*	肠系膜
nasal mucus	鼻涕
nose / nəʊz / *n.*	鼻净色；鼻
not to get what one desires	求不得
nutriment / ˈnjuːtrɪmənt / *n.*	食色；营养物
odour / ˈəʊdə(r) / *n.*	香；气味
origin / ˈɒrɪdʒɪn / *n.*	起源
perceive / pəˈsiːv / *vt.*	觉知；观察到
phenomena / fəˈnɒmɪnə / *n.*	现象（phenomenon 的复数）
phlegm / flem / *n.*	痰
physical basis of mind	心所依处
predominate / prɪˈdɒmɪneɪt / *vi.*	统治；支配
priest / priːst / *n.*	婆罗门
pus / pʌs / *n.*	脓
radiation / reɪdɪˈeɪʃ(ə)n / *n.*	辐射；暖；发光
reality / rɪˈælɪtɪ / *n.*	实相；真实
saliva / səˈlaɪvə / *n.*	唾液
sense / sens / *n.*	根；感觉；官能
Solid Element	地大
Sorrow, Lamentation, Pain, Grief, Despair / *n.*	悲，哀，痛，恼，绝望
sound / saʊnd / *n.*	声；声音
space / speɪs / *n.*	空界；空间
speech / spiːtʃ / *n.*	语表；讲话
spleen / spliːn / *n.*	脾
sublime / səˈblaɪm / *adj.*	殊妙的；庄严的
subtle / ˈsʌtl / *adj.*	微妙的；微细的
suffering of not getting what one desires	求不得苦
taste / teɪst / *n.*	味；味道
the Noble Truth of Suffering	苦圣谛
tongue / tʌŋ / *n.*	舌净色；舌
tranquilizing / ˈtræŋkwɪlaɪzɪŋ / *pr.* / *p.*	寂静；使……安静
true wisdom	真实智
Vibrating (Windy) Element	风大

visible form	色
vital force	命；命的根；生命力
vitality / vaɪˈtæləti / *n.*	命根色；生命力；活力
wail / weɪl / *n.* / *vi.*	痛哭；哀号
woe / wəʊ / *n.*	悲哀；悲苦；苦恼

Grammar

●佛教关键概念往往是以"数词 + 名词"的形式表示的，如：

四圣谛，三法印，五蕴，十二因缘，八正道，四念处，七觉支等。

翻译为英语时，有以下几种情况：

（1）多习惯直接使用巴利（梵）文的，如：

三藏：Ti-piṭaka（Three Baskets），三宝：ti-ratana（Three Jewels），三皈依：Ti-sarana（Threefold Refuge）。

（2）习惯译为"数词 + 名词"词组的，如：

The Four Noble Truths（四圣谛）；

Five（Moral）Precepts（五戒）。

（3）使用"数词 + fold + 单数名词"的形式，如：

"Threefold Refuge"（三皈依）。

为什么不是"three refuges"？

这是因为，巴利文的"ti-sarana"是单数，不是复数，而且，"三皈依"是一个整体的概念，不是三个互相独立的"庇护所"。

"八圣道"（ariya-atthangika-magga）英文译为"Noble eightfold path"（单数），也是同样的道理。

●数词和表示"度量单位"的词构成词组，可修饰另一个名词，如：

A three-year project, a 3-year period, a 5-year loan, seven-year itch（七年之痒）。

It's a five-minute walk from the library to the playground.

从图书馆到操场需要走五分钟。

She's a sixteen-year-old girl.

她是个十六岁的女孩。

Laura is a 30-year-old mother of three.

劳拉是个 30 岁的母亲，有三个孩子。

I'll need a five-hundred-dollar retainer.

我将收取 500 美元的定金。

This model is powered by a 1.8-litre petrol engine.

这一型号用 1.8 升汽油发动机驱动。

可参考以下网页：http://www.yygrammar.com/Article/201303/3151_2.html。

●注意：数词和名词（形容词）中间用连字符，词组中的名词不用复数。
《佛言》课文中的："After a six year's quest…"

现代英语中要说 "After six years' quest…" 或 "After a six-year quest…"。

Five and forty years.

这是古英语（Middle English）数词的语序。

e.g. eahta and twentiġ（twenty-eight）。

在《圣经》较早的版本中，也有这种用法。

e.g. And Arphaxad lived five and thirty years, and begat Salah.… And Eber lived four and thirty years, and begat Peleg.（旧约创世纪）美国天主教会新版圣经则改为 "When Eber was thirty-four years old, he became the father of Peleg"。

顺便提一下，英语属日耳曼语系，其数词与德语数词同源。直到今天，现代德语还是同样的语序。e.g. Fünf und Vierzig Jahre.（45 years）

Exercises

1. Why is life suffering?

2. List the aspects or phases of life, from birth to death, and explain why they cause suffering?

THE WORD OF THE BUDDHA

3. How do you understand the statement "The five groups of existence are suffering"?

4. Name the Four Primary Elements, and explain how they relate to our body.

5. How do you define "body"?

6. Compare the following compound words:

   Ti-pitaka: three baskests (pl.)

   Ti-ratana: three jewels (pl.)

   Ti-sarana: threefold refuge (sing.)

   Why is "threefold refuge"singular,and not plural?

7. Do yo agree that every corporeal element in the body is karmically acquired?

   Could there be any material component of the body that is not karmically acquired?

Unit Three

The Group of Feeling (vedanā-khandha)

S.XXXVI, 1

There are three kinds of Feeling: pleasant, unpleasant, and neither pleasant nor unpleasant (indifferent).

The Group of Perception (saññā-khandha)

S. XXII, 56

What, now, is Perception? There are six classes of perception: perception of forms, sounds, odors, tastes, bodily impressions, and of mental objects.

The Group of Mental Formations (saṅkhāra-khandha)

What, now, are Mental Formations? There are six classes of volitions (cetanā): will directed to forms (rūpa-cetanaa), to sounds, odors, tastes, bodily impressions, and to mental objects.

The 'group of Mental Formations' (saṅkhāra-khandha) is a collective term for numerous functions or aspects of mental activity which, in addition to feeling and perception, are present in a single moment of consciousness. In the Abhidhamma, fifty Mental Formations are distinguished, seven of which are constant factors of mind. The number and composition of the rest varies according to the character of the respective class of consciousness (see Table in B. Dict). In the Discourse on Right Understanding (M.9) three main representatives of the Group of Mental Formations are mentioned: volition (cetanā), sense impression (phassa), and attention (manasikāra). Of these again, it is volition which, being a principal 'formative' factor, is particularly characteristic of the Group of Formations, and therefore serves to exemplify it in the passage given above.

For other applications of the term saṅkhāra see B. Dict.

The Group of Consciousness (viññāṇa-khandha)

S. XXII. 56

What, now, is consciousness? There are six classes of consciousness: consciousness of forms, sounds, odors, tastes, bodily impressions, and of mental objects (lit.: eye-conscious-ness, ear-consciousness, etc.).

Dependent Origination of Consciousness
M. 28

Now, though one's eye be intact, yet if the external forms do not fall within the field of vision, and no corresponding conjunction (of eye and forms) takes place, in that case there occurs no formation of the corresponding aspect of consciousness. Or, though one's eye be intact, and the external forms fall within the field of vision, yet if no corresponding conjunction takes place; in that case also there occurs no formation of the corresponding aspect of consciousness. If, however, one's eye is intact, and the external forms fall within the field of vision, and the corresponding conjunction takes place, in that case there arises the corresponding aspect of consciousness.

M. 38

Hence I say: the arising of consciousness is dependent upon conditions; and without these conditions, no consciousness arises. And upon whatsoever conditions the arising of consciousness is dependent, after these it is called.

Consciousness, whose arising depends on the eye and forms, is called 'eye-consciousness' (cakkhu-viññāṇa).

Consciousness, whose arising depends on the ear and sounds, is called 'ear-consciousness' (sota-viññāṇa).

Consciousness, whose arising depends on the olfactory organ and odors, is called 'nose-consciousness' (ghāna-viññāṇa).

Consciousness, whose arising depends on the tongue and taste, is called 'tongue-consciousness' (jivhā-viññāṇa).

Consciousness, whose arising depends on the body and bodily contacts, is called 'body-consciousness' (kāya-viññāṇa).

Consciousness, whose arising depends on the mind and mind objects, is called 'mind-consciousness' (mano-viññāṇa).

M. 28

Whatsoever there is of 'corporeality' (rūpa) on that occasion, this belongs to the Group of Corporeality. Whatsoever there is of 'feeling' (vedanā), this belongs to the Group of Feeling. Whatsoever there is of 'perception' (saññā), this belongs to the Group of Perception. Whatsoever there are of 'mental formations' (saṅkhāra), these belong to the Group of Mental Formations. Whatsoever there is of consciousness (viññāṇa), this belongs to the Group of Consciousness.

Dependency of Consciousness on the Four Other Khandhas
S. XXII. 53

And it is impossible that any one can explain the passing out of one existence, and the entering into a new existence, or the growth, increase and development of consciousness, independently of corporeality, feeling, perception, and mental formations.

The Three Characteristics of Existence (ti-lakkhaṇa)

A. III. 134

All formations are 'transient' (anicca); all formations are 'subject to suffering' (dukkha); all things are 'without a self' (anattā).

S. XXII, 59

Corporeality is transient, feeling is transient, perception is transient, mental formations are transient, consciousness is transient.

And that which is transient, is subject to suffering; and of that which is transient and subject to suffering and change, one cannot rightly say: 'This belongs to me; this am I; this is my Self'.

Therefore, whatever there be of corporeality, of feeling, perception, mental formations, or consciousness, whether past, present or future, one's own or external, gross or subtle, lofty or low, far or near, one should understand according to reality and true wisdom: 'This does not belong to me; this am I not; this is not my Self'.

The Anatta Doctrine

Individual existence, as well as the whole world, is in reality nothing but a process of ever-changing phenomena which are all comprised in the five Groups of Existence. This process has gone on from time immemorial, before one's birth, and also after one's death it will continue for endless periods of time, as long, and as far, as there are conditions for it. As stated in the preceding texts, the five Groups of Existence—either taken separately or combined—in no way constitute a real Ego-entity or subsisting personality, and equally no self, soul or substance can be found outside of these Groups as their 'owner'. In other words, the five Groups of Existence are 'not-self' (anattā), nor do they belong to a Self (anattaniya). In view of the impermanence and conditionality of all existence, the belief in any form of Self must be regarded as an illusion.

Just as what we designate by the name of 'chariot' has no existence apart from axle, wheels, shaft, body and so forth: or as the word 'house' is merely a convenient designation for various materials put together after a certain fashion so as to enclose a portion of space, and there is no separate house-entity in existence: in exactly the same way, that which we call a 'being' or an 'individual' or a 'person', or by the name 'I', is nothing but a changing combination of physical and psychical phenomena, and has no real existence in itself.

This is, in brief, the Anattā Doctrine of the Buddha, the teaching that all existence is void (suñña) of a permanent self or substance. It is the fundamental Buddhist doctrine not found in any other religious teaching or philosophical system. To grasp it fully, not only in an abstract and intellectual way, but by constant reference to actual experience, is an indispensable condition for the true understanding of the Buddha-Dhamma and for the realization of its goal. The Anattā-Doctrine is the necessary outcome of the thorough analysis of actuality, undertaken, e.g. in the Khandha Doctrine of which only a bare indication can be given by means of the texts included here.

For a detailed survey of the Khandhas see B. Dict.

S. XXII. 95

Suppose a man who was not blind beheld the many bubbles on the Ganges as they drove along, and he watched them and carefully examined them; then after he had carefully examined them they would appear to him empty, unreal and unsubstantial. In exactly the same way does the monk behold all the corporeal phenomena, feelings, perceptions, mental formations, and states of consciousness—whether they be of the past, or the present, or the future, far or near. And he watches them, and examines them carefully; and, after carefully examining them, they appear to him empty, void and without a Self.

S. XXII. 29

Whoso delights in corporeality, or feeling, or perception, or mental formations, or consciousness, he delights in suffering; and whoso delights in suffering, will not be freed from suffering. Thus I say.

Dhp. 146-48

How can you find delight and mirth
Where there is burning without end?
In deepest darkness you are wrapped!

Why do you not seek for the light?

Look at this puppet here, well rigged,

A heap of many sores, piled up,

Diseased, and full of greediness,

Unstable, and impermanent!

Devoured by old age is this frame,

A prey to sickness, weak and frail;

To pieces breaks this putrid body,

All life must truly end in death.

The Three Warnings
III. 35

Did you never see in the world a man, or a woman, eighty, ninety, or a hundred years old, frail, crooked as a gable-roof, bent down, resting on crutches, with tottering steps, infirm, youth long since fled, with broken teeth, grey and scanty hair or none, wrinkled, with blotched limbs? And did the thought never come to you that you also are subject to decay, that you also cannot escape it?

Did you never see in the world a man, or a woman who, being sick, afflicted, and grievously ill, wallowing in his own filth, was lifted up by some and put to bed by others? And did the thought never come to you that you also are subject to disease, that you also cannot escape it?

Did you never see in the world the corpse of a man, or a woman, one or two or three days after death, swollen up, blue-black in color, and full of corruption? And did the thought never come to you that you also are subject to death, that you also cannot escape it?

Saṃsāra
S. XV. 3

Inconceivable is the beginning of this Saṃsāra; not to be discovered is any first beginning of beings, who obstructed by ignorance, and ensnared by craving, are hurrying and hastening through this round of rebirths.

Saṃsāra—the wheel of existence, lit, the 'Perpetual Wandering'—is the name given in the Pali scriptures to the sea of life ever restlessly heaving up and down, the symbol of this continuous process of ever again and again being born, growing old, suffering, and dying. More precisely put: Saṃsāra is the unbroken sequence of the fivefold Khandha-combinations, which, constantly changing from moment to moment, follow continually one upon the other through inconceivable periods of time. Of this Saṃsāra a single life time constitutes only a tiny fraction. Hence, to be able to comprehend the first Noble Truth, one must let one's gaze rest upon the Saṃsāra, upon this frightful sequence of rebirths, and not merely upon one single life time, which, of course, may sometimes be not very painful.

The term 'suffering' (dukkha), in the first Noble Truth refers therefore, not merely to painful bodily and mental sensations due to unpleasant impressions, but it comprises in addition everything productive of suffering or liable to it. The Truth of Suffering teaches that, owing to the universal law of impermanence, even high and sublime states of happiness are subject to change and destruction, and that all states of existence are therefore unsatisfactory, without exception carrying in themselves the seeds of suffering.

Which do you think is more: the flood of tears, which weeping and wailing you have shed upon this long way—hurrying and hastening through this round of rebirths, united with the undesired, separated from the desired-this, or the waters of the four oceans?

Long have you suffered the death of father and mother, of sons, daughters, brothers, and sisters. And whilst you were thus suffering, you have indeed shed more tears upon this long way than there is water in the four oceans.

S. XV. 13

Which do you think is more: the streams of blood that, through your being beheaded, have flowed upon this long way, these, or the waters of the four oceans?

Long have you been caught as robbers, or highway men or adulterers; and, through your being beheaded, verily more blood has flowed upon this long way than there is water in the four oceans.

But how is this possible?

Inconceivable is the beginning of this Saṃsāra; not to be discovered is any first beginning of beings, who, obstructed by ignorance and ensnared by craving, are hurrying and hastening through this round of rebirths.

S. XV. 1

And thus have you long undergone suffering, undergone torment, undergone misfortune, and filled the graveyards full; truly, long enough to be dissatisfied with all the forms of existence, long enough to turn away and free yourselves from them all.

New Words and Expressions

all states of existence — 一切有；一切存在；一切境有
Anatta Doctrine — 无我说
attention / ə'tenʃn / *n.* — 作意；注意力
be ensnared by — 为……所缚
behead / bi'hed / *vt.* — 斩首
behold / bi'həʊld / — 注视；看
body-consciousness — 身识
Buddha-Dhamma — 佛法
conditionality / kəndiʃən'æliti / *n.* — 缘起；缘；条件
conditions / kən'dɪʃnz / *n.* — 诸缘
constant factors of mind — 遍一切心心所
craving / 'kreɪvɪŋ / *n.* — 贪
Death / dɛθ / *n.* — 死；死亡
delight (in) / dɪ'laɪt / *vi.* — 对……很喜欢；喜于……
devour / di'vauə / *vt.* — 吞噬；毁灭
disease / di'ziːz / *n.* — 病；疾病
distinguish / dɪ'stɪŋgwɪʃ / *vt.* — 辨别；区别

ear-consciousness	耳识
Ego-entity	实我；我
empty, void / *adj.*	空的
ensnare / ɪn'sneə(r) / *vt.*	进入；落网
examine / ɪg'zæmɪn / *vt.*	审视；检查
eye-consciousness	眼识
Fivefold Khandha-combinations	五蕴和合
from time immemorial	从无始时来
greediness / griːdinis / *n.*	贪欲
ignorance / 'ɪgnərəns / *n.*	无明；痴；愚痴
illusion / ɪ'luːʒn / *n.*	虚妄；幻觉；错觉
impermanence / im'pəːmənəns / *n.*	无常；暂时性
inconceivable / ˌɪnkən'siːvəbl / *adj.*	不可思议的；不能想象的
intellectual / inti'lektʃuəl / *adj.*	智慧的；理性的；知识的
mental activity	心理活动
mental formations	心行
mental objects	心法
mind-consciousness	意识
mirth / mɜːθ / *n.*	欢笑；欢乐；高兴
misfortune / mis'fɔːtʃən / *n.*	不幸；灾祸
neither pleasant nor unpleasant	非苦非乐
nose-consciousness	鼻识
not-self	无我；无我的
obstruct / əb'strʌkt / *vt.*	阻碍；障碍
perpetual wandering	轮回
personality, self, soul or substance / *n.*	个体，自我，灵魂或实质
puppet / 'pʌpit / *n.*	傀儡；木偶；被操纵的人
putrid / 'pjuːtrid / *adj.*	腐烂的；令人厌恶的
reality / rɪ'ælɪtɪ / *n.*	事实；现实；实际
rebirth / riː'bɜːθ / *n.*	再生
restlessly / 'restləsli / *adv.*	不安地
rigged / rigd / *pp.*	被操纵的；被控制的
round of rebirths	轮回
Samsara / səm'saːrə /	轮回
scripture / 'skriptʃə / *n.*	经；经文；经典

Self / self / *n.* 　　　　　　　　　　　　　　　　我

sensation / sen'seɪʃən / *n.* 　　　　　　　　　感受；感觉

sense impression 　　　　　　　　　　　　　　触；

separated from the desired 　　　　　　　　爱别离

subject to suffering 　　　　　　　　　　　　苦的；受制于苦

subsisting / səb'sɪstɪŋ / *pr.* /*p.* 　　　　　　存在的；实在的

the First Noble Truth 　　　　　　　　　　　第一圣谛

the Ganges / *n.* 　　　　　　　　　　　　　　恒河

the Three Characteristics Of Existence 　三法印

the Three Warnings 　　　　　　　　　　　　三示戒

the Truth of Suffering 　　　　　　　　　　苦谛

the wheel of existence 　　　　　　　　　　轮回

tongue-consciousness 　　　　　　　　　　　舌识

torment / 'tɔːment / *n.* 　　　　　　　　　　折磨

transient / 'trænzɪənt / *adj.* 　　　　　　　无常；短暂的

united with the undesired 　　　　　　　　怨憎会

unpleasant impressions 　　　　　　　　　　非乐触

unreal / ʌn'rɪəl / *adj.* 　　　　　　　　　　非真；假的

unstable / ʌn'steɪb(ə)l / *adj.* 　　　　　　不稳定的；易变的

unsubstantial / ʌnsəb'stænʃ(ə)l / *adj.* 　非实；无实质的；不坚固的

volition / və'lɪʃ(ə)n / *n.* 　　　　　　　　思；意

watch / wɒtʃ / *vt.* 　　　　　　　　　　　观察；注视

weak / wiːk / *adj.* 　　　　　　　　　　　虚弱的

will / wɪl / *n.* 　　　　　　　　　　　　　意；意志；意图

will directed to forms 　　　　　　　　　色思

without a Self 　　　　　　　　　　　　　无我

Grammar

话语标志（Discourse Marker）并不是传统语法的词类，而是包括了具有相似的语法功能的几类词或短语。它们在文章中的作用，通俗地讲，就是提示文章思路的"起承转合"。

《佛言》中最具标志性的 Discourse Marker 就是"now"。例如：

What, now, is the Noble Truth of Suffering?

这里的 "now", 只是表示 "下面, 要开始讲一个新观点", 或者, "下面讲的东西很重要", 提醒听众（读者）注意：（= I want to call your attention now）。

类似的 "话语标志" 还有：

thus, truly, verily, or, therefore, but, indeed, hence, yet, in brief, I tell you, and further...

Discourse Marker 的大量使用是佛祖（经）语言特点之一。有时, 在一个短短的句子中, 会出现几个 Discourse Marker：

Now, Right Speech, I tell you, is of two kinds.

短短的一句话, 竟被 Discourse Marker 分成了 4 个部分, 中间要停顿 3 次。此处的话语标志使节奏放慢, 目的是强调, 加强读者的印象。试想, 如果不用 "话语标志", 句子就会变得非常平直：

Right Speech is of two kinds.

类似的例子在《佛言》中比比皆是。在这些句子中, 我们可以听到一种 "教戒" 的语气和 "不容置疑" 的威严气势。

Exercises

1. What are the three characteristics of existence?

2. Elaborate on the "Anatta" doctrine. Give examples of bodily and mentale suffering.

3. What do you think are the "high and sublime states of happiness"? (Can you give examples?)

   Will they last forever?

4. What is Samsara? How is it related to the First Noble Truth?

5. All formations are 'transient' (anicca); all formations are 'subject to suffering' (dukkha); all things are 'without a self' (anatta).

   Can we say "all formations are 'suffering'"? Why?

Unit Four

The Noble Truth of the Origin of Suffering

D. 22

What, now, is the Noble Truth of the Origin of Suffering? It is craving, which gives rise to fresh rebirth, and, bound up with pleasure and lust, now here, now there, finds ever-fresh delight.

The Threefold Craving

There is the 'Sensual Craving' (kāma-taṇhā), the 'Craving for (Eternal) Existence' (bhava-taṇhā), the 'Craving for Self-Annihilation' (vibhava-taṇhā).

'Sensual Craving' (kāma-taṇhā) is the desire for the enjoyment of the five sense objects.

'Craving for Existence' (bhava-taṇhā) is the desire for continued or eternal life, referring in particular to life in those higher worlds called Fine-material and Immaterial Existences (rūpa-, and arūpa-bhava). It is closely connected with the so-called 'Eternity-Belief' (bhava- or sassata-diṭṭhi), i.e. the belief in an absolute, eternal Ego-entity persisting independently of our body.

'Craving for Self-Annihilation' (lit., 'for non-existence', vibhava-taṇhā) is the outcome of the 'Belief in Annihilation' (vibhava- or uccheda-diṭṭhi), i.e. the delusive materialistic notion of a more or less real Ego which is annihilated at death, and which does not stand in any causal relation with the time before death and the time after death.

Origin of Craving

But where does this craving arise and take root? Wherever in the world there are delightful and pleasurable things, there this craving arises and takes root. Eye, ear, nose, tongue, body, and mind, are delightful and pleasurable: there this craving arises and takes root.

Visual objects, sounds, smells tastes, bodily impressions, and mind objects, are delightful and pleasurable: there this craving arises and takes root.

Consciousness, sense impression, feeling born of sense impression, perception, will, craving, thinking, and reflecting, are delightful and pleasurable: there this craving arises and takes root.

This is called the Noble Truth of the Origin of Suffering.

Dependent Origination of All Phenomena

M. 38

If, whenever perceiving a visual object, a sound, odour, taste, bodily impression, or a mind-object, the object is pleasant, one is attracted; and if unpleasant, one is repelled.

Thus, whatever kind of 'Feeling' (vedanā) one experiences-pleasant, unpleasant or indifferent-if one approves of, and cherishes the feeling, and clings to it, then while doing so, lust springs up; but lust for feelings means 'Clinging' (upādāna), and on clinging depends the (present) 'process of Becoming'; on the process of becoming (bhava; here kamma-bhava, Karma-process) depends (future) 'Birth' (jāti); and dependent on birth are 'Decay and Death', sorrow, lamentation, pain, grief and despair. Thus arises this whole mass of suffering.

The formula of the Dependent Origination (paṭicca-samuppāda) of which only some of the twelve links have been mentioned in the preceding passage, may be regarded as a detailed explanation of the Second Truth.

Present Karma-Results

M. 13

Truly, due to sensuous craving, conditioned through sensuous craving, impelled by sensuous craving, entirely moved by sensuous craving, kings fight with kings, princes with princes, priests with priests, citizens with citizens; the mother quarrels with the son, the son with the mother, the father with the son, the son with the father; brother quarrels with brother, brother with sister, sister with brother, friend with friend. Thus, given to dissension, quarrelling and fighting, they fall upon one another with fists, sticks, or weapons. And thereby they suffer death or deadly pain.

And further, due to sensuous craving, conditioned through sensuous craving, impelled by sensuous craving, entirely moved by sensuous craving, people break into houses, rob, plunder, pillage whole houses, commit highway robbery, seduce the wives of others. Then, the rulers have such people caught, and inflict on them various forms of punishment. And thereby they incur death or deadly pain. Now, this is the misery of sensuous craving, the heaping up of suffering in this present life, due to sensuous craving, conditioned through sensuous craving, caused by sensuous craving, entirely dependent on sensuous craving.

Future Karma-Results

And further, people take the evil way in deeds, the evil way in words, the evil way in thoughts; and by taking the evil way in deeds, words and thoughts, at the dissolution of the body, after death, they fall into a downward state of existence, a state of suffering, into an unhappy destiny, and the abysses of the hells. But this is the misery of sensuous craving, the heaping up of suffering in the future life, due to sensuous craving, conditioned through sensuous craving, caused by sensuous craving, entirely dependent on sensuous craving.

Dhp. 127

> Not in the air, nor ocean-midst,
>
> Nor hidden in the mountain clefts,
>
> Nowhere is found a place on earth,
>
> Where man is freed from evil deeds.

Karma as Volition

A.VI. 63

It is volition (cetanā) that I call 'Karma' (action). Having willed, one acts by body, speech, and mind.

There are actions (kamma) ripening in hells… ripening in the animal kingdom… ripening in the domain of ghosts… ripening amongst men… ripening in heavenly worlds.

The result of actions (vipāka) is of three kinds: ripening in the present life, in the next life, or in future lives.

Inheritance of Deeds (Karma)

A.X. 206

All beings are the owners of their deeds (kamma, Skr: karma), the heirs of their deeds: their deeds are the womb from which they sprang, with their deeds they are bound up, their deeds are their refuge. Whatever deeds they do—good or evil—of such they will be the heirs.

A. III. 33

And wherever the beings spring into existence, there their deeds will ripen; and wherever their deeds ripen, there they will earn the fruits of those deeds, be it in this life, or be it in the next life, or be it in any other future life.

S. XXII. 99

There will come a time when the mighty ocean will dry up, vanish, and be no more. There will come a time when the mighty earth will be devoured by fire, perish, and be no more. But yet there will be no end to the suffering of beings, who, obstructed by ignorance, and ensnared by craving, are hurrying and hastening through this round of rebirths.

Craving (taṇhā), however, is not the only cause of evil action, and thus of all the suffering and misery produced thereby in this and the next life; but wherever there is craving, there, dependent on craving, may arise envy, anger, hatred, and many other evil things productive of suffering and misery. And all these selfish, life-affirming impulses and actions, together with the various kinds of misery produced thereby here or thereafter, and even all the five groups of phenomena constituting life—everything is ultimately rooted in blindness and ignorance (avijjā).

Karma

The second Noble Truth serves also to explain the causes of the seeming injustices in nature, by teaching that nothing in the world can come into existence without reason or cause, and that not only our latent tendencies, but our whole destiny, all weal and woe, result from causes (Karma), which we have to seek partly in this life, partly in former states of existence.

These causes are the life-affirming activities (kamma, Skr: karma) produced by body, speech and mind. Hence it is this threefold action (kamma) that determines the character and destiny of all beings. Exactly defined Karma denotes those good and evil volitions (kusala-akusala-cetanā), together with rebirth. Thus existence, or better the Process of Becoming (bhava), consists of an active and conditioning 'Karma Process' (kamma-bhava), and of its result, the 'Rebirth Process' (upapatti-bhava).

Here, too, when considering Karma, one must not lose sight of the impersonal nature (anattatā) of existence. In the case of a storm-swept sea, it is not an identical wave that hastens over the surface of the ocean, but it is the rising and falling of quite different masses of water. In the same way it should be understood that there are no real Ego-entities hastening through the ocean of rebirth, but merely life-waves, which, according to their nature and activities (good or evil), manifest themselves here as men, there as animals, and elsewhere as invisible beings.

Once more the fact may be emphasized here that correctly speaking, the term 'Karma' signifies only the aforementioned kinds of action themselves, and does not mean or include their results.

For further details about Karma see Fund. and B. Dict.

New Words and Expressions

abysses of the hells	地狱深渊
activities / æk'tivitiz / *n.*	业
animal kingdom	畜生道；傍生趣
be dependent on	以……为缘；依赖于
Birth / bɜːθ / *n.*	生
bodily impression	身触
body, speech, and mind	身口意
causal relation	因果关系
cause / kɔːz / *n.*	因；原因；事业
causes / 'kɔːzəz / *n.*	业
cling (to) / klɪŋ / *vi.*	执取；执着；附着；坚持
Clinging / 'klɪŋɪŋ / *n.*	取
condition / kən'dɪʃn / *n.*	缘；条件；
vt.	决定；以……为条件
Craving for (Eternal) Existence	有爱；贪有

Craving for Self-Annihilation	无有爱；断灭贪
Decay and Death / *n.*	老死
deeds / diːdz / *n.*	业；行为；行动
delusive / dɪ'luːsɪv / *adj.*	迷惑的
depend on…	以……为缘；依赖于
dissension / dɪ'senʃn / *n.*	纠纷；意见不合
domain of ghosts	鬼道；鬼趣
Ego / 'iːgəʊ / *n.*	我；自我
Eternity-Belief	常见
Feeling / 'fiːlɪŋ / *n.*	受
Fine-material Existence	色界
fruits / fruːts / *n.*	果
Future Karma-Results	未来的业果（业报）
future life	未来世；来世；来生
good and evil volitions	善不善思
heavenly worlds	天道；天趣
hell / hel / *n.*	地狱
Immaterial Existence	无色界
Inheritance of Deeds (Karma)	业行之承负
Karma / 'kaːmə / *n.*	业
Karma Process	业有
Karma-Result	业果；业报
life-affirming	执着生命的
Lust / lʌst / *n.*	贪；强烈的欲望
mass of suffering	苦蕴
men / men / *n.*	人；人道 man 的复数形式
misery / 'mɪzərɪ / *n.*	痛苦；不幸
Origin of Craving	贪爱之集
pleasant, unpleasant or indifferent	苦、乐或不苦不乐
Present Karma-Results	现生业果（业报）
present life	现世；今生
Process of Becoming	有

reason / 'riːzn / *n.*	因；理由；动机
Rebirth / ˌriː'bɜːθ / *n.*	再生
Rebirth Process	转生的过程
result / rɪ'zʌlt / *n.*	果；结果
ripen / 'raɪpən / *vi.*	成熟；异熟
sense objects	尘；境；感官对象
Sensual Craving	爱欲；欲贪
sensuous / 'senʃuəs / *adj.*	感觉（上）的；感官的
spring / sprɪŋ / *vi.*	生长；涌出
take root	住；生根
the Belief in Annihilation	断见
the Noble Truth of The Origin of Suffering	集圣谛
twelve links	十二支
visual objects	色尘；色
womb / wuːm / *n.*	子宫；发源地
	执着于无（断见）

Grammar

课文中出现的倒装句，可分为两类：

1. 完全倒装，即把句子谓语全部置于主语之前。

2. 部分倒装，即把句子部分谓语（助动词或者情态动词）置于句子主语之前。

例如：

This am I not; …（完全倒装）

Inconceivable is the beginning of this Saṃsāra; …（完全倒装）

Long have you been caught as robbers, or highway men or adulterers.（部分倒装）

Thus arises this whole mass of suffering.（完全倒装）

On clinging depends the process of becoming; on the process of becoming depends birth ….（完全倒装）

Nowhere is found a place on earth where man is freed from evil deeds.（完全倒装）

Thus does the disciple dwell in contemplation of the body.（部分倒装）

※使用倒装句，是为了突出、强调某一句子成分，或是为了平衡句子结构，或是与上文相呼应。例如：讲"缘起"的一段：

On clinging depends "the process of becoming"; on "the process of becoming" depends "birth"; and dependent on birth are "Decay and Death" …

※为了更好地表现因果之间的联系和突出上下句之间的呼应，倒装句将主语（果）置于句末，并在下一句首重复同一词语；但此处，同一因素已从"果"变成了"因"。反复重复同一结构，就造成逻辑推演层层叠加，步步深入的效果，更好地表达了"缘起"的诸环节之间，依次互为因果，环环相扣的道理。

试将倒装句改为正常语序：

"The process of becoming" depends on clinging; "birth" depends on "the process of becoming"; and "Decay and Death" are dependent on "birth"…

改后的句子还是同样的意思，但正常语序的句子明显缺乏倒装句的表现力。

Exercises

1. Why do we have sensuous craving?

2. Explain the following concepts:

Feeling, lust, clinging, becoming, birth, decay, death

How do they relate to each other?

3. How do you account for the seeming injustice in the world? (e.g. some are rich, some are poor, etc.)

4. Why is everything (craving, envy, anger, hatred) "ultimately rooted in ignorance"?

5. What is Karma? How does Karma determine our lives? What can we do about our Karma? Can we change it?

6. Where does craving arise and take root?

Unit Five

The Noble Truth of the Extinction of Suffering

D.22

What, now, is the Noble Truth of the Extinction of Suffering? It is the complete fading away and extinction of this craving, its forsaking and abandonment, liberation and detachment from it.

But where may this craving vanish, where may it be extinguished? Wherever in the world there are delightful and pleasurable things, there this craving may vanish, there it may be extinguished.

S. XII. 66

Be it in the past, present, or future, whosoever of the monks or priests regards the delightful and pleasurable things in the world as impermanent (anicca), miserable (dukkha), and without a self (anattā), as diseases and cankers, it is he who overcomes craving.

Dependent Extinction of All Phenomena

S. XII. 43

And through the total fading away and extinction of Craving (taṇhā), Clinging (upādāna) is extinguished; through the extinction of clinging, the Process of Becoming (bhava) is extinguished; through the extinction of the (karmic) process of becoming, Rebirth (jāti) is extinguished; and through the extinction of rebirth, Decay and Death, sorrow, lamentation, suffering, grief and despair are extinguished. Thus comes about the extinction of this whole mass of suffering.

S. XXII. 30

Hence the annihilation, cessation and overcoming of corporeality, feeling, perception, mental formations, and consciousness: this is the extinction of suffering, the end of disease, the overcoming of old age and death.

The undulatory motion which we call a wave-and which in the ignorant spectator creates the illusion of one and the same mass of water moving over the surface of the lake-is produced and fed by the wind, and maintained by the stored-up energies. Now, after the wind has ceased, and if no fresh wind again whips up the water of the lake, the stored-up energies will gradually be consumed, and thus the whole undulatory motion will come to an end. Similarly, if fire does not get new fuel, it will, after consuming all the old fuel, become extinct.

Just in the same way this Five-Khandha-process—which in the ignorant worldling creates the illusion of an Ego-entity—is produced and fed by the life-affirming craving (taṇhā), and maintained for some time by means of the stored-up life energies. Now, after the fuel (upādāna), i.e. the craving and clinging to life, has ceased, and if no new craving impels again this Five-Khandha-process, life will continue as long as there are still life-energies stored up, but at their destruction at death, the Five-Khandha -process will reach final extinction.

Thus, Nibbāna, or 'Extinction' (Sanskrit: nirvāna; from nir +root vā to cease blowing, become extinct) may be considered under two aspects, namely as:

1. 'Extinction of Impurities' (kilesa-parinibbāna), reached at the attainment of Arahatship, or Holiness, which generally takes place during life-time; in the Suttas it is called 'saupādisesa-nibbāna', i.e. 'Nibbāna with the Groups of Existence still remaining'.

2. 'Extinction of the Five-Khandha-process' (khandha-parinibbāna), which takes place at the death of the Arahat, called in the Suttas: 'an-upādisesa-nibbāna' i.e. 'Nibbāna without the Groups remaining'.

Nibbana

A. III. 32

This, truly, is Peace, this is the Highest, namely the end of all Karma formations, the forsaking of every substratum of rebirth, the fading away of craving, detachment, extinction, Nibbāna.

A. III. 55

Enraptured with lust, enraged with anger, blinded by delusion, overwhelmed, with mind ensnared, man aims at his own ruin, at the ruin of others, at the ruin of both, and he experiences mental pain and grief.

But, if lust, anger, and delusion are given up, man aims neither at his own ruin, nor at the ruin of others, nor at the ruin of both and he experiences no mental pain and grief. Thus is Nibbāna immediate, visible in this life, inviting, attractive, and comprehensible to the wise.

S.XXXVIII.1

The extinction of greed, the extinction of hate, the extinction of delusion: this, indeed, is called Nibbāna.

The Arahat, or Holy One

A. VI. 55

And for a disciple thus freed, in whose heart dwells peace, there is nothing to be added to what has been done, and naught more remains for him to do. Just as a rock of one solid mass remains unshaken by the wind, even so neither forms, nor sounds, nor odors, nor tastes, nor contacts of any kind, neither the desired nor the undesired, can cause such a one to waver. Steadfast is his mind, gained is deliverance.

Snp. 1048

And he who has considered all the contrasts on this earth, and is no more disturbed by anything whatever in the world, the peaceful One, freed from rage, from sorrow, and from longing, he has passed beyond birth and decay.

The Immutable

Ud. VIII. 1

Truly, there is a realm, where there is neither the solid, nor the fluid, neither heat, nor motion, neither this world, nor any other world, neither sun nor moon.

This I call neither arising, nor passing away, neither standing still, nor being born, nor dying. There is neither foothold, nor development, nor any basis. This is the end of suffering.

Ud. VIII. 3

There is an Unborn, Unoriginated, Uncreated, Unformed. If there were not this Unborn, this Unoriginated, this Uncreated, this Unformed, escape from the world of the born, the originated, the created, the formed, would not be possible.

But since there is an Unborn, Unoriginated, Uncreated, Unformed, therefore is escape possible from the world of the born, the originated, the created, the formed.

The Noble Truth of the Path That Leads to the Extinction of Suffering

The Two Extremes, and the Middle Path

S. LVI. 11

To give oneself up to indulgence in Sensual Pleasure, the base, common, vulgar, unholy, unprofitable; or to give oneself up to Self-mortification, the painful, unholy, unprofitable: both these two extremes, the Perfect One has avoided, and has found out the Middle Path, which makes one both to see and to know, which leads to peace, to discernment, to enlightenment, to Nibbāna.

The Eightfold Path

It is the Noble Eightfold Path, the way that leads to the extinction of suffering, namely:

1.	Right Understanding (Sammā-diṭṭhi)	III. Wisdom (Paññā)
2.	Right Thought (Sammā-saṅkappa)	
3.	Right Speech (Sammā-vācā)	I. Morality (Sīla)
4.	Right Action (Sammā-kammanta)	
5.	Right Livelihood (Sammā-ājīva)	

续表

6.	Right Effort (Sammā-vāyāma)	
7.	Right Mindfulness (Sammā-sati)	II. Concentration (Samādhi)
8.	Right Concentration (Sammā-samādhi)	

This is the Middle Path which the Perfect One has found out, which makes one both see and know, which leads to peace, to discernment, to enlightenment, to Nibbāna.

The Noble Eightfold Path (Ariya-aṭṭhaṅgikamagga)

The figurative expression 'Path' or 'Way' has been sometimes misunderstood as implying that the single factors of that Path have to be taken up for practice, one after the other, in the order given. In that case, Right Understanding, i.e. the full penetration of Truth, would have to be realized first, before one could think of developing Right Thought, or of practising Right Speech, etc. But in reality the three factors (3~5) forming the section 'Morality' (Sīla) have to be perfected first; after that one has to give attention to the systematic training of mind by practising the three factors (6~8) forming the section 'Concentrations' (samādhi); only after that preparation, man's character and mind will be capable of reaching perfection in the first two factors (1~2) forming the section of 'Wisdom' (Paññā).

An initial minimum of Right Understanding, however, is required at the very start, because some grasp of the facts of suffering, etc., is necessary to provide convincing reasons, and an incentive, for a diligent practice of the Path. A measure of Right Understanding is also required for helping the other Path factors to fulfil intelligently and efficiently their individual functions in the common task of liberation. For that reason, and to emphasize the importance of that factor, Right Understanding has been given the first place in the Noble Eightfold Path.

This initial understanding of the Dhamma, however, has to be gradually developed, with the help of the other Path factors, until it reaches finally that highest clarity of Insight (vipassanā) which is the immediate condition for entering the four Stages of Holiness (see" The Noble Ones") and for attaining Nibbāna.

Right Understanding is therefore the beginning as well as the culmination of the Noble Eightfold Path.

M. 139

Free from pain and torture is this path, free from groaning and suffering: it is the perfect path.

Dhp. 274-75

Truly, like this path there is no other path to the purity of insight. If you follow this path, you will put an end to suffering.

Dhp. 276

But each one has to struggle for himself, the Perfect Ones have only pointed out the way.

M. 26

Give ear then, for the Deathless is found. I reveal, I set forth the Truth. As I reveal it to you, so act! And that supreme goal of the holy life, for the sake of which sons of good families rightly go forth from home to the homeless state: this you will, in no long time, in this very life, make known to yourself, realize, and make your own.

New Words and Expressions

abandonment / ə'bændənmənt / n.　　　抛弃；放纵
annihilation / ə,naɪə'leɪʃn / n.　　　断灭 灭绝；消灭
base / beɪs / adj.　　　卑鄙的；低劣的
cessation / se'seɪʃn / n.　　　灭；停止；中止；中断

concentration / ˌkɒnsn'treɪʃn / *n.*	定
dependent / dɪ'pendənt / *adj.*	依靠的；从属的；取决于……的；
n.	依赖他人者；受赡养者
Dependent Extinction	缘灭
detachment / dɪ'tætʃmənt / *n.*	无著；无住；分离
diligent / 'dɪlɪdʒənt / *adj.*	勤奋的；精进的
discernment / dɪ'sɜːnmənt / *n.*	有智；识别；洞察力
enrage / ɪn'reɪdʒ / *vt.*	使暴怒
enrapture / ɪn'ræptʃə(r) / *vt.*	使狂喜
Extinction / ɪk'stɪŋkʃn / *n.*	寂灭
Extinction of Impurities	不净（烦恼）之灭尽
Extinction of the Five-Khandha-process	五蕴之灭尽
extinguish / ɪk'stɪŋgwɪʃ / *vt.*	使熄灭；扑灭；使不复存在
factor / 'fæktə(r) / *n.*	道支；因素；要素
fading away	逐渐消失
foothold / 'fʊthəʊld / *n.*	立足处；据点
forsaking / fə'seikɪŋ /	放弃；断念；forsake 的动名词
four Stages of Holiness / *n.*	四种果位
groan / grəʊn / *vi.*	呻吟；受折磨
Holiness / 'həʊlɪnəs / *n.*	圣
Holy One	圣者：佛陀、阿罗汉
immutable / ɪ'mjuːtəbl / *adj.*	常；不变的
incentive / ɪn'sentɪv / *n.*	动机
indulgence / ɪn'dʌldʒəns / *n.*	沉湎；放纵
Insight / 'ɪnsaɪt / *n.*	观；毗婆舍那
Middle Path / *n.*	中道
miserable / 'mɪzrəbl / *adj.*	苦；痛苦的；悲惨的
Morality / mə'ræləti / *n.*	戒
naught / nɔːt / *n.*	无；零
Nibbāna with the Groups of Existence Still Remaining	有余涅槃
Nibbāna without the Groups (of Existence) Remaining	无余涅槃

Noble Eightfold Path		八正道
Noble Truth of the Extinction of Suffering		灭谛
overcome / ˌəʊvəˈkʌm /	*vt.*	舍离；克服；胜过
peace / piːs /	*n.*	寂静
penetration / ˌpenɪˈtreɪʃn /	*n.*	彻底洞悉；完全洞察
practice / ˈpræktɪs /	*n. / v.*	修习；实践；练习
rage / reɪdʒ /	*n.*	嗔；愤怒
realm / relm /	*n.*	界；领域；范围
reveal / rɪˈviːl /	*vt.*	展现；揭示
Right Action		正业
Right Concentration		正定
Right Effort		正精进
Right Livelihood		正命
Right Mindfulness		正念
Right Speech		正语
Right Thought		正思维
Right Understanding		正见
ruin / ˈruːɪn /	*n. / vt.*	毁灭；毁坏
Sensual Pleasure		欲乐
spectator / spekˈteitə /	*n.*	观众；旁观者
steadfast / ˈstedfɑːst /	*adj.*	坚定的；不动摇的
substratum / ˈsʌbˌstreɪtəm /	*n.*	基础；根据；底层
supreme / suːˈpriːm /	*adj.*	至高的；极度的
Sutta /	*n.*	经；契经；修多罗
the Third Truth		第三圣谛
Two Extremes		两边
undulatory / ˈʌndjʊlətərɪ /	*adj.*	波动的；起伏的
unprofitable / ʌnˈprɒfɪtəbl /	*adj.*	无利益的；无用的
vanish / ˈvænɪʃ /	*vi.*	消失
vulgar / ˈvʌlɡə(r) /	*adj.*	低俗的
Wisdom / ˈwɪzdəm /	*n.*	慧

Grammar

《佛言》中使用了很多强调句（it is … that…），其结构是：

It is（was）+ 被强调部分（主语、宾语或状语）+ that（who）…

一般来说，被强调部分指人时，用 who，其他情况用 that，美国英语中则常用 which，但 that，which 也可用来指人。

例如：

It is volition that I call "Karma"（action）.（强调宾语）

我说思为"业"。

It is through not understanding, not realizing four things, that I, Disciples, as well as you, had to wander so long through this round of rebirths.（强调状语）

因不觉知、不通达四种法，我与汝等如是长久流转于轮回。

Hence it is this threefold action（kamma）that determines the character and destiny of all beings.（强调主语）

因此，是此三业决定了众生的特性和命运。

It is concord that he spreads by his words.（强调宾语）。

他以言传播的是和合。

It is through the simple act of reciting this formula three times that one declares oneself a Buddhist.（强调状语）

只要三诵此誓词，即可宣布自己为佛教徒。

Of these again, it is volition which, being a principal 'formative' factor, is particularly characteristic of the Group of Formations, and therefore serves to exemplify it in the passage given above.（强调主语）

其中，"思"作为首要的"造作"因素，又是"行蕴"的典型代表。（p.12）

It is craving, which gives rise to fresh rebirth, and, bound up with pleasure and lust, now here, now there, finds ever-fresh delight.（强调主语）

是爱导致了再生，它有俱喜贪，到处不断寻求新的欲乐。

It is correct to say that not only all the sankhaaras（= sankhata-dhamma）, but that all the dhammas（including the asankhata-dhamma）lack an Ego（an-attaa）.（强调主语）

说诸行无我，且诸法也无我，这是正确的。

It is my Self that feels, my Self that has the faculty of feeling.（强调主语）

是我之自我在感受，是我之自我有感受的能力。

It is by a mere figure of speech that one says: "I go", "I stand" and so forth'.（强调状语）

人们说"我走"，"我站立"，这仅仅是个比喻罢了。

"形式主语"与强调句在结构上很相似，但也很容易区别：

1. 形式主语"it"指代的是一个"that"从句，本身意思完整，而强调句中被强调的部分只是主语、宾语或状语等句子成分，本身意思不完整。

2. "强调句"复原为正常语序后，"it"和"that（which, who）"都要去掉，而形式主语"it"取消后，"that"必须保留。

例如：

It is untrue that you have not been.（形式主语）

That you have not been is untrue.（正常语序）

说你过去不存在是不正确的。

It is he who overcomes craving.（强调句）

He overcomes craving.（正常语序）他战胜了贪爱。

另外，"强调句"一般可以复原为正常语序。而"形式主语"句则往往无法复原，如复原，则很不自然。

例如：

And it is impossible that a being possessed of right understanding should regard anything as the Self.（形式主语）

That a being possessed of right understanding should regard anything as the Self is impossible.

具足正见之有情，不视任何法为我。

And it is impossible that any one can explain the passing out of one existence, and the entering into a new existence, or the growth, increase and development of consciousness, independently of corporeality, feeling, perception, and mental formations.（形式主语）

若离于色受想行而施设命之死生，识之生长，增益，广大者，无有是处。

Exercises

1. How is suffering extinguished?
2. Explain how the extinction of one of the following leads to the extinction of the next:

   Craving, clinging, becoming, birth, decay, death

3. In what way(s) is life similar to a wave?

4. What is the Middle Path? How is it different from the two extremes? And where does it lead to?

5. Name the eight factors of the Path, and explain how they relate to each other.

6. Why is Right Understanding placed at the beginning of the Eightfold Path? Why is Right Understanding "the beginning as well as culmination"?

Unit Six

FIRST FACTOR

Right Understanding
(Sammā-diṭṭhi)

D.24

What, now, is Right Understanding?

Understanding the Four Truths

1. To understand suffering; 2. to understand the origin of suffering; 3. to understand the extinction of suffering; 4. to understand the path that leads to the extinction of suffering. This is called Right Understanding.

Understanding Merit and Demerit

M. 9

Again, when the noble disciple understands what is karmically wholesome, and the root of wholesome karma, what is karmically unwholesome, and the root of unwholesome karma, then he has Right Understanding.

What, now, is 'karmically unwholesome' (akusala)?

1.	Destruction of living beings is karmically unwholesomex	Bodily Action (kāya-kamma)
2.	Stealing is karmically unwholesome	
3.	Unlawful sexual intercourse is karmically unwholesome	
4.	Lying is karmically unwholesome	Verbal Action (vacī-kamma)
5.	Tale-bearing is karmically unwholesome	
6.	Harsh language is karmically unwholesome	
7.	Frivolous talk is karmically unwholesome	
8.	Covetousness is karmically unwholesome	Mental Action (mano-kamma)
9.	Ill-will is karmically unwholesome	
10.	Wrong views are karmically unwholesome.	

These ten are called 'Evil Courses of Action' (akusala-kammapatha).

And what are the roots of unwholesome karma? Greed (lobha) is a root of unwholesome karma; Hatred (dosa) is a root of unwholesome karma; Delusion (moha) is a root of unwholesome karma.

Therefore, I say, these demeritorious actions are of three kinds: either due to greed, or due to hatred, or due to delusion.

As 'karmically unwholesome' (a-kusala) is considered every volitional act of body, speech, or mind, which is rooted in greed, hatred, or delusion. It is regarded as akusala, i.e. unwholesome or unskillful, as it produces evil and painful results in this or some future existence. The state of will or volition is really that which counts as action (kamma). It may manifest itself as action of the body, or speech; if it does not manifest itself outwardly, it is counted as mental action.

The state of greed (lobha), as also that of hatred (dosa), is always accompanied by ignorance (or delusion; moha), this latter being the primary root of all evil. Greed and hatred, however, cannot co-exist in one and the same moment of consciousness.

What, now, is 'karmically wholesome' (kusala)?

1.	To abstain from killing is karmically wholesome	Bodily Action (kāya-kamma)
2.	To abstain from stealing is karmically wholesome	
3.	To abstain from unlawful sexual intercourse is karmically wholesome	
4.	To abstain from lying is karmically wholesome	Verbal Action (vacī-kamma)
5.	To abstain from tale-bearing is karmically wholesome	
6.	To abstain from harsh language is karmically wholesome	
7.	To abstain from frivolous talk is karmically wholesome	
8.	Absence of covetousness is karmically wholesome	Mental Action (mano-kamma)
9.	Absence of ill-will is karmically wholesome	
10.	Right understanding is karmically wholesome	

These ten are called 'Good Courses of Action' (kusala-kamma-patha).

And what are the roots of wholesome karma? Absence of greed (a-lobha = unselfishness) is a root of wholesome karma; absence of hatred (a-dosa = kindness) is a root of wholesome karma; absence of delusion (a-moha = wisdom) is a root of wholesome karma.

Understanding the Three Characteristics (Ti-lakkhaṇa)

S. XXII. 51

Again, when one understands that corporeality, feeling, perception, mental formations and consciousness are transient (subject to suffering, and without a self), also in that case one possesses Right Understanding.

Unprofitable Questions

M. 63

Should anyone say that he does not wish to lead the holy life under the Blessed One, unless the Blessed One first tells him whether the world is eternal or temporal, finite or infinite: whether the life-principle is identical with the body or something different; whether the Perfect One continues after death, etc.—such a one would die ere the Perfect One could tell him all this.

It is as if a man were pierced by a poisoned arrow and his friends, companions or near relations should send for a surgeon; but that man should say: 'I will not have this arrow pulled out, until I know, who the man is that has wounded me: whether he is a noble man, a priest, a tradesman, or a servant'; or: 'what his name is, and to what family he belongs'; or: 'whether he is tall, or short, or of medium height'. Truly, such a man would die ere he could adequately learn all this.

Snp. 592

Therefore, the man who seeks his own welfare, should pull out this arrow—this arrow of lamentation, pain, and sorrow.

M. 63

For, whether the theory exists, or whether it does not exist, that the world is eternal, or temporal, or finite or infinite—yet certainly, there exists birth, there exists decay, there exist death, sorrow, lamentation, pain, grief, and despair, the extinction of which, attainable even in this present life, I make known unto you.

Five Fetters (Saṃyojana)

M. 64

Suppose for instance, that there is an unlearned worldling, void of regard for holy men, ignorant of the teaching of holy men, untrained in the noble doctrine. And his heart is possessed and overcome by Self-illusion, by Skepticism, by Attachment to mere Rule and Ritual, by Sensual Lust, and by Ill-will; and how to free himself from these things, he does not in reality know.

Self-Illusion (sakkāya-diṭṭhi) may reveal itself as:

1. 'Eternalism': bhava- or sassata- diṭṭhi, lit. 'Eternity-Belief', i.e. the belief that one's Ego, Self or Soul exists independently of the material body, and continues even after the dissolution of the latter.

2. 'Annihilationism': vibhava- or uccheda-diṭṭhi, lit. 'Annihilation-Belief', i.e. the materialistic belief that this present life constitutes the Ego, and hence that it is annihilated at the death of the material body.

For the ten 'Fetters' (saṃyojana), see 'The Ten Fetters'.

Unwise Considerations

M. 2

Not knowing what is worthy of consideration, and what is unworthy of consideration, he considers the unworthy, and not the worthy.

And unwisely he considers thus: 'Have I been in the past? Or, have I not been in the past? What have I been in the past? How have I been in the past? From what state into what state did I change in the past?

Shall I be in the future? Or, shall I not be in the future? What shall I be in the future? How shall I be in the future? From what state into what state shall I change in the future?'

And the present also fills him with doubt; 'Am I? Or, am I not? What am I? How am I? This being, whence has it come? Whither will it go?'

The Six Views about the Self

And with such unwise considerations, he adopts one or other of the six views, and it becomes his conviction and firm belief: 'I have a Self', or: 'I have no Self', or: 'With the Self I perceive the Self', or: 'With that which is no Self, I perceive the Self'; or: 'With the Self I perceive that which is no Self'. Or, he adopts the following view: 'This my Self, which can think and feel, and which, now here, now there, experiences the fruit of good and evil deeds: this my Self is permanent, stable, eternal, not subject to change, and will thus eternally remain the same'.

M. 22

If there really existed the Self, there would also exist something which belonged to the Self. As, however, in truth and reality neither the Self, nor anything belonging to the Self, can be found, is it not therefore really an utter fools 'doctrine to say: 'This is the world, this am I; after death I shall be permanent, persisting, and eternal'?

M. 2

These are called mere views, a thicket of views, a puppet-show of views, a toil of views, a snare of views; and ensnared in the fetter of views the ignorant worldling will not be freed from rebirth, from decay, and from death, from sorrow, pain, grief and despair; he will not be freed, I say, from suffering.

Wise Considerations

The learned and noble disciple, however, who has regard for holy men, knows the teaching of holy men, is well trained in the noble doctrine; he understands what is worthy of consideration, and what is unworthy. And knowing this, he considers the worthy, and not the unworthy. What suffering is, he wisely considers; what the origin of suffering is, he wisely considers; what the extinction of suffering is, he wisely considers; what the path is that leads to the extinction of suffering, he wisely considers.

New Words and Expressions

absence of ...   无……

Annihilationism / ə,naɪəˈleɪʃənɪzəm / *n.*   断见；断灭论

Attachment to Mere Rule and Ritual   戒禁取；对戒和仪轨的执着

attainable / əˈteɪnəbl / *adj.*   可证的；可得的

Bodily Action   身业

conviction and firm belief   定解

covetousness / ˈkʌvitəsnis / *n.*   悭贪

delusion / dɪˈluːʒn / *n.*   痴

eternal / ɪˈtɜːnl / *adj.*   永恒的

Eternalism / ɪˈtɜːnəlɪzəm / *n.*   常见

experience the fruit of good and evil deeds   受善恶业的果报

fetter / ˈfetə(r) / *n.*   结；系缚；桎梏

First Factor   第一道支

Five Fetters   五下分结

free...from...	使……从……解脱
frivolous talk	绮语
Good Courses of Action	善业道
harsh Language	恶口；粗恶语
ill-will	嗔；嗔恚；恶意
karmically unwholesome	不善业
karmically wholesome	善业
killing / 'kɪlɪŋ / n.	杀生
life-principle	命
lying / 'laɪŋ / n.	妄语
manifest / 'mænɪfest / vt.	显现；现行
material body	肉身；肉体
Mental Action	意业
mere views	戏论
noble man	刹帝利
Scepticism / 'skeptɪsɪzəm / n.	疑
Self-illusion	身见
Sensual Lust	欲贪
servant / n.	首陀罗
Six Views about the Self	六种我见
stealing / 'stiːlɪŋ / n.	偷盗
subject to suffering	苦的
tale-bearing	两舌
the Blessed One	世尊
the Four Truths / n.	四谛
the noble doctrine	圣人教法；圣人教理
Three Characteristics	三法印
tradesman / 'treɪdzmən / n.	吠舍
transient / 'trænzɪənt / n.	无常
unlawful sexual intercourse	邪淫

unlearned / ʌn'ləːnid / *adj.*	无学问的
unlearned worldling	无知的凡夫
Unprofitable Questions	不记说；无益的问题
unwise considerations	非理作意
Verbal Action	语业
wise considerations	如理作意
without a Self	无我

Grammar

《佛言》中有大量的问句，可分为三种情况：

1. 设问句：在篇（段）首的问句，用自问自答的形式来提示主题。例如：

What, now, is the Noble Truth of Suffering? 何为苦圣谛？

What, now, is Consciousness? 何为 "识" ？

2. 反问句：用来指出某种观点的不合常理或荒谬性，或提醒读者（听者）注意显而易见的道理，事实。例如：

反问句实际上已经包含了答案——肯定反问句暗示否定的答案，而否定反问句则隐含了肯定的答案。

A. 肯定反问句：主要用于破斥论敌的邪见，一般是用 "归谬法"，即以对方观点为前提，引导出一个不合理的结论。例如：

...now, if after the extinction of feelings, no feeling whatever exists there, is it possible to say, "This am I"?

答案是否定的："If that is the case, it is not possible to say 'This am I'"。如果是那种情况，就无法说 "这是我"。

B. 否定反问句：主要用于指出显而易见的道理，事实。例如：

"And did the thought never come to you that you are also subject to decay…"?

难道你从未想过你也会变老吗？隐含的答案是：你肯定想到过你也会变老。

Is it not therefore really an utter fool's doctrine to say: "This is the world, this am I: after death I shall be permanent, persisting, and eternal"?

如果有人断言："此是世界，此是我：我死之后可得常驻，常恒，久远"，这难道不是愚蠢之极的见解吗？隐含的答案是：这很明显是个愚蠢的见解。

注意：反问句在现代英语中一般否定助动词。

"Did you never see…the corpse of a man…"?

在现代英语中一般要说："Didn't you ever see…"

再如：Didn't your mother ever tell you not to talk with your mouth full?

你妈妈没告诉过你吃饭时不要说话吗？

3. 选择问句：既不是肯定句，也不是否定句。例如：

Which do you think is more: the stream of blood that, through your being beheaded, have flowed upon this long way, these or the waters of the four oceans?

这个问句也隐含了一个答案：

The stream of blood is more than the waters of the four oceans.

（在往世轮回中你被杀头流的血比四海的水还要多。）

修辞性问句的使用，不仅使论述具有很强的论战性，而且还是叙述主体与读者交流的积极手段。通过修辞性问句，读者的批判性思维被唤起，随叙述主体加入推论的过程，被动的阅读变成主动的诘问和质疑。

Exercises

1. List all the wholesome Karma, and classify them into the three groups of actions.
2. How do the three groups of actions relate to each other?
3. Give one example of the unprofitable questions. Why are the questions unprofitable?
4. What are the ten fetters? What will happen if you are able to overcome them?

Unit Seven

The Sotāpanna or 'Stream-Enterer'

And by thus considering, three fetters vanish, namely; Self-illusion, Scepticism, and Attachment to mere Rule and Ritual.

M. 22

But those disciples, in whom these three fetters have vanished, they all have 'entered the Stream' (sotāpanna).

Dhp. 178

> More than any earthly power,
> More than all the joys of heaven,
> More than rule o'er all the world,
> Is the Entrance to the Stream.

The Ten Fetters (Saṃyojana)

There are ten 'Fetters'—saṃyojana—by which beings are bound to the wheel of existence. They are:

Self-Illusion (sakkāya-diṭṭhi)

Scepticism (vicikicchā)

Attachment to mere Rule and Ritual (sīlabbata-parāmāsa)

Sensual Lust (kāma-rāga)

Ill-Will (vyāpāda)

Craving for Fine-Material Existence (rūpa-rāga)

Craving for Immaterial Existence (arūpa-rāga)

Conceit (māna)

Restlessness (uddhacca)

Ignorance (avijjā)

The Noble Ones (Ariya-puggala)

One who is freed from the first three Fetters is called a 'Stream-Enterer' (in Pali: Sotāpanna) i.e. one who has entered the stream leading to Nibbaana. He has unshakable faith in the Buddha, Dhamma, and Sangha, and is incapable of breaking the five Moral Precepts. He will be reborn seven times, at the utmost, and not in a state lower than the human world.

One who has overcome the fourth and the fifth Fetters in their grosser form, is called a Sakadāgāmi, lit. 'Once-Returner' i.e. he will be reborn only once more in the Sensuous Sphere (kāma-loka), and thereafter reach Holiness.

An Anāgāmi, lit. 'Non-Returner', is wholly freed from the first five Fetters which bind one to rebirth in the Sensuous Sphere; after death, while living in the Fine-Material Sphere (rūpa-loka), he will reach the goal.

An Arahat, i.e. the perfectly 'Holy One', is freed from all the ten Fetters.

Each of the aforementioned four stages of Holiness consists of the 'Path' (magga) and the 'Fruition', e.g. 'Path of Stream Entry' (sotāpatti-magga) and 'Fruition of Stream Entry' (sotāpatti-phala). Accordingly there are eight types, or four pairs, of 'Noble Individuals' (ariya-puggala).

The 'Path' consists of the single moment of entering the respective attainment. By 'Fruition' are meant those moments of consciousness which follow immediately thereafter as the result of the 'Path', and which under certain circumstances, may repeat innumerable times during life-time.

For further details, see B. Dict.: ariya-puggala, sotāpanna, etc.

Mundane and Supermundane Right Understanding

M.117

Therefore, I say, Right Understanding is of two kinds:

1. The view that alms and offerings are not useless; that there is fruit and result, both of good and bad actions; that there are such things as this life, and the next life; that father and mother, as also spontaneously born beings (in the heavenly worlds), are no mere words; that there are in the world monks and priests, who are spotless and perfect, who can explain this life and the next life, which they themselves have understood: this is called the 'Mundane Right Understanding' (lokiya-sammā-diṭṭhi), which yields worldly fruits and brings good results.

2. But whatsoever there is of wisdom, of penetration, of right understanding conjoined with the 'Path' (of the Sotāpanna, Sakadāgāmi, Anāgāmi, or Arahat)—the mind being turned away from the world and conjoined with the path, the holy path being pursued: this is called the 'Supermundane Right Understanding' (lokuttara-sammā-diṭṭhi), which is not of the world, but is supermundane and conjoined with the path.

Thus, there are two kinds of the Eightfold Path:

(1) The 'mundane' (lokiya), practised by the 'Worldling' (puthujjana), i.e. by all those who have not yet reached the first stage of Holiness.

(2) The 'supermundane' (lokuttara) practised by the 'Noble Ones' (ariya-puggala).

Conjoined with Other Steps

Now, in understanding wrong understanding as wrong and right understanding as right, one practises 'Right Understanding' (1st factor); and in making efforts to overcome wrong understanding, and to arouse right understanding, one practises 'Right Effort' (6th factor); and in overcoming wrong understanding with attentive mind, and dwelling with attentive mind in the possession of right understanding one practises 'Right Mindfulness' (7th factor). Hence, there are three things that accompany and follow upon right understanding, namely: Right Understanding, Right Effort, and Right Mindfulness.

Free from All Theories

M. 72

Now, if any one should put the question, whether I admit any theory at all, he should be answered thus: The Perfect One is free from any theory, for the Perfect One has understood what corporeality is, and how it arises and passes away. He has understood what feeling is, and how it arises and passes away. He has understood what perception is, and how it arises and passes away. He has understood what the mental formations are, and how they arise and pass away. He has understood what consciousness is, and how it arises and passes away. Therefore I say, the Perfect One has won complete deliverance through the extinction, fading-away, disappearance, rejection, and getting rid of all opinions and conjectures, of all inclination to the vain-glory of 'I' and 'mine'.

The Three Characteristics

A. III. 134

Whether Perfect Ones (Buddhas) appear in the world, or whether Perfect Ones do not appear in the world, it still remains a firm condition, an immutable fact and fixed law: that all formations are impermanent (anicca), that all formations are subject to suffering (dukkha); that everything is without a Self (an-attā).

In Pali: Sabbe saṅkhārā aniccā, Sabbe saṅkhārā dukkhā, Sabbe dhammā anattā.

The word 'saṅkhārā' (formations) comprises here all things that are conditioned or 'formed' (saṅkhata-dhamma), i.e. all possible physical and mental constituents of existence. The word 'dhamma', however, has a still wider application and is all-embracing, as it comprises also the so-called Unconditioned ('unformed', asaṅkhata), i.e. Nibbāna.

For this reason, it would be wrong to say that all dhammas are impermanent and subject to change, for the Nibbāna-dhamma is permanent and free from change. And for the same reason, it is correct to say that not only all the saṅkhāras (=saṅkhata-dhamma), but that all the dhammas (including the asaṅkhata-dhamma) lack an Ego (an-attā).

S. XXII. 94

A corporeal phenomenon, a feeling, a perception, a mental formation, a consciousness, which is permanent and persistent, eternal and not subject to change, such a thing the wise men in this world do not recognize; and I also say that there is no such thing.

A. I. 15

And it is impossible that a being possessed of right understanding should regard anything as the Self.

Views and Discussions about the Ego

D. 15

Now, if someone should say that feeling is his Self, he should be answered thus: 'There are three kinds of feeling: pleasurable, painful, and indifferent feeling. Which of these three feelings do you consider as your Self?' Because, at the moment of experiencing one of these feelings, one does not experience the other two. These three kinds of feeling are impermanent, of dependent origin, are subject to decay and dissolution, to fading-away and extinction. Whosoever, in experiencing one of these feelings, thinks that this is his Self, must after the extinction of that feeling, admit that his Self has become dissolved. And thus he will consider his Self already in this present life as impermanent, mixed up with pleasure and pain, subject to arising and passing away.

If anyone should say that feeling is not his Ego, and that his Self is inaccessible to feeling, he should be asked thus: 'Now, where there is no feeling, is it then possible to say: "This am I?"

Or, another might say: 'Feeling, indeed, is not my Self, but it also is untrue that my Self is inaccessible to feeling, for it is my Self that feels, my Self that has the faculty of feeling'. Such a one should be answered thus: 'Suppose that feeling should become altogether totally extinguished; now, if after the extinction of feeling, no feeling whatever exists there, is it then possible to say: "This am I'?"

M. 148

To say that the mind, or the mind-objects, or the mind-consciousness, constitute the Self, such an assertion is unfounded. For an arising and a passing away is seen there; and seeing the arising and passing away of these things, one would come to the conclusion that one's Self arises and passes away.

S. XII. 62

1t would be better for the unlearned worldling to regard his body, built up of the four elements, as his Self, rather than his mind. For it is evident that the body may last for a year, for two years, for three, four, five, or ten years, or even for a hundred years and more; but that which is called thought, or mind, or consciousness, arises continuously, during day and night, as one thing, and passes away as another thing.

S. XXII. 59

Therefore, whatsoever there is of corporeality, of feeling, of perception, of mental formations, of consciousness whether past, present or future, one's own or external, gross or subtle, lofty or low, far or near: of this one should understand according to reality and true wisdom: 'This does not belong to me; this am I not; this is not my Self.'

To show the impersonality and utter emptiness of existence, Visuddhi-Magga
XVI quotes the following verse:

> *Mere suffering exists, no sufferer is found,*
> *The deed is, but no doer of the deed is there.*
> *Nirvāna is, but not the man that enters it.*
> *The path is, but no traveller on it is seen'.*

New Words and Expressions

conceit / kən'siːt / *n.*	慢；骄慢
Craving for Fine-material Existence	色界爱
Craving for Immaterial Existence	无色界爱
Eightfold Path	八正道
emptiness / 'emptinis / *n.*	空性
Fine-material Sphere	色界

Formations / fɔː'meɪʃnz / *n. (pl.)*	行；造作
formed / fɔːmd / *n.*	有为法
Fruition of Stream Entry	须陀洹果；初果
immutable / ɪ'mjuːtəbl / *adj.*	不变的；永恒的
impermanent / ɪm'pɜːmənənt / *adj.*	无常的
indifferent feeling	不苦不乐受
mental formations	行蕴；心行
mind-consciousness	心识
mind-object	心法
mundane / mʌn'deɪn / *adj.*	世间的
Non-Returner	不还；阿那含
Once-Returner	一来；斯陀含
Path of Stream Entry	预流果道；须陀洹果道
Restlessness / 'restləsnəs / *n.*	掉举
sensual passion	贪爱
Sensuous Sphere	欲界
Stream Enterer	须陀洹
supermundane / ˌsuːpə'mʌndeɪn / *adj.*	出世间的
Supermundane Right Understanding	出世间的正见
The Noble Ones	圣者
the Unconditioned / ˌʌnkən'dɪʃnd / *n.*	无为法

Grammar

较多使用被动句，这是科技、哲学论著的一般特征。《佛言》中使用被动句，主要是为了客观地陈述事实，宣说哲理；被动句强调行为及其对象，而不是"动作主体"（agent of action）。

有时，被动句的动作主体也可以用介词"by"引入：

The state of greed（lobha）, as also that of hatred（dosa）, is always accompanied by igonorance（moha）.

贪（lobha）和嗔（dosa）一样，总是为痴（moha）所随。

但在更多情况下，被动句的动作主体都被省略掉了，其原因，或是动作主体不明确，或是动作主体不言自明，例如：

An Anāgami... is wholly **freed** from the first five Fetters....

阿那含已断五上分结。（动作主体是其本人）

Mere suffering exists, no sufferer is **found**.

有苦而无受苦者。（动作主体不明确）

Through the extinction of feeling, "craving" is **extinguished**.

受灭则爱灭。（动作主体不明确）

It is **regarded** as akusala, i.e., unwholesome or unskillful, as it produces evil and painful results.

它被视为不善，即有害或愚笨的，因为它会产生恶果和苦果。（动作主体不明确）

Thus, these five Groups of Existence must be wisely **penetrated**; Ignorance and Craving must be wisely **abandoned**; Tranquility and Insight must be wisely **developed**.

如是之五取蕴，应所证知而谛观察；无明与贪爱，应所证知而断除；止与观，应所证知而修习。［行为者（佛弟子）是不言自明的。］

The figurative expression "Path" or "Way" has been sometimes **misunderstood** as implying the single factors of that Path have to be taken up for practice, one after the other, in the order given.

道路或途径这种比喻的说法有时会使人误解——以为八正道的每一支必须按照给定的顺序，一支一支地次第修习。（动作主体不明确）

在被动句中，由于"行为者"的缺位，一般就没有第一人称主语（"我"）。被动句与"无我"，这常常是同一个问题的两个方面。

Exercises

1. What are the four levels of nobleness? How can a disciple attain such goals? How can a disciple "enter the stream"?

2. Is there an Ego or Self that continues after death? Why do you think people believe in the existence of Ego or Self? How do they prove the existence of an Ego or Self?

3. If there is no Ego or Self that continues after death, how do you explain the next life or rebirth?

4. Accordingly there are eight types, or four pairs, of 'Noble Individuals' (ariya-puggala).

   Please explain this sentence.

Unit Eight

Past, Present and Future

D. 9

If now, any one should ask: 'Have you been in the past, and is it untrue that you have not been? Will you be in the future, and is it untrue that you will not be? Are you, and is it untrue that you are not?' —you may reply that you have been in the past, and that it is untrue that you have not been; that you will be in the future, and that it is untrue that you will not be; that you are, and that it is untrue that you are not.

In the past only that past existence was real, but unreal the future and present existence. In the future only the future existence will be real, but unreal the past and the present existence. Now only the present existence is real, but unreal, the past and future existence.

M. 28

Verily, he who perceives the 'Dependent Origination' (paṭicca-samuppāda), perceives the truth; and he who perceives the truth, perceives the Dependent Origination.

D. 8

For just as from the cow comes milk, from milk curd, from curd butter, from butter ghee, from ghee the skim of ghee; and when it is milk, it is not counted as curd, or butter, or ghee, or skim of ghee, but only as milk; and when it is curd, it is only counted as curd: just so was my past existence at that time real, but unreal the future and present existence; and my future existence will be at that time real, but unreal the past and present existence; and my present existence is now real, but unreal the past and future existence. All these are merely popular designations and expressions, mere conventional terms of speaking, mere popular notions. The Perfect One indeed makes use of these, without however clinging to them.

S. XLIV 4

Thus, he who does not understand corporeality, feeling, perception, mental formations and consciousness according to reality (i.e. as void of a personality, or Ego) nor understands their arising, their extinction, and the way to their extinction, he is liable to believe, either that the Perfect One continues after death, or that he does not continue after death, and so forth.

The Two Extremes (Annihilation and Eternity Belief) and the Middle Doctrine

S. XII. 25

Truly, if one holds the view that the vital principle (jīva; 'Soul') is identical with this body, in that case a holy life is not possible; and if one holds the view that the vital principle is something quite different from the body, in that case also a holy life is not possible. Both these two extremes the Perfect One has avoided, and he has shown the Middle Doctrine, which says:

Dependent Origination (paṭicca-samuppāda)

S. XII. 1

On Ignorance (avijjā) depend the 'Karma-formations' (saṅkhārā).

On the Karma-formations depends 'Consciousness' (viññāṇa; starting with rebirth-consciousness in the womb of the mother).

On Consciousness depends the 'Mental and Physical Existence' (nāma-rūpa).

On the mental and physical existence depend the 'Six Sense-Organs' (saḷāyatana).

On the six sense-organs depends 'Sensorial Impression' (phassa).

On sensorial impression depends 'Feeling' (vedanā).

On feeling depends 'Craving' (taṇhā).

On craving depends 'Clinging' (upādāna).

On clinging depends the 'Process of Becoming' (bhava).

On the process of becoming (here: kamma-bhava, or karma-process) depends 'Rebirth' (jāti).

On rebirth depend 'Decay and Death' (jarā-maraṇa), sorrow, lamentation, pain, grief and despair.

Thus arises this whole mass of suffering. This is called the noble truth of the origin of suffering.

" *No god, no Brahma can be called*

The maker of this wheel of life:

Empty phenomena roll on,

Dependent on conditions all. "

(Quoted in Visuddhi-Magga XIX).

S. XII. 51

A disciple, however, in whom Ignorance (avijjā) has disappeared and wisdom arisen, such a disciple heaps up neither meritorious, nor demeritorious, nor imperturbable Karma-formations.

The term saṅkhāra has been rendered here by 'Karma Formations' because, in the context of the Dependent Origination, it refers to karmically wholesome and unwholesome volition (cetanā), or volitional activity, in short, Karma.

The threefold division of it, given in the preceding passage, comprises karmic activity in all spheres of existence, or planes of consciousness. The 'meritorious

karma-formations' extend also to the Fine-Material Sphere (rūpāvacara), while the 'imperturbable karma-formations' (aneñjābhisaṅkhāra) refer only to the Immaterial Sphere (arūpāvacara).

S. XII. 1

Thus, through the entire fading away and extinction of this 'Ignorance', the 'Karma-formations' are extinguished. Through the extinction of Karma-formations, 'Consciousness' (rebirth) is extinguished. Through the extinction of consciousness, the 'Mental and Physical Existence' is extinguished. Through the extinction of the mental and physical existence, the 'Six Sense-Organs' are extinguished. Through the extinction of the six sense-organs, 'Sensorial Impression' is extinguished. Through the extinction of sensorial impression, 'Feeling' is extinguished. Through the extinction of feeling, 'Craving' is extinguished. Through the extinction of craving, 'Clinging' is extinguished. Through the extinction of clinging, the 'Process of Becoming' is extinguished. Through the extinction of the process of becoming, 'Rebirth' is extinguished. Through the extinction of rebirth, 'Decay and Death', sorrow, lamentation, pain, grief and despair are extinguished. Thus takes place the extinction of this whole mass of suffering. This is called the noble truth of the extinction of suffering.

Rebirth-Producing Karma

M. 43

Truly, because beings, obstructed by ignorance (avijjā) and ensnared by craving (taṇhā) seek ever fresh delight, now here, now there, therefore fresh rebirth continually comes to be.

III. 33

And the action (kamma) that is done out of greed, hatred and delusion (lobha, dosa, moha), that springs from them, has its source and origin in them: this action ripens wherever one is reborn, and wherever this action ripens there one experiences the fruits of this action, be it in this life, or the next life, or in some future life.

Cessation of Karma

M. 43

However, through the fading away of ignorance, through the arising of wisdom, through the extinction of craving, no future rebirth takes place again.

A .III. 33

For the actions which are not done out of greed, hatred and delusion, which have not sprung from them, which have not their source and origin in them: such actions, through the absence of greed, hatred and delusion, are abandoned, rooted out, like a palm-tree torn out of the soil, destroyed, and not able to spring up again.

A .VIII. 12

In this respect one may rightly say of me: that I teach annihilation, that I propound my doctrine for the purpose of annihilation, and that I herein train my disciples; for certainly I do teach annihilation-the annihilation, namely, of greed, hatred and delusion, as well as of the manifold evil and unwholesome things.

The Paṭicca samuppāda, lit, the Dependent Origination, is the doctrine of the conditionality of all physical and mental phenomena, a doctrine which, together with that of Impersonality (anattā), forms the indispensable condition for the real understanding and realization of the Buddha's teaching. It shows that the various physical and mental life-processes, conventionally called personality, man, animal, etc., are not a mere play of blind chance, but the outcome of causes and conditions. Above all, the Paṭicca-samuppāda explains how the arising of rebirth and suffering is dependent upon conditions; and, in its second part, it shows how, through the removal of these conditions, all suffering must disappear. Hence, the Paṭicca-samuppāda serves to elucidate the second and the third Noble Truths, by explaining them from their very foundations upwards, and giving them a fixed philosophical form.

The following diagram shows at a glance how the twelve links of the formula extend over three consecutive existences, past, present, and future:

Past Existence	1. Ignorance (avijjā)	Karma Process (kamma-bhava) 5 causes: 1, 2, 8, 9, 10
	2. Karma-Formations (saṅkhārā)	
Present Existence	3. Consciousness (viññāṇa)	Rebirth-Process (upapatti-bhava) 5 results: 3~7
	4. Mental and Physical Existence (nāma-rūpa)	
	5. 6 Sense Organs (saḷ-āyatana)	
	6. Sense-Impression (phassa)	
	7. Feeling (vedanā)	
	8. Craving (taṇhā)	Karma Process (kamma-bhava) 5 causes: 1, 2, 8, 9, 10
	9. Clinging (upādāna)	
	10. Process of Existence (bhava)	
Future Existence	11. Rebirth (jāti)	Rebirth-Process (upapatti-bhava) 5 results: 3~7
	12. Decay and Death (jarā-maraṇa)	

The links 1~2, together with 8~10, represent the Karma-Process, containing the five karmic causes of rebirth.

The links 3~7, together with 11~12, represent the Rebirth-Process, containing the five Karma-Results.

Accordingly it is said in the Patisambhidā-Magga:

Five causes were there in past,

Five fruits we find in present life.

Five causes do we now produce,

Five fruits we reap in future life.

(Quoted in Vis. M. XVII)

For a full explanation see Fund. III and B. Dict.

New Words and Expressions

Conditionality / kən'dɪʃə'nælətɪ / *n.*	缘起性
Consciousness / 'kɒnʃəsnəs / *n.*	识
Delusion / dɪ'luːʒn / *n.*	痴
demeritorious / di,merɪ'tɔːriəs / *adj.*	不善的
demeritorious actions	不善业
Dependent Origination	缘起
Four Elements	四大
greed / griːd / *n.*	贪
grief / griːf / *n.*	忧；忧伤
hatred / 'heɪtrɪd / *n.*	嗔
impersonality / ɪm'pɜːsə'nælətɪ / *n.*	无我
imperturbable karma-formations	静业
Karma-Formations	业行
Karma-Process	业有
Mental and Physical Existence	名色
meritorious / ,merɪ'tɔːriəs / *adj.*	善的
meritorious Karma-formations	善业
Middle Doctrine	中道法
past existence	前生；过去世
popular designations and expressions	世间立言
popular notions	世俗义
Process of Becoming	有；形成的过程
Rebirth / ,riː'bɜːθ / *n.*	生；再生；轮回
Rebirth-Process	生有
Sense-Impression	触
sensorial impression	触
Six Sense-Organs	六根

sphere / sfɪə / *n.*	界
The Perfect One / *n.*	如来
Unwholesome / ˌʌnˈhəʊlsəm / *adj.*	不善的
Wholesome / ˈhəʊlsəm / *adj.*	善的

Grammar

情态动词 "should" 经常表示假设的情况，或对方可能提出的不合常理或荒谬的观点，例如：

If anyone should say that… he should be answered thus…

如果有人说……就该这样回答他……

If anyone should say that… he should be asked thus…

如果有人说……就该这样问他……

※注意： 以上例句中，"should" 的不同意义。

第一个 "should" 作为情态动词，表示意外，或者在说话人看来 "不可思议，有违常理"，常译为 "竟会" "居然"。

第二个 "should" 表示 "应该"。

※下面这两个例子也是类似第一个 "should" 的用法：

It is impossible that a being possessed of right understanding should regard anything as the Self.

一个持有正见的人竟然会认为什么东西是 "自我"，这是绝不可能的。

Suppose that feeling should become altogether totally extinguished.

设想 "受" 居然会完全彻底地消失。

※顺便提一下，《佛言》中的情态动词 "should" 很多都是从巴利原文的 "祈愿式"（opt.）动词翻译来的。

Exercises

1. What is the purpose of the "milk-cream-butter" analogy? Do you see any similarities between a "milk-cream-butter" analogy and a "past- present-future" existence?

2. In view of the "milk-cream-butter" analogy, explain why Annihilation and Eternity Believes are wrong.

3. Name the twelve links of "Dependent Origination". What is the purpose of the theory of "Dependent Origination"?

4. "Five causes were there in the past,

    Five fruits we find in present life.

    Five causes do we now produce,

    Five fruits we reap in future life."

Identify the "five causes" and "five fruits" in the above verse, in the past, present and future.

What is the relationship between the "five fruits" in the future life and the "11~12" links (Future Birth, Decay and Death)? Are they different names for the same process? If not, how are they different?

Unit Nine

SECOND FACTOR

Right Thought (Sammā-saṅkappa)

D. 22

What, now, is Right Thought?

Thought free from lust (nekkhamma-saṅkappa).

Thought fr ee from ill-will (avyāpāda-saṅkappa).

Thought free from cruelty (avihiṃsā-saṅkappa).

This is called Right Thought.

Mundane and Supermundane Right Thought

M. 117

Now, Right Thought, I tell you, is of two kinds:

1. Thought free from lust, from ill-will, and from cruelty—this is called 'Mundane Right Thought' (lokiya-sammā-saṅkappa), which yields worldly fruits and brings good results.

2. But, whatsoever there is of thinking, considering, reasoning, thought, ratiocination, application—the mind being holy, being turned away from the world, and conjoined with the path, the holy path being pursued—these

'verbal operations' of the mind (vacī-saṅkhārā) are called the 'Supermundane Right Thought' (lokuttara-sammā-saṅkappa), which is not of the world, but is supermundane, and conjoined with the path.

Conjoined with other Factors

Now, in understanding wrong thought as wrong, and right thought as right, one practises Right Understanding (1st factor); and in making efforts to overcome evil thought and to arouse right thought, one practises Right Effort (6th factor); and in overcoming evil thought with attentive mind, and dwelling with attentive mind in possession of right thought, one practises Right Mindfulness (7th factor). Hence there are three things that accompany and follow upon Right Thought, namely: Right Understanding, Right Effort, and Right Mindfulness.

THIRD FACTOR

Right Speech(Sammā-vācā)

What now, is Right Speech?

Abstaining from Lying

A. X. 176

1. Herein someone avoids lying and abstains from it. He speaks the truth, is devoted to the truth, reliable, worthy of confidence, not a deceiver of men. Being at a meeting, or amongst people, or in the midst of his relatives, or in a society, or in the king's court, and called upon and asked as witness to tell what he knows, he answers, if he knows nothing: 'I know nothing', and if he knows, he answers: 'I know'; if he has seen nothing, he answers: 'I have seen nothing', and if he has seen, he answers: 'I have seen'. Thus he never knowingly speaks a lie, either for the sake of his own advantage, or for the sake of another person's advantage, or for the sake of any advantage whatsoever.

Abstaining from Tale-bearing

2. He avoids tale-bearing, and abstains from it. What he has heard here, he does not repeat there, so as to cause dissension there; and what he has heard there, he does not repeat here, so as to cause dissension here. Thus he unites those that are divided; and those that are united, he encourages. Concord gladdens him, he delights and rejoices in concord; and it is concord that he spreads by his words.

Abstaining from Harsh Language

3. He avoids harsh language, and abstains from it. He speaks such words as are gentle, soothing to the ear, loving, such words as go to the heart, and are courteous, friendly, and agreeable to many.

In Majjhima-Nikāya No. 21, the Buddha says: 'Even, O monks, should robbers and murderers saw through your limbs and joints, whosoever should give way to anger thereat would not be following my advice. For thus ought you to train yourselves:

'Undisturbed shall our mind remain, no evil words shall escape our lips; friendly and full of sympathy shall we remain, with heart full of love, and free from any hidden malice; and that person shall we penetrate with loving thoughts, wide, deep, boundless, freed from anger and hatred'.

Abstaining from Vain Talk

A. X. 176

4. He avoids vain talk, and abstains from it. He speaks at the right time, in accordance with facts, speaks what is useful, speaks of the law and the discipline: his speech is like a treasure, uttered at the right moment, accompanied by arguments, moderate and full of sense.

This is called Right Speech.

Mundane and Supermundane Right Speech

M. 117

Now, Right Speech, I tell you, is of two kinds:

1. Abstaining from lying, from tale-bearing, from harsh language, and from vain talk; this is called 'Mundane Right Speech' (lokiya-sammā-vācā), which yields worldly fruits and brings good results.

2. But the avoidance of the practice of this fourfold wrong speech, the abstaining, desisting. refraining therefrom—the mind being holy, being turned away from the world, and conjoined with the path, the holy path being pursued—this is called the 'Supermundane Right Speech' (lokuttara-sammā-vācā), which is not of the world, but is supermundane, and conjoined with the path.

Conjoined with Other Factors

Now, in understanding wrong speech as wrong, and right speech as right, one practises Right Understanding (1st factor); and in making efforts to overcome evil speech and to arouse right speech, one practises Right Effort (6th factor); and in overcoming wrong speech with attentive mind, and dwelling with attentive mind in possession of right speech, one practises Right Mindfulness (7th factor). Hence, there are three things that accompany and follow upon Right Speech, namely: Right Understanding, Right Effort, and Right Mindfulness.

New Words and Expressions

application / ˌæplɪ'keɪʃn / *n.*	用（心）；专注；思量
arouse / ə'raʊz / *vt.*	生；引起
attentive mind	专注的心念
concord / 'kɒŋkɔːd / *n.*	和合；和谐
Conjoined with Other Factors	与其他道支俱行
conjoined with the path	与道相合
conscientious / ˌkɒnʃi'enʃəs / *adj.*	认真负责的；本着良心的；谨慎的
considering / kən'sɪdərɪŋ / *n.*	寻
dwell with...in...	以……住于……
free from	离；摆脱；除去
Karma-results	业果
malice / 'mælɪs / *n.*	怨恨；恶意
ratiocination / ˌrætiˌɒsɪ'neɪʃn / *n.*	推理
refrain from	抑制；避免

Supermundane / ˌsjuːpə'mʌndeɪn / *adj.*	出世间的
Sympathy / 'sɪmpəθɪ / *n.*	同情；怜悯
tale-bearing / *n.*	两舌
thinking / 'θɪŋkɪŋ / *n.*	思
thought / θɔːt / *n.*	想
undisturbed / ˌʌndɪ'stɜːbd / *adj.*	不受干扰的
vain talk	绮语
welfare / 'welfeə(r) / *n.*	福利；福祉
wrong speech	邪语

Grammar

动词的名词化，包括 "-ing" 形式的动名词，也包括由动词派生的 "-tion, -ment" 等形式的名词。

《佛言》中经常使用这类词。例如：

What, now, is the Noble Truth of the Extinction of Suffering? It is the complete fading away and extinction of this craving, its forsaking and abandonment, liberation and detachment from it.（p.24）

1. 一般来说，这类词比相关动词要更抽象，使用这类词，比直接使用相关动词显得更为正式。这也是《佛言》文体的一个特点。

2. 需注意动词名词化所表示的动作的"方向"。

物主代词之后的这类词，如果是"及物"词性，其动作的方向，可指向另一个词，此时，这个词是主格；也可指向该物主代词，此时，该物主代词是宾格。

例如：

…its forsaking and abandonment.

"its" 是 "forsaking and abandonment" 逻辑上的宾语

"…their conception and springing into existence…"

They 是 conception 逻辑上的宾语，是 springing into existence 逻辑上的主语。

"…their destruction, disappearance…"

他们的灭亡（宾格），消失（主格）。

以上分析也适用于由 "of" 构成的 "所有格"。

Exercises

1. What is the difference between Right Thought and Right Understanding? Is Right Thought part of Right Understanding?

2. What is the difference between Mundane and Supermundane Right Thought?

3. Should we tell a person the unfavorable comments or accusations made by other people behind his back? Should we warn a friend against an evil plot against him?

4. What is the relation between Right Thought and Right Speech?

Unit Ten

FOURTH FACTOR

Right Action (Sammā-kammanta)

X. 176

What, now, is Right Action?

Abstaining from Killing

1. Herein someone avoids the killing of living beings, and abstains from it. Without stick or sword, conscientious, full of sympathy, he is desirous of the welfare of all living beings.

Abstaining from Stealing

2. He avoids stealing, and abstains from it; what another person possesses of goods and chattels in the village or in the wood, that he does not take away with thievish intent.

Abstaining from Unlawful Sexual Intercourse

3. He avoids unlawful sexual intercourse, and abstains from it. He has no intercourse with such persons as are still under the protection of father, mother, brother, sister or relatives, nor with married women, nor female convicts, nor lastly, with betrothed girls.

This is called Right Action.

Mundane and Supermundane Right Action

M. 117

Now, Right Action, I tell you, is of two kinds:

1. Abstaining from killing, from stealing, and from unlawful sexual intercourse: this is called the 'Mundane Right Action' (lokiya-sammā-kammanta) which yields worldly fruits and brings good results.

2. But the avoidance of the practice of this threefold wrong action, the abstaining, desisting, refraining therefrom—the mind being holy, being turned away from the world, and conjoined with the path, the holy path being pursued—this is called the 'Supermundane Right Action' (lokuttara-sammā-kammanta), which is not of the world, but is supermundane, and conjoined with the path.

Conjoined with Other Factors

Now, in understanding wrong action as wrong, and right action as right, one practises Right Understanding (1st factor): and in making efforts to overcome wrong action, and to arouse right action, one practises Right Effort (6th factor); and in overcoming wrong action with attentive mind, and dwelling with attentive mind in possession of right action, one practises Right Mindfulness (7th factor). Hence, there are three things that accompany and follow upon Right Action, namely: Right Understanding, Right Effort and Right Mindfulness.

FIFTH FACTOR

Right Livelihood
(Sammā-ājīva)

D. 22

What, now, is Right Livelihood?

1. When the noble disciple, avoiding a wrong way of living, gets his livelihood by a right way of living, this is called Right Livelihood.

In the Majjhima-Nikāya, No. 117, it is said: 'To practise deceit, treachery, soothsaying, trickery, usury: this is wrong livelihood.'

And in the Aṅguttara-Nikāya, V. 177, it is said: 'Five trades should be avoided by a disciple: trading in arms, in living beings, in flesh, in intoxicating drinks, and in poison'.

Included are the professions of a soldier, a fisherman, a hunter, etc.

Mundane and Supermundane Right Livelihood ✎

M. 117

Now, Right Livelihood, I tell you, is of two kinds:

1. When the noble disciple, avoiding wrong living, gets his livelihood by a right way of living: this is called 'Mundane Right Livelihood' (lokiya-sammā-

ājīva), which yields worldly fruits and brings good results.

2. But the avoidance of wrong livelihood, the abstaining, desisting, refraining therefrom—the mind being holy, being turned away from the world, and conjoined with the path, the holy path being pursued—this is called the 'Supermundane Right Livelihood' (lokuttara-sammā-ājīva), which is not of the world, but is supermundane, and conjoined with the path.

Conjoined with Other Factors

Now, in understanding wrong livelihood as wrong, and right livelihood as right, one practises Right Understanding (1st factor); and in making efforts to overcome wrong livelihood, to establish right livelihood, one practises Right Effort (6th factor); and in overcoming wrong livelihood with attentive mind, and dwelling with attentive mind in possession of right livelihood, one practises Right Mindfulness (7th factor). Hence, there are three things that accompany and follow upon Right Livelihood, namely: Right Understanding, Right Effort, and Right Mindfulness.

SIXTH FACTOR

Right Effort
(Sammā-vāyāma)

IV. 13, 14

What, now, is Right Effort?

There are Four Great Efforts; the effort to avoid, the effort to overcome, the effort to develop, and the effort to maintain.

The Effort to Avoid (Saṃvara-ppadhāna)

What, now, is the effort to Avoid? Herein the disciple rouses his will to avoid the arising of evil, unwholesome things that have not yet arisen; and he makes efforts, stirs up his energy; exerts his mind and strives.

Thus, when he perceives a form with the eye, a sound with the ear, and an odor with the nose, a taste with the tongue, an impression with the body, or an object with the mind, he neither adheres to the whole, nor to its parts. And he strives to ward off that through which evil and unwholesome things, greed and sorrow, would arise, if he remained with unguarded senses; and he watches over his senses, restrains his senses.

Possessed of this noble 'Control over the Senses' he experiences inwardly a feeling of joy, into which no evil thing can enter.

This is called the effort to avoid.

The Effort to Overcome (Pahāna-ppadhāna)

What, now, is the effort to Overcome? There the disciple rouses his will to overcome the evil, unwholesome things that have already arisen; and he makes effort, stirs up his energy, exerts his mind and strives.

He does not retain any thought of sensual lust, ill-will or grief, or any other evil and unwholesome states that may have arisen; he abandons them, dispels them, destroys them, causes them to disappear.

Five Methods of Expelling Evil Thoughts

M. 20

If, whilst regarding a certain object, there arise in the disciple, on account of it, evil and unwholesome thoughts connected with greed, hatred and delusion, then the disciple (1) should, by means of this object, gain another and wholesome object. (2) Or, he should reflect on the misery of these thoughts; 'Unwholesome, truly, are these thoughts! Blamable are these thoughts! Of painful result are these thoughts!' (3) Or he should pay no attention to these thoughts. (4) Or, he should consider the compound nature of these thoughts. (5) Or, with teeth clenched and tongue pressed against the gums, he should with his mind restrain, suppress and root out these thoughts; and in doing so these evil and unwholesome thoughts of greed, hatred and delusion will dissolve and disappear; and the mind will inwardly become settled and calm, composed and concentrated.

This is called the effort to overcome.

The Effort to Develop (Bhāvanā-ppadhāna)

IV. 13, 14

What, now, is the effort to Develop? Herein the disciple rouses his will to arouse wholesome things that have not yet arisen; and he makes effort, stirs up his energy, exerts his mind and strives.

Thus he develops the 'Elements of Enlightenment' (bhojjhaṅga), based on solitude, on detachment, on extinction, and ending in deliverance, namely: 'Mindfulness' (sati), 'Investigation of the Law' (dhamma-vicaya), 'Energy' (viriya), 'Rapture' (pīti), 'Tranquillity' (passaddhi), 'Concentration' (samādhi) and 'Equanimity' (upekkhā).

This is called the effort to develop.

The Effort to Maintain (Anurakkhaṇa-ppadhāna)

What, now, is the effort to Maintain? Herein the disciple rouses his will to maintain the wholesome things that have already arisen, and not to allow them to disappear, but to bring them to growth, to maturity and to the full perfection of development (bhāvanā); and he makes effort, stirs up his energy, exerts his mind and strives.

Thus, for example, he keeps firmly in his mind a favorable object of concentration that has arisen, such as the mental image of a skeleton, of a corpse infested by worms, of a corpse blue-black in color, of a festering corpse, of a corpse riddled with holes, of a corpse swollen up.

This is called the effort to maintain.

M. 70

Truly, for a disciple who is possessed of faith and has penetrated the Teaching of the master, it is fit to think: 'Though skin sinews and bones wither away, though flesh and blood of my body dry up, I shall not give up my efforts till I have attained whatever is attainable by manly perseverance, energy and endeavour.'

This is called Right Effort.

A.IV. 14

The effort of Avoiding, Overcoming,

Of Developing and Maintaining:

These four great efforts have been shown

By him, the scion of the sun.

And he who firmly clings to them,

May put an end to suffering.

New Words and Expressions

calm / kɑːm / *adj.*   平静的

composed / kəm'pəʊzd / *adj.*   镇定的

compound nature   因缘和合性；复合性

concentrated / 'kɒnsntreɪtɪd / *adj.*   入定的；专一的

control over the Senses   摄诸根

corpse blue-black in colour   青淤（相）

corpse infested by worms   虫聚（相）

corpse riddled with holes   穿孔（相）

corpse swollen up   膨胀（相）

development / dɪ'veləpmənt / *n.*   修行

dispel / dɪ'spel / *vt.*   打消；祛除

dissolve / dɪ'zɒlv / *vt.*   消散；消失

Effort to Avoid	律仪勤；勤防护；未生恶令不生
Effort to Develop	修勤；勤增长；未生善令生
Effort to Maintain	随护勤；已生善令增长
Effort to Overcome	断勤；生恶令断
endeavour / ɪn'devə(r) / *vt.*	努力；奋进
faith / feɪθ / *n.*	信；信心
form with the eye	眼根对色尘
Four Great Efforts	四正勤
good results	好的果报
impression with the body	身根对触尘
inwardly / 'ɪnwədliː / *adv.*	向内；内心地
maturity / mə'tʃʊərɪtɪ / *n.*	成熟
mental image / *adj.*	心相：
	心随诸缘而生种种对境之相
Mundane Right Livelihood	世间正命
object of concentration	所观境
object with the mind	意根对法尘
odor with the nose	鼻根对香尘
painful result	苦果
penetrate / 'penətreɪt / *vt.*	洞察
restrain / rɪ'streɪn / *vt.*	抑制；阻止
root out	根除；拔除
rouse / raʊz / *vt.*	激发；唤醒；引起
sensual lust	情欲
settled / 'setld / *adj.*	安稳的
skeleton / 'skelɪtn / *n.*	骸骨（相）
solitude / 'sɒlɪtjuːd / *n.*	隐居；独处
sound with the ear	耳根对声尘
stir up	激起；唤起
strive / straɪv / *vi.*	努力；进取
Supermundane Right Livelihood	出世间正命
suppress / sə'pres / *vt.*	压制；压服
taste with the tongue	舌根对味尘
worldly fruits	世间的果报
wrong livelihood	邪命

Grammar

《佛言》中有很多长句，有时整个段落就是一句话。这是为了更准确，全面地表述思想：对某命题的适用范围加以限定，列举某一现象的各种表现形式，历数某一状态（事实）存在的全部条件，对命题作补充说明，或从反面再次表述同样的思想，等等。而所有这些，都是通过在长句中，主干（骨架）结构之外的附属成分（限定成分）实现的。

※ 附属成分包括：同位语短语（从句），状语短语（从句），定语短语（从句）。

（1）同位结构：

长句中的同位结构是《佛言》标志性的语言特点之一。反复叠加的同位结构往往会造成"排比，递进"等修辞效果，不仅增强了论述的说服力，还造成了篇章结构中特殊的节奏感和韵律。

（What is birth?）The birth of beings belonging to this or that order of beings，their being born，their conception and springing into existence，the manifestation of the Groups of Existence，the arising of sense activity: **this is called birth**（主句，this 指代前面 4 个并列成分构成的主语）.

The only way（主语）that leads to（介词"to"引导 5 个并列成分）the attainment of purity, to the overcoming of sorrow and lamentation, to the end of pain and grief, to the entering upon the right path, and the realization of Nibbana, **is by these four foundations of mindfulness**（表语）.

（2）状语短语（从句）：

Should anyone say that he does not wish to lead the holy life, under the Blessed One, unless the Blessed One first tells him whether the world is eternal or temporal, finite or infinite: whether the life-principle is identical with the body, or something different; whether the Perfect One continues after death, etc. （以上是条件句状语从句，其中又嵌套了一个二阶状语从句）—such a one would die ere the Perfect One could tell him all this. （主句）

（3）定语短语（从句）

All corporeal phenomena（主语）, whether past, present or future, one's own or external, gross or subtle, loft or low, far or near（以上为定语）, all belong to the Group of Corporeality. （谓语）

（4）为了强调佛法的"普遍适应性"，佛法的"真理性"，在长句的附属成分中，经常使用"whatever"（whatsoever）, "whenever", "whosoever", "whether…, or", "be it…, be it…"（= whether it be…or）"等关系代词和关系副词。这些限定成分的共同特点是：它们都表示逻辑上的"全称判断"，即：某命题的适用范围无限制，包罗万象，放之四海而皆准。

例如：

But whatsoever there is of corporeality, feeling, perception, mental formations, or consciousness: all these phenomena he regards as "impermanent"（anicca）, "subject to pain"（dukkha）.

Whenever the disciple dwells in contemplation of body, feeling, mind and mind-objects, strenuous, clearly comprehending them, mindful, after subduing worldly greed and grief—at such a time his mindfulness is undisturbed…

Exercises

1. Give examples of modern professions that would have been considered "Wrong Livelihood", e.g. banker, novelist, poet, etc. Is it all right for a

Buddhist to invest in the stock market?

2. Why is Right Effort an important element in the other factors of the Path?

3. What is the difference between Right Effort and Attachment (clinging, grasping)? Can there be "too much" efforts (obsession, stubbornness, etc.) that actually obstruct your progress? Have you ever been in a situation where even the greatest efforts won't get you anywhere?

4. Compare the Five Precepts and Right Action. What is (are) the difference(s)?

Unit Eleven

SEVENTH FACTOR

Right Mindfulness (Sammā-sati)

What, now, is Right Mindfulness?

The Four Foundations of Mindfulness (Satipaṭṭhāna)

D. 22

The only way that leads to the attainment of purity, to the overcoming of sorrow and lamentation, to the end of pain and grief, to the entering upon the right path and the realization of Nibbāna, is by the 'Four Foundations of Mindfulness'. And which are these four?

Herein the disciple dwells in contemplation of the Body, in contemplation of Feeling, in contemplation of the Mind, in contemplation of the Mind-Objects; ardent, clearly comprehending them and mindful, after putting away worldly greed and grief.

Contemplation of the Body (kāyanupassanā)

But how does the disciple dwell in contemplation of the body?

Watching over In- and Out-Breathing (ānāpāna-sati)

Herein the disciple retires to the forest, to the foot of a tree, or to a solitary place, seats himself with legs crossed, body erect, and with mindfulness fixed before him, mindfully he breathes in, mindfully he breathes out. When making a long inhalation, he knows: 'I make a long inhalation'; when making a long exhalation, he knows: 'I make a long exhalation'. When making a short inhalation, he knows: 'I make a short inhalation': when making a short exhalation, he knows: 'I make a short exhalation'. 'Clearly perceiving the entire (breath-) body, I shall breathe in': thus he trains himself;

'Clearly perceiving the entire (breath-) body, I shall breathe out': thus he trains himself. 'Calming this bodily function (kāya-saṅkhāra), I shall breathe in': thus he trains himself; 'Calming this bodily function. I shall breathe out': thus he trains himself.

Thus he dwells in contemplation of the body, either with regard to his own person, or to other persons, or to both, he beholds how the body arises; beholds how it passes away; beholds the arising and passing away of the body. A body is there—

'A body is there, but no living being, no individual, no woman, no man, no self, and nothing that belongs to a self; neither a person, nor anything belonging to a person.' (Comm.)

this clear awareness is present in him, to the extent necessary for knowledge and mindfulness, and he lives independent, unattached to anything in the world. Thus does the disciple dwell in contemplation of the body.

'Mindfulness of Breathing' (ānāpāna-sati) is one of the most important meditative exercises. It may be used for the development of Tranquillity (samatha-bhāvanā), i.e. for attaining the four Absorptions (jhāna; see" The Four Absorptions"), for the development of Insight (vipassanā-bhāvanā) or for a combination of both practices. Here, in the context of satipaṭṭhāna, it is principally intended for tranquillization and concentration preparatory to the practice of Insight, which may be undertaken in the following way.

After a certain degree of calm and concentration, or one of the Absorptions, has been attained through regular practice of mindful breathing, the disciple proceeds to examine the origin of breath. He sees that the inhalations and exhalations are conditioned by the body consisting of the four material elements and the various corporeal phenomena derived from them, e.g. the five sense organs, etc. Conditioned by fivefold sense-impression arises consciousness, and together with it the three other 'Groups of Existence', i.e. Feeling, Perception, and mental Formations. Thus the meditator sees clearly: 'There is no ego-entity or self in this so called personality, but it is only a corporeal and mental process conditioned by various factors'. Thereupon he applies the Three Characteristics to these phenomena, understanding them thoroughly as impermanent, subject to suffering, and impersonal.

For further details about Ānāpāna-sati, see M. 118.62, Visuddhi-Magga VIII. 3.

The Four Postures

And further, whilst going, standing, sitting, or lying down, the disciple understands (according to reality) the expressions; 'I go'; 'I stand'; 'I sit'; 'I lie down'; he understands any position of the body.

'The disciple understands that there is no living being, no real Ego, that goes, stands, etc., but that it is by a mere figure of speech that one says:" I go";" I stand" and so forth.' (Comm.)

Mindfulness and Clear Comprehension (sati-sampajañña)

And further, the disciple acts with clear comprehension in going and coming; he acts with clear comprehension in looking forward and backward; acts with clear comprehension in bending and stretching (any part of his body); acts with clear comprehension in carrying alms bowl and robes; acts with clear comprehension in eating, drinking, chewing and tasting; acts with clear comprehension in discharging excrement and urine; acts with clear comprehension in walking, standing, sitting, falling asleep, awakening; acts with clear comprehension in speaking and keeping silent.

In all that the disciple is doing, he has a clear comprehension: 1. of his intention, 2. of his advantage, 3. of his duty, 4. of the reality. (Comm.)

Contemplation of Loathsomeness (paṭikkūla-sañña)

And further, the disciple contemplates this body from the sole of the foot upward, and from the top of the hair downward, with a skin stretched over it, and filled with manifold impurities: 'This body has hairs of the head and of the body, nails, teeth, skin, flesh, sinews, bones, marrow, kidneys, heart, liver, diaphragm, spleen, lungs, stomach, bowels, mesentery, and excrement; bile, phlegm, pus, blood, sweat, lymph, tears, skin-grease, saliva, nasal mucus, oil of the joints, and urine.'

Just as if there were a sack, with openings at both ends, filled with various kinds of grain—with paddy, beans, sesamum and husked rice—and a man not blind opened it and examined its contents, thus: 'That is paddy, these are beans, this is sesamum, this is husked rice': just so does the disciple investigate this body.

Analysis of Four Elements (dhātu)

And further, the disciple contemplates this body, however it may stand or move, with regard to the elements; 'This body consists of the solid element, the liquid element, the heating element and the vibrating element'. Just as if a skilled butcher or butcher's apprentice, who had slaughtered a cow and divided it into separate portions, were to sit down at the junction of four highroads: just so does the disciple contemplate this body with regard to the elements.

In Visuddhi-Magga XIII. 2 this simile is explained as follows:

When a butcher rears a cow, brings it to the place of slaughter, binds it to a post, makes it stand up, slaughters it and looks at the slaughtered cow, during all that time he has still the notion 'cow'. But when he has cut up the slaughtered cow, divided it into pieces, and sits down near it to sell the meat, the notion, 'cow' ceases in his mind, and the notion 'meat' arises. He does not think that he is selling a cow or that people buy a cow, but that it is meat that is sold and bought. Similarly, in an ignorant worldling, whether monk or layman, the concepts 'being', 'man', 'personality', etc., will not cease until he has mentally dissected this body of his, as it stands and moves, and has contemplated it according to its component elements. But when he has done so, the notion 'personality', etc., will disappear, and his mind will become firmly established in the Contemplation of the Elements.

Cemetery Meditations

1. And further, just as if the disciple were looking at a corpse thrown on a charnel-ground, one, two, or three days dead, swollen up, blue-black in color, full of corruption—so he regards his own body: 'This body of mine also has this nature, has this destiny, and cannot escape it.'

2. And further, just as if the disciple were looking at a corpse thrown on a charnel-ground, eaten by crows, hawks or vultures, by dogs or jackals, or devoured by all kinds of worms—so he regards his own body; 'This body of mine also has this nature, has this destiny, and cannot escape it.'

3. And further, just as if the disciple were looking at a corpse thrown on a charnel-ground, a framework of bones, flesh hanging from it, bespattered with blood, held together by the sinews;

4. A framework of bone, stripped of flesh, bespattered with blood, held together by the sinews;

5. A framework of bone, without flesh and blood, but still held together by the sinews;

6. Bones, disconnected and scattered in all directions, here a bone of the hand, there a bone of the foot, there a shin bone, there a thigh bone, there a pelvis, there the spine, there the skull—so he regards his own body: 'This body of mine also has this nature, has this destiny, and cannot escape it.'

7. And further, just as if the disciple were looking at bones lying in the charnel-ground, bleached and resembling shells;

8. Bones heaped together, after the lapse of years;

9. Bones weathered and crumbled to dust—so he regards his own body: 'This body of mine also has this nature, has this destiny, and cannot escape it.'

Thus he dwells in contemplation of the body, either with regard to his own person, or to other persons, or to both.

He beholds how the body arises; beholds how it passes away; beholds the arising and passing away of the body. 'A body is there': this clear awareness is present in him, to the extent necessary for knowledge and mindfulness; and he lives independent, unattached to anything in the world. Thus does the disciple dwell in contemplation of the body.

Assured of Ten Blessings
M. 119

Once the contemplation of the body is practised, developed, often repeated, has become one's habit, one's foundation, is firmly established, strengthened and perfected; the disciple may expect ten blessings:

1. Over delight and discontent he has mastery; he does not allow himself to be overcome by discontent; he subdues it, as soon as it arises.

2. He conquers fear and anxiety; he does not allow himself to be overcome by fear and anxiety; he subdues them, as soon as they arise.

3. He endures cold and heat, hunger and thirst; wind and sun, attacks by gadflies, mosquitoes and reptiles; patiently he endures wicked and malicious speech, as well as bodily pains that befall him, though they be piercing, sharp, bitter, unpleasant, disagreeable, and dangerous to life.

4. The four Absorptions' (jhāna) which purify the mind, and bestow happiness even here, these he may enjoy at will, without difficulty, without effort.

Six 'Psychical Powers' (Abhiñña)

5. He may enjoy the different 'Magical Powers (iddhi-vidhā).

6. With the 'Heavenly Ear' (dibba-sota), the purified, the super-human,

he may hear both kinds of sounds, the heavenly and the earthly, the distant and the near.

7. With the mind he may obtain 'Insight into the Hearts of Other Beings' (parassa-cetopariya-ñāṇa), of other persons.

8. He may obtain 'Remembrances of many Previous Births' (pubbe-nivāsānussati-ñāṇa).

9. With the 'Heavenly Eye' (dibba-cakkhu), purified and super-human, he may see beings vanish and reappear, the base and the noble, the beautiful and the ugly, the happy and the unfortunate; he may perceive how beings are reborn according to their deeds.

10. He may, through the 'Cessation of Passions' (āsavakkhaya), come to know for himself, even in this life, the stainless deliverance of mind, the deliverance through wisdom.

The last six blessings (5~10) are the 'Psychical Powers' (abhiññā). The first five of them are mundane (lokiya) conditions, and may therefore be attained even by a 'worldling' (puthujjana), whilst the last Abhiññā is super-mundane (lokuttara) and exclusively the characteristic of the Arahat, or Holy One. It is only after the attainment of all the four Absorptions (jhāna) that one may fully succeed in acquiring the five worldly 'Psychical Powers'. There are four iddhipāda, or 'Bases for obtaining Magical Powers', namely: concentration of Will, concentration of Energy, concentration of Mind, and concentration of Investigation.

New Words and Expressions

Absorptions / əb'sɔːpʃnz / *n.*   禅；禅那

advantage / əd'vaːntɪdʒ / *n.*   益处

agreeable feeling   乐受

anxiety / æŋ'zaɪəti / *n.*   焦虑

attainment / ə'teɪnmənt / *n.*   证得；达到；获得

Bases for obtaining Magical Powers (Four iddhipada)	四神足；四如意足
bodily function	身行（入出息）
cemetery meditations	冢间观
Cessation of Passions	漏尽通
comprehend / ˌkɒmprɪ'hend / *vt.*	理解；领悟
Concentration of Energy	勤神足；精进如意足
Concentration of Investigation	观神足；思维如意足
Concentration of Mind	心神足；念如意足
Concentration of Will	欲神足；欲如意足
Contemplation of Loathsomeness	厌恶想；不净观
Contemplation of the Body	观身；身念处
Contemplation of the Elements	四界分别观
Contemplation of the Feelings	观受；受念处
Contemplation of the Mind	观心；心念处
Contemplation of the Mind-Objects	观法；法念处
corporeal and mental process	物质及精神过程
destiny / 'destənɪ / *n.*	命运
development of Insight	修观；修毗婆舍那
development of Tranquility	修止；修定；修奢摩他
disagreeable feeling	苦受
dissect / dɪ'sekt / *vt.*	剖析；仔细分析
dwell in	住于
escape / ɪ'skeɪp / *vt.*	逃避
figure of speech	比喻；修辞格
five sense organs	五根；五种感官
fivefold sense-impression	五尘触
Four Absorptions	四禅；四禅那
Four Postures	四威仪
heavenly ear	天耳（通）

heavenly eye	天眼（通）
impurities / ɪmˈpjʊərɪtɪs / n.	不净；秽物
Insight into the Hearts of Other Beings	他心通
intention / ɪnˈtenʃn / n.	念头；动机；意图
layman	在家众；居士
lead to	趣向；导归
magical powers	神变；神通
meditative exercises	禅修训练
meditator / ˈmedɪteɪtə / n.	禅修者
Mindfulness and Clear Comprehension	正念正知
mindfulness of breathing	观（念）入出息；数息观
personality / ˌpɜːsəˈnæləti / n.	个人；个体
psychical powers	神通；神通力
Reborn according to one's deeds	随业转生（轮回／流转）
Remembrances of many Previous Births	宿命通
simile / ˈsɪməlɪ / n.	喻；比喻
superhuman / ˌsuːpəˈhjuːmən / adj.	超人的
Ten Blessings	十种功德
the heavenly and the earthly	天道与人道
unattached to	不执着于

Grammar

　　《佛言》中有大量的"圆周句"（Periodic Sentence）。"圆周句"是一种修辞手段，其特点是：句子的语法结构，直到句末才变得完整，关键词，往往保留到句末才出现，句子的意思，直到最后才表达清楚。

　　例如：Whosoever, in experiencing one of these feelings, thinks that this is his Self, must after the extinction of that feeling, admit that his Self already has become dissolved.

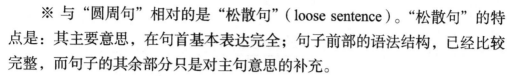

※ 与"圆周句"相对的是"松散句"（loose sentence）。"松散句"的特点是：其主要意思，在句首基本表达完全；句子前部的语法结构，已经比较完整，而句子的其余部分只是对主句意思的补充。

例如：The Sangha is the Order of Bhikkhus or Mendicant Monks（主句），founded by the Buddha and still existing in its original form in Burma, Siam, Ceylon, Cambodia, Laos and Chitagong.（松散句）

"松散句"（loose sentence）的意思比较容易理解，读者不感到压力（阅读的张力）。一般文章中，大部分句子都是"松散句"。

而"圆周句"则较难读懂，往往要放慢节奏，甚至要反复读几遍，才能理解意义。因此，"圆周句"在一般文章中的数量要大大少于"松散句"。

※ "圆周句"的作用：

（1）促使读者高度集中注意力，并要记住前半句的观点、事实，甚至句法结构。

（2）持有不同意见的人，也会暂时中止主观"判断""反驳"，而集中于对观点、事实的理解。

（3）"悬念"（阅读的张力），在句末解决，紧张感得到释放，阅读达到高潮。

"圆周句"并非英语特有的语言现象。2000 年前的古希腊人就已经注意到这种句子。"圆周句"（Periodic Sentence）一词，就源于希腊语。宗教经典，哲学论文中经常使用"Periodic Sentence"，特别是在表达重要思想、对讨论进行总结时。

例如：

And though I have the gift of prophecy, and understand all mysteries, and all knowledge; and though I have all faith, so that I could remove mountains, and have not charity, I am nothing.（The King James Bible）

《佛言》中大量的"圆周句"，既反映了文体的特点，也是佛祖个人的语言表达习惯。

Exercises

1. What are the Four Foundations of Mindfulness?
2. What is the purpose of Right Mindfulness?
3. Explain the statement—"A body is there." What kind of body is meant in that statement?
4. Name the Ten Blessings as the outcome of practicing Contemplation of the Body. Are these Blessings the final goals of Holy life?

Unit Twelve

Contemplation of the Feelings (vedanānupassanā)

D. 22

But how does the disciple dwell in contemplation of the feelings?

In experiencing feelings, the disciple knows: 'I have an agreeable feeling'; or: 'I have a disagreeable feeling', or: 'I have an indifferent feeling'; or: 'I have a worldly agreeable feeling', or: 'I have an unworldly agreeable feeling', or: 'I have a worldly disagreeable feeling', or: 'I have an unworldly disagreeable feeling', or: 'I have a worldly indifferent feeling', or: 'I have an unworldly indifferent feeling'.

Thus he dwells in contemplation of the feelings, either with regard to his own person, or to other persons, or to both. He beholds how the feelings arise; beholds how they pass away; beholds the arising and passing away of the feelings. 'Feelings are there': this clear awareness is present in him, to the extent necessary for knowledge and mindfulness; and he lives independent, unattached to anything in the world. Thus does the disciple dwell in contemplation of the feelings.

The disciple understands that the expression 'I feel' has no validity except as a conventional expression (vohāra-vacana); he understands that, in the absolute sense (paramattha), there are only feelings, and that there is no Ego, no experiencer of the feelings.

Contemplation of the Mind (Cittānupassanā)

But how does the disciple dwell in contemplation of the mind?

Herein the disciple knows the greedy mind as greedy, and the not greedy mind as not greedy; knows the hating mind as hating, and the not hating mind as not hating: knows the deluded mind as deluded and the undeluded mind as undeluded. He knows the cramped mind as cramped, and the scattered mind as scattered; knows the developed mind as developed, and the undeveloped mind as undeveloped; knows the surpassable mind as surpassable and the unsurpassable mind as unsurpassable; knows the concentrated mind as concentrated, and the unconcentrated mind as unconcentrated; knows the freed mind as freed, and the unfreed mind as unfreed.

Citta (mind) is here used as a collective term for the cittas, or moments of consciousness. Citta being identical with viññāṇa, or consciousness, should not be translated by 'thought'. 'Thought' and 'thinking' correspond rather to the 'verbal operations of the mind': vitakka (thought-conception) and vicāra (discursive thinking), which belong to the saṅkhāra-kkhandha.

Thus he dwells in contemplation of the mind, either with regard to his own person, or to other persons, or to both. He beholds how consciousness arises; beholds how it passes away; beholds the arising and passing away of consciousness. 'Mind is there'; this clear awareness is present in him, to the extent necessary for knowledge and mindfulness; and he lives independent, unattached to anything in the world. Thus does the disciple dwell in contemplation of the mind.

Contemplation of the Mind-Objects (dhammānupassanā)

But how does the disciple dwell in contemplation of mind-objects?

Herein the disciple dwells in contemplation of the mind-objects, namely of the 'Five Hindrances.'

The Five Hindrances (nīvaraṇa)

He knows when there is 'Lust' (kāmacchanda) in him: 'In me is lust'; knows when there is 'Anger' (vyāpāda) in him: 'In me is anger'; knows when there is 'Torpor and Sloth' (thīna-middha) in him: 'In me is torpor and sloth'; knows when there is 'Restlessness and Mental Worry' (uddhacca-kukkucca) in him: 'In me is restlessness and mental worry'; knows when there are 'Doubts' (vicikkicchā) in him: 'In me are doubts'. He knows when these hindrances are not in him: 'In me these hindrances are not'. He knows how they come to arise; knows how, once arisen, they are overcome; and he knows how they do not rise again in the future.

For example, 'Lust' arises through unwise thinking on the agreeable and delightful. It may be suppressed by the following six methods: fixing the mind upon an idea that arouses disgust; contemplation of the loathsomeness of the body; controlling one's six senses; moderation in eating; friendship with wise and good men; right instruction. Lust and anger are forever extinguished upon attainment of Anāgāmīship; 'Restlessness' is extinguished by reaching Arahatship; 'Mental Worry', by reaching Sotāpanship.

The Five Groups of Existence (khandha)

And further: the disciple dwells in contemplation of the mind-objects, namely of the five 'Groups of Existence'. He knows what 'Corporeality' (rūpa) is, how it arises, how it passes away; knows what 'Feeling' (vedanā) is, how it arises, how it passes away; knows what 'Perception' (saññā) is, how it arises, how it passes away; knows what the 'Mental Formations' (saṅkhāra) are, how they arise, how they pass away; knows what 'Consciousness' (viññāṇa) is, how it arises, how it passes away.

The Sense-Bases (āyatana)

And further: the disciple dwells in contemplation of the mind-objects, namely of the six 'Subjective-Objective Sense-Bases'. He knows the eye and visual objects, ear and sounds, nose and odors, tongue and tastes, body and bodily impressions, mind and mind-objects; and the fetter that arises in dependence on them, he also knows. He knows how the fetter comes to arise, knows how the fetter is overcome, and how the abandoned fetter does not rise again in future.

The Seven Elements of Enlightenment (bojjhanga)

And further: the disciple dwells in contemplation of the mind-objects, namely of the seven 'Elements of Enlightenment', He knows when there is in him 'Mindfulness' (sati), 'Investigation of the Law' (dhammavicaya), 'Energy' (viriya), 'Enthusiasm' (pīti), 'Tranquillity' (passaddhi), 'Concentration' (samādhi), and 'Equanimity' (upekkhā). He knows when it is not in him, knows how it comes to arise, and how it is fully developed.

The Four Noble Truths (ariya-sacca)

And further: the disciple dwells in contemplation of the mind-objects, namely of the 'Four Noble Truths'. He knows according to reality, what Suffering is; knows according to reality, what the Origin of suffering is; knows according to reality what the Extinction of suffering is; knows according to reality, what the Path is that leads to the extinction of suffering.

Thus he dwells in contemplation of the mind-objects either with regard to his own person, or to other persons or to both. He beholds how the mind-objects arise, beholds how they pass away, beholds the arising and passing away of the mind-objects. 'Mind-objects are there': this clear awareness is present in him, to the extent necessary for knowledge and mindfulness; and he lives independent, unattached to anything in the world. Thus does the disciple dwell in contemplation of the mind-objects.

The only way that leads to the attainment of purity, to the overcoming of sorrow and lamentation, to the end of pain and grief, to the entering upon the right path, and the realization of Nibbāna, is by these four foundations of mindfulness.

These four contemplations of Satipaṭṭhāna relate to all the five Groups of Existence, namely: 1. the contemplation of corporeality relates to rūpakkhandha;

2. the contemplation of feeling, to vedanākkhandha; 3. the contemplation of mind, to viññāṇakkhandha; 4. the contemplation of mind-objects, to sañña- and saṅkhāra-kkhandha.

For further details about Satipaṭṭhāna see the Commentary to the discourse of that name, translated in The Way of Mindfulness, by Bhikkhu Soma (Kandy 1967, Buddhist Publication Society).

New Words and Expressions

absolute sense	胜义；究竟法义
attainment of purity	获清净
awareness / ə'weənəs / *n.*	觉察；觉知
behold / bɪ'həʊld / *vt.*	观照
concentrated mind	专注心；定心
concentration / ˌkɒnsn'treɪʃn / *n.*	定
discursive thinking / *adj.*	伺：心的随属，即专注在所缘上
Doubt / daʊt / *n.*	疑盖
Energy / 'enədʒɪ / *n.*	精进（觉支）
entering upon the right path	进入正道
Enthusiasm / ɪn'θjuːziæzəm / *n.*	喜（觉支）；禅悦
Equanimity / ˌekwə'nɪməti / *n.*	舍（觉支）；平静
expression / ɪk'spreʃn / *n.*	言说
Five Hindrances	五盖：覆盖心性的五种烦恼；即：贪欲盖、嗔恚盖、惛沉睡眠盖、掉举恶作盖和疑盖
Four Foundations of Mindfulness	四念处；四念住
indifferent feeling	舍受
mind-objects	心法；心所对之境
moderation in eating	节制饮食
realization of Nibbana	证得涅槃
restlessness and mental worry	掉举恶作盖

scattered mind	散乱心
sense-bases	根；处
Seven Elements of Enlightenment	七觉支；七菩提分
Six Subjective-Objective Sense-Bases	六根对六尘（境）
thought-conception	寻：最初的心专注；念头的开端
Torpor and Sloth	惛沉睡眠盖
Tranquility / træŋ'kwɪlɪtɪ / *n.*	轻安（觉支）
watching over in-and-out-breathing	观（念）出入息；数息观

Grammar

（1）as long as 只要，引导条件状语从句。

例句：Life will continue as long as there are still life-energies stored up.

只要生命的能量存储起来，生命就会继续。

（2）as 作介词，意思是"作为"，"以……身份"。也常和某些动词例如 regard, consider 等连用，表达把……当作、称作、认作……

例句：He was born in the 6th century B.C., at Kapilavatthu, as the son of the king who ruled the Sakya country, a principality situated in the border area of modern Nepal.

他于公元前 6 世纪诞生在迦毗罗卫，是释迦国王之子，释迦国位于现今尼泊尔疆界一带。

（3）As if 似乎、好像，譬如，犹如；通常引导的从句都为虚拟语气，表与事实相反或者假设。

例句：It is as if a man were pierced by a poisoned arrow and his friends, companions or near relations should send for a surgeon...

如是犹如有人被涂厚毒之箭所射，彼之亲友、同伴、亲族为彼请医疗治…

（4）Just as + 从句　正如 / 就好像……

例句：Just as one calls 'hut' the circumscribed space which comes to be by means of wood and rushes, reeds, and clay, even so we call 'body' the circumscribed space that comes to be by means of bones and sinews, flesh and skin.

譬如小木屋由木头、灯心草、茅草和泥土搭建起来，同样的，我们所名之身体，是由骨、腱、肉和皮肤包覆的空间。

as 引导原因状语从句

例句：The word 'dhamma', however, has a still wider application and is all embracing, as it comprises also the so-called Unconditioned（'unformed', asankhata）, i.e. Nibbāna.

然而"法"一词应用更广，圆融无碍，亦包括无为，亦即涅槃。

惯用语：as well as 与……一样……；不但……而且；还……

例句：…for certainly I do teach annihilation—the annihilation, namely, of greed, hatred and delusion, as well as of the manifold evil and unwholesome things.

我为弟子说断灭法，我说贪嗔痴之断灭，说种种恶不善法之断灭。

such…as… 例如……比如……

例句：He speaks such words as are gentle, soothing to the ear, loving, such words as go to the heart, and are courteous, friendly, and agreeable to many.（p.48）

是人说诸清美、顺耳、可爱、悦意、如此多人谓之有礼、友善、得体之语。

（5）As soon as… 引导时间状语从句，一……就……

例句：But as soon as the absolute true knowledge and insight as regards these Four Noble Truths had become perfectly clear in me, there arose in me the assurance that I had won that supreme Enlightenment unsurpassed.

然我于此四圣谛，如是如实智见已达、悉皆清净故，我敢言我已证无上正等觉。

（6）As 的代词用法

…as regards…

As long as the absolute true knowledge and insight as regards these Four Noble Truths was not quite clear in me…

只要我对四圣谛的认识尚不完全透彻……

But as soon as the absolute truth knowledge and insight as regards these Four Noble Truths had become perfectly clear in me…

一旦我对四圣谛的认识完全透彻……

"…such words as are gentle, …such words as go to the heart…"

Exercises

1. What are the Five Hindrances? How are they overcome? And what will happen if the Five Hindrances are overcome?

2. How are the Four Foundations of Mindfulness related to the Five Groups of Existence?

3. Why can't 'citta' be translated as 'thought'?

Unit Thirteen

Nibbāna through Ānāpāna-Sati

M. 118

Watching over In- and Out-breathing (ānāpāna-sati), practised and developed, brings the Four 'Foundations of Mindfulness' to perfection; the four foundations of mindfulness, practised and developed, bring the seven 'Elements of Enlightenment' to perfection; the seven elements of enlightenment, practised and developed, bring 'Wisdom and Deliverance' to perfection.

But how does Watching over In- and Out-breathing, practised and developed, bring the four 'Foundations of Mindfulness' (Satipaṭṭhāna) to perfection?

I. Whenever the disciple (1) mindfully makes a long inhalation or exhalation, or (2) makes a short inhalation or exhalation, or (3) trains himself to inhale or exhale whilst experiencing the whole (breath-) body, or (4) whilst calming down this bodily function (i.e. the breath)—at such a time the disciple dwells in 'contemplation of the body', full of energy, comprehending it, mindful, after subduing worldly greed and grief. For, inhalation and exhalation I call one amongst the corporeal phenomena.

II. Whenever the disciple trains himself to inhale or exhale (1) whilst feeling rapture (pīti), or (2) joy (sukha), or (3) the mental functions (cittasaṅkhāra), or (4) whilst calming down the mental functions—at such a time he dwells in 'contemplation of the feelings', full of energy, clearly comprehending them, mindful, after subduing worldly greed and grief. For, the full awareness of In- and Out-breathing I call one amongst the feelings.

III. Whenever the disciple trains himself to inhale or exhale (1) whilst experiencing the mind, or (2) whilst gladdening the mind, or (3) whilst concentrating the mind, or (4) whilst setting the mind free—at such a time he dwells in 'contemplation of the mind', full of energy, clearly comprehending it, mindful, after subduing worldly greed and grief. For, without mindfulness and clear comprehension, I say, there is no Watching over In- and Out-breathing.

IV. Whenever the disciple trains himself to inhale or exhale whilst contemplating (1) impermanence, or (2) the fading away of passion, or (3) extinction, or (4) detachment—at such a time he dwells in 'contemplation of the mind-objects', full of energy, clearly comprehending them, mindful, after subduing worldly greed and grief. Having seen, through understanding, what is the abandoning of greed and grief, he looks on with complete equanimity.

Watching over In- and Out-breathing, thus practised and developed, brings the four Foundations of Mindfulness to perfection.

But how do the four Foundations of Mindfulness, practised and developed, bring the seven 'Elements of Enlightenment' (bojjhaṅga) to full perfection?

1. Whenever the disciple dwells in contemplation of body, feelings, mind and mind-objects, strenuous, clearly comprehending them, mindful, after subduing worldly greed and grief—at such a time his mindfulness is undisturbed; and whenever his mindfulness is present and undisturbed, at such a time he has gained and develops the Element of Enlightenment 'Mindfulness' (sati-sambojjhaṅga); and thus this element of enlightenment reaches fullest perfection.

2. And whenever, whilst dwelling with mindfulness, he wisely investigates, examines and thinks over the 'Law' (dhamma)—at such a time he has gained and develops the Element of Enlightenment 'Investigation of the Law' (dhammavicaya-sambojjhaṅga); and thus this element of enlightenment reaches fullest perfection.

3. And whenever, whilst wisely investigating, examining and thinking

over the law, his energy is firm and unshaken—at such a time he has gained and develops the Element of Enlightenment 'Energy' (viriya-sambojjhaṅga); and thus this element of enlightenment reaches fullest perfection.

4. And whenever in him, whilst firm in energy, arises super-sensuous rapture—at such a time he has gained and develops the Element of Enlightenment 'Rapture' (pīti-sambojjhaṅga); and thus this element of enlightenment reaches fullest perfection.

5. And whenever, whilst enraptured in mind, his spiritual frame and his mind become tranquil—at such a time he has gained and develops the Element of Enlightenment 'Tranquillity' (passaddhi-sambojjhaṅga); and thus this element of enlightenment reaches fullest perfection.

6. And whenever, whilst being tranquillized in his spiritual frame and happy, his mind becomes concentrated—at such a time he has gained and develops the Element of Enlightenment 'Concentration' (samādhi-sambojjhaṅga); and thus this element of enlightenment reaches fullest perfection.

7. And whenever he looks with complete indifference on his mind thus concentrated—at such a time he has gained and develops the Element of Enlightenment 'Equanimity' (upekkhā-sambojjhaṅga); and thus this element of enlightenment reaches fullest perfection.

The four Foundations of Mindfulness, thus practised and developed, bring the seven elements of enlightenment to full perfection.

And how do the seven elements of enlightenment, practised and developed, bring Wisdom and Deliverance (vijjā-vimutti) to full perfection?

Herein the disciple develops the elements of enlightenment: Mindfulness, Investigation of the Law, Energy, Rapture, Tranquillity, Concentration and Equanimity, based on detachment, on absence of desire, on extinction and renunciation.

The seven elements of enlightenment thus practised and developed, bring wisdom and deliverance, to full perfection.

M. 125

Just as the elephant hunter drives a huge stake into the ground and chains the wild elephant to it by the neck, in order to drive out of him his wonted forest ways and wishes, his forest unruliness, obstinacy and violence, and to accustom him to the environment of the village, and to teach him such good behavior as is required amongst men: in like manner also should the noble disciple fix his mind firmly to these four Foundations of Mindfulness, so that he may drive out of himself his wonted worldly ways and wishes, his wonted worldly unruliness, obstinacy and violence, and win to the True, and realize Nibbāna.

New Words and Expressions

abandoning of greed and grief	断除贪忧
Calming (down) this bodily function	安定身行；安定出入息
calming down the mental functions	安定心行
clearly comprehending	正知；清楚地觉照
corporeal phenomena	色法；物质现象
Detachment / dɪ'tætʃmənt / *n.*	出离；舍弃；无住；不执着
fading away of passion	离贪
Foundations of Mindfulness	念处；念住：念的住立或现起处
mental functions	心行
obstinacy / 'ɒbstɪnəsɪ / *n.*	顽固；执拗
practice and develop	修习及多修
renunciation / rɪ,nʌnsi'eɪʃn / *n.*	舍弃
Setting the mind free	令心解脱
Subduing worldly greed and grief	调伏世间的贪与忧
Wisdom and Deliverance	慧解脱

Grammar

英语句子结构的中心（灵魂）是动词，而其他成分，都是围绕动词而生成、组织、展开的。

《佛言》（佛教英语）里主要使用了哪些动词呢？这些动词的语义特点是什么呢？

以下是《佛言》里使用的动词（包括名词性的动词）的不完全统计：

（1）离，失，灭：

Extinction（extinct），detachment, fading away, forsaking, abandonment, liberate（liberation）from, destruction（destroy），dissolution（dissolve），discard, loss, depart, vanish, extinguish, overcome, annihilation, cessation, comes to an end, put an end to, the end of, cease, give up, disappearance, escape, free from, reach（reach final extinction），turn away from, absence of, abstaining from, avoidance of, ward off, dispel, suppress, root out, etc.

（2）坚持、住于：adhere to, attach to（attachment），cling to, grasp "dwell with…； dwell in …"（安住于……）注意：这是个"中性"的概念。既可"住于"观身，也可"住于"互相攻击。

（3）达到，成就，证得：
只有"arise, gain, reach, attain, realize, enter（into），lead to, win, penetrate"等少数几个。

观察以上动词，可得到以下初步印象：

"得"与"失"严重不对称。表示"失去，灭"的动词的数量远远多于表示"得"的动词，其语义也更丰富，更具体，更具表现力。句型也更多样化。

如何理解"得"与"失"不对称的现象呢?
这些语义特征与佛经的内容、佛教思想、修行体系有什么关系?

Exercises

1. Is it possible to attain Nibbana by watching over In-and-out Breathing alone?

2. Explain how the practice and development of the "Four Foundations of Mindfulness" will lead to perfection in Wisdom and Deliverance (vijjā-vimutti).

3. What is the elephant compared to in the "Taming Wild Elephant" example?
   And what is the function of the "huge stake" in the story?

4. And whenever, whilst enraptured in mind, his spiritual frame and his mind become tranquil-at such a time he has gained and develops the Element of Enlightenment 'Tranquillity' (passaddhi-sambojjhanga); and thus this element of enlightenment reaches fullest perfection.
   What is the exact meaning of 'spiritual frame' in the above sentence?

5. How can we best translate 'upadana' into English? By 'attachment', 'clinging' or 'grasping'?

Unit
Fourteen

EIGHTH FACTOR

Right Concentration
(Sammā-samādhi)

M. 44

What, now, is Right Concentration?

Its Definition

Having the mind fixed to a single object (cittekaggatā, lit. 'One-pointedness of mind'): this is concentration.

'Right Concentration' (sammā-samādhi), in its widest sense, is the kind of mental concentration which is present in every wholesome state of consciousness (kusala-citta), and hence is accompanied by at least Right Tho ught (2nd factor), Right Effort (6th factor) and Right Mindfulness (7th factor). 'Wrong Concentration' is present in unwholesome states of consciousness, and hence is only possible in the sensuous, not in a higher sphere. Samādhi, used alone, always stands in the Sutta, for sammā-samādhi, or Right Concentration.

Its Objects

The four 'Foundations of Mindfulness' (7th factor): these are the objects of concentration.

Its Requisites

The four 'Great Efforts' (6th factor): these are the requisites for concentration.

Its Development

The practising, developing and cultivating of these things: this is the development (bhāvanā) of concentration.

Right Concentration (sammā-samādhi) has two degrees of development; 1. 'Neighborhood Concentration' (upacāra-samādhi), which approaches the first absorption without, however, attaining it; 2. 'Attainment Concentration' (appanāsamādhi), which is the concentration present in the four Absorptions (jhāna). These Absorptions are mental states beyond the reach of the fivefold sense-activity, attainable only in solitude and by unremitting perseverance in the practice of concentration. In these states all activity of the five senses is suspended. No visual or audible impressions arise at such a time, no bodily feeling is felt. But, although all outer sense-impressions have ceased, yet the mind remains active, perfectly alert, fully awake.

The attainment of these Absorptions, however, is not a requisite for the realization of the four Supermundane Paths of Holiness; and neither Neighborhood-Concentration nor Attainment-Concentration, as such, possesses the power of conferring entry to the four Supermundane Paths: hence they really have no power to free one permanently from evil things. The realization of the Four Supermundane Paths is possible only at the moment of deep 'Insight' (vipassanā) into the Impermanency (aniccatā), Miserable Nature (dukkhatā) and Impersonality (anattatā) of this whole phenomenal process of existence. This Insight, again, is attainable only during Neighborhood-Concentration, not during Attainment Concentration.

He who has realized one or other of the Four Supermundane Paths without ever having attained the Absorptions, is called Sukkha-vipassaka, or Suddha-vipassana-yānika, i.e. 'one who has taken merely Insight (vipassanā) as his vehicle'. He, however, who, after cultivating the Absorptions, has reached one of the Supermundane Paths, is called Samatha-yānika, or 'one who has taken Tranquillity (samatha) as his vehicle (yāna)'.

For samatha and vipassanā see Fund. IV and B. Dict.

The Four Absorptions (jhāna)

D.22

Detached from sensual objects, detached from evil things, the disciple enters into the first Absorption, which is accompanied by Thought Conception and Discursive Thinking, is born of detachment, and filled with Rapture and Happiness.

This is the first of the Absorptions belonging to the Fine-Material Sphere (rūpāvacarajjhāna). It is attained when, through the strength of concentration, the fivefold sense activity is temporarily suspended, and the five Hindrances are likewise eliminated.

See B. Dict.: kasina, nimitta, samādhi.

M. 43

This first Absorption is free from five things, and five things are present. When the disciple enters the first Absorption, there have vanished (the five Hindrances): Lust, Ill-Will, Torpor and Sloth, Restlessness and Mental Worry, Doubts; and there are present: Thought Conception (vitakka), Discursive Thinking (vicāra), Rapture (pīti), Happiness (sukha), Concentration (citt'ekaggatā = samādhi).

These five mental factors present in the first Absorption, are called Factors (or Constituents) of Absorption (jhānaṅga). Vitakka (initial formation of an abstract thought) and vicāra (discursive thinking, rumination) are called 'verbal functions' (vacī-saṅkhāra) of the mind; hence they are something secondary compared with consciousness.

In Visuddhi-Magga, vitakka is compared with the taking hold of a pot, and vicāra with the wiping of it. In the first Absorption both are present, but are exclusively focussed on the subject of meditation, vicāra being here not discursive, but of an 'exploring' nature. Both are entirely absent in the following Absorptions.

D. 22

And further: after the subsiding of Thought-Conception and Discursive Thinking, and by the gaining of inner tranquillity and oneness of mind, he enters into a state free from Thought-Conception and Discursive Thinking, the second Absorption, which is born of concentration (samādhi), and filled with Rapture (pīti) and Happiness (sukha).

In the second Absorption, there are three Factors of Absorption: Rapture, Happiness, and Concentration.

And further: after the fading away of Rapture, he dwells in equanimity, mindful, with clear awareness: and he experiences in his own person that feeling of which the Noble Ones say: 'Happy lives he who is equanimous and mindful'— thus he enters the third Absorption.

In the third Absorption there are two Factors of Absorption: equanimous Happiness (upekkhā-sukha) and Concentration (citt'ekaggatā).

And further: after the giving up of pleasure and pain, and through the disappearance of previous joy and grief, he enters into a state beyond pleasure and pain, into the fourth Absorption, which is purified by equanimity and mindfulness.

In the fourth Absorption there are two Factors of Absorption: Concentration and Equanimity (upekkhā).

In Visuddhi-magga forty subjects of meditation (kammaṭṭhāna) are enumerated and treated in detail. By their successful practice the following Absorptions may be attained:

All four Absorptions: through Mindfulness of Breathing (see Vis. M. VIII. 3), the ten Kasina-exercises (Vis. M. IV, V and B. Dict.); the contemplation of Equanimity (upekkhā), being the practice of the fourth Brahma-vihāra (Vis. M. IX. 4).

The first three Absorptions: through the development of Loving-Kindness (mettā), Compassion (karunā) and Sympathetic Joy (muditā), being the practice of the first three Brahma-vihāras (Vis. M. IX. 1-3).

The first Absorption: through the ten Contemplations of Impurity (asubha-bhāvanā; i.e. the Cemetery Contemplations, which are ten according to the enumeration in Vis. M. VI); the contemplation of the Body (i.e. the 32 parts of the body; Vis. M. VIII. 2); 'Neighborhood-Concentration' (upacāra-samādhi): through the Recollections on Buddha, Dhamma and Sangha, on Morality, Liberality, Heavenly Beings, Peace (=Nibbāna) and death (Vis. M. VI. VII); the Contemplation on the Loathsomeness of Food (Vis. M. XI. 1); the Analysis of the Four Elements (Vis. M. IX. 2).

The four Immaterial Absorptions (arūpa-jjhāna or āruppa), which are based on the fourth Absorption, are produced by meditating on their respective objects from which they derive their names; Sphere of Unbounded Space, of Unbounded Consciousness, of Nothingness, and of Neither-Perception-Nor-Non-Perception.

The entire object of concentration and meditation is treated in Vis M. III-XIII; see also Fund. IV.

S. XXII. 5

Develop your concentration: for he who has concentration, understands things according to their reality. And what are these things? The arising and passing away of corporeality, of feeling, perception, mental formations and consciousness.

M. 149

Thus, these five Groups of Existence must be wisely penetrated; Ignorance and Craving must be wisely abandoned; Tranquillity (samatha) and Insight (vipassanā) must be wisely developed.

S. LVI. II

This is the Middle Path which the Perfect One has discovered, which makes one both to see and to know, and which leads to peace, to discernment, to enlightenment, to Nibbāna.

Dhp. 275

And following upon this path, you will put an end to suffering.

New Words and Expressions

Analysis of the Four elements	四界分别观
Attainment Concentration	安止定
Compassion / kəmˈpæʃn / *n.*	悲：四无量心之一
Concentration / ˌkɒnsnˈtreɪʃn / *n.*	心一境之定
contemplation of Equanimity	舍心想；舍：四无量心之一
contemplation of the body (32 parts)	观 32 身分
Contemplation on the Loathsomeness of Food	食厌想
cultivate / ˈkʌltɪveɪt / *vt.*	培养
development of concentration	定之修习
discernment / dɪˈsɜːnmənt / *n.*	敏锐；洞察力
discursive / dɪˈskɜːsɪv / *adj.*	推论的；论证的
Discursive Thinking	伺；伺察：一种心行，即专注在所缘上
eliminate / ɪˈlɪmɪneɪt / *vt.*	消除；熄灭
enumerate / ɪˈnjuːməreɪt / *vt.*	枚举
Equanimity / ˌekwəˈnɪməti / *n.*	舍（禅支）
Equanimous Happiness	舍乐（禅支）
Factors (Constituents) of Absorption	禅支
First Absorption	初禅
fivefold sense activity	五根的活动
forty subjects of meditation	四十业处
Four Immaterial Absorptions	四无色定（禅）
Happiness / ˈhæpɪnəs / *n.*	乐（禅支）
impermanency / ˈɪmpɜːmənənsɪ / *n.*	无常性
initial formation of an abstract thought	寻：一种心行，即把心安置在所缘上
Loving-Kindness	慈：四无量心之一
miserable nature	苦
neighborhood Concentration	近行定
objects of concentration	所观法（境）
Sphere of Unbounded Space	空无边处

Sphere of Neither-Perception-Nor-Non Perception	非想非非想处
Sphere of Nothingness	无所有处
Sphere of Unbounded Consciousness	识无边处
one who has taken Tranquility as his vehicle	止行者；定乘者
oneness of mind	一心；心一境性
One-pointedness of Mind	心一境性
Rapture / 'ræptʃə(r) / n.	喜（禅支）
requisite / 'rekwɪzɪt / n.	必要条件
requisites for concentration	定的资粮；定的条件
rumination / ˌruːmɪ'neɪʃn / n.	思路；沉思
sensual objects	所缘境（尘）；感官对象
solitude / 'sɒlɪtjuːd / n.	独处
subside / səb'saɪd / vi.	平息；止息
suspend / sə'spend / vt.	中止
Sympathetic Joy	喜：四无量心之一
Contemplations of Impurity	不净观
the ten Kasina-Excercises	十遍
Thought Conception	寻
Tranquility / træŋ'kwɪlɪtɪ / n.	止；奢摩他
Unwholesome States of Consciousness	不善心识
vehicle / 'viːəkl / n.	乘；交通工具
verbal functions of the mind	心之语行
visual or audible impressions	眼触或耳触
wholesome state of consciousness	善心识
Wrong Concentration	邪定

Grammar

段落内，句子之间常用并列 / 排比结构：

例段：

And further, the disciple acts with clear comprehension in going and coming;

157

he acts with clear comprehension in looking forward and backward; acts with clear comprehension in bending and stretching; acts with clear comprehension in carrying alms bowls and robes; acting with clear comprehension in eating, drinking, chewing and tasting; acts with clear comprehension in discharging excrement and urine; acts with clear comprehension in walking, standing, sitting, falling asleep, awakening; acts with clear comprehension in speaking and keeping silent.

复次，佛弟子于去、来时，以正知而行；彼于前瞻、后视时，以正知而行；于屈、伸（肢体任何部位）时，以正知而行；于持钵、着衣时，以正知而行；于啖、饮、嚼、味时，以正知而行；于大小便时，以正知而行，于行、住、坐、寐、寤时，以正知而行；于语、默时，以正知而行。

And further: the disciple dwells in contemplation of the mind-objects, namely of the five 'Groups of Existence'. He knows what 'Corporeality' (rū pa) is, how it arises, how it passes away; knows what 'Feeling' (vedanā) is, how it arises, how it passes away; knows what 'Perception' (saññā) is, how it arises, how it passes away; knows what the 'Mental Formations' (sankhāra) are, how they arise, how they pass away; knows what 'Consciousness' (viññāna) is, how it arises, how it passes away.

复次，弟子于法，名"五蕴"者，观法而住。彼知"如是色，如是色之生起、灭尽；知如是受，如是受之生起、灭尽；知如是想，如是想之生起、灭尽；知如是行，如是行之生起、灭尽；知如是识，如是识之生起、灭尽。"

不同段落也常有大段重复文字：
例文：
…'A body is there': this clear awareness is present in him, to the extent necessary for knowledge and mindfulness; and he lives independent, unattached to anything in the world. Thus does the disciple dwell in contemplation of the body.

……"有身"之念现前，足以生起智与念。彼无所依而住，不执着世间一切法。弟子如是，于身观身而安住。

　　…'Feelings are there': this clear awareness is present in him, to the extent necessary for knowledge and mindfulness; and he lives independent, unattached to anything in the world. Thus does the disciple dwell in contemplation of the feelings.

　　……"有受"之念现前，足以生起智与念。彼无所依而住，不执着世间一切法。弟子如是，于受观受而安住。

　　…'Mind is there'; this clear awareness is present in him, to the extent necessary for knowledge and mindfulness; and he lives independent, unattached to anything in the world. Thus does the disciple dwell in contemplation of the mind.

　　……"有心"之念现前，足以生起智与念。彼无所依而住，不执着世间一切法。行者如是于心观心而住。

　　根据 Thanissaro Bhikkhu 对《转法轮经》的注释，佛经中大段重复的文字，如三转、十二行相这种表述方式就叫作"轮"（cakka），是古印度哲学、法律论著的一种传统论辩手段和表达方式。在口头传承的古代，文本中的大量重复有助于记忆，而重复造成的平行排比结构还有修辞的功能，就像音乐中的"refrain"。在重复表述中加入变化因素，不断扩展，层层深入，也利于更全面、系统地表述思想，给读者（论敌）以严谨，滴水不漏的印象。

　　但"轮"也有其局限性。特别是在现代媒介中。"轮"中的重复冗余部分不仅降低了信息量和传输效率，对习惯现代思维方式的读者，"轮"的存在也易使阅读失去挑战性和兴趣。既然不用口头传承，过多重复的文字也就显得没有必要。

　　在佛经中有大量的"轮"，如何处理这些重复的文字，这对译经者是个挑战。有些译者，如 Nyanatiloka 就对这些"轮"进行了适当的归纳、缩写。这样的好处是更精炼，条理更清晰，坏处是失去了"原汁原味"。

Thanissaro Bhikkhu 对《转法轮经》的注释：

The discussion in the four paragraphs beginning with the phrase, "Vision arose…," takes two sets of variables—the four noble truths and the three levels of knowledge appropriate to each—and lists their twelve permutations. In ancient Indian philosophical and legal traditions, this sort of discussion is called a wheel. Thus, this passage is the Wheel of Dhamma from which the discourse takes its name.

关于"轮"的更多资料：

Dhammacakka（Dharma Cakra）　http://oaks.nvg.org/dharmacakra.html

Richard Gombrich remarks: "We do not really know what the Buddha said in his first sermon… and it has even been convincingly demonstrated that the language of the text as we have it is in the main a set of formulae, expressions which are by no means self-explanatory but refer to already established doctrines. Nevertheless, the compilers of the Canon put in the first sermon what they knew to be the very essence of theBuddha's Enlightenment." - [Gombrich, Richard. Theravada Buddhism: A Social History from Ancient Benares to Modern Colombo. London: Routledge, 1988, repr. 2002, p.61. -A second edition from 2006 exists too.]

The Gombrich quotation helps us to understand something vital about the first old documents of Buddhism. First they were orally transmitted, and the very many repetitions in them help in such circumstances. After a period of oral transmittion they were put down in writing and apparently translated into such as Pali.

Many of the sutra repetitions occur through fixed schemas that statements are put into, maybe with slight variations. For the most part repetitions have been omitted here, as the new media seldom call for them. "Keep It Sweet and Short" is largely fit nowadays. Even so, there are a lot of views to go through or look into. - TK

The exposition in the four paragraphs that begin with the phrase, "Vision arose ..., " uses two sets of variables—the four noble truths and the three levels of knowledge applied to each—and lists twelve combinations of them. In ancient Indian philosophical and legal traditions, such a sort of discussion is called a wheel [cf. schema above]. Thus, the Wheel of Dharma that the discourse takes its name from, refers to the ancient presentation method. It also relates to the Buddhist Wheel symbol.

Exercises

1. What is the difference between Mindfulness and Concentration?
2. How many different states of Concentration are there?
3. What are the differences between different stages of Concentration (Absorptions)?
4. How are the absorptions achieved?
5. What is the relationship between Concentration and Insight?

Unit Fifteen

Gradual Development of the Eightfold Path in the Progress of the Disciple

Confidence and Right Thought (Second Factor)

M. 38

Suppose a householder, or his son, or someone reborn in a good family, hears the law; and after hearing the law he is filled with confidence in the Perfect One. And filled with this confidence, he thinks: 'Full of hindrances is household life, a refuse heap; but the homeless life (of a monk) is like the open air. Not easy is it, when one lives at home, to fulfil in all points the rules of the holy life. How if now I were to cut off hair and beard, put on the yellow robe and go forth from home to the homeless life?' And in a short time, having given up his possessions, great or little, having forsaken a large or small circle of relations, he cuts off hair and beard, puts on the yellow robe, and goes forth from home to the homeless life.

Morality (Third, Fourth, Fifth Factor)

Having thus left the world, he fulfils the rules of the monks. He avoids the killing of living beings and abstains from it. Without stick or sword, conscientious, full of sympathy, he is desirous of the welfare of all living beings.—He avoids stealing, and abstains from taking what is not given to him. Only what is given to him he takes, waiting till it is given; and he lives with a heart honest and pure.—He avoids unchastity, living chaste, celibate and aloof from the vulgar practice of sexual intercourse.—He avoids lying and abstains from it. He speaks the truth, is devoted to the truth, reliable, worthy of confidence, no deceiver of men.—He avoids tale-bearing and abstains from it. What he has heard here, he does not repeat there, so as to cause dissension there; and what he has heard there, he does not repeat here, so as to cause dissension here. Thus he unites those that are divided, and those that are united he encourages; concord gladdens him, he delights and rejoices in concord; and it is concord that he spreads by his words.—He avoids harsh language and abstains from it. He speaks such words as are gentle, soothing to the ear, loving, such words as go to the heart, and are courteous, friendly, and agreeable to many.—He avoids vain talk and abstains from it. He speaks at the right time, in accordance with facts, speaks what is useful, speaks of the law and the discipline; his speech is like a treasure, uttered at the right moment, accompanied by arguments, moderate and full of sense.

He takes food only at one time of the day (forenoon), abstains from food in the evening, does not eat at improper times. He keeps aloof from dance, song, music and the visiting of shows; rejects flowers, perfumes, ointment, as well as every kind of adornment and embellishment. High and gorgeous beds he does not use. Gold and silver he does not accept.—He does not accept raw corn and flesh, women and girls, male and female slaves, or goats, sheep, fowls, pigs, elephants, cows or horses, or land and goods. He does not go on errands and do the duties of a messenger. He eschews buying and selling things. He has nothing to do with false measures, metals and weights. He avoids the crooked ways of bribery, deception and fraud. He has no part in stabbing, beating, chaining, attacking, plundering and oppressing.

He contents himself with the robe that protects his body, and with the alms bowl by means of which he keeps himself alive. Wherever he goes, he is provided with these two things; just as a winged bird in flying carries his wings along with him. By fulfilling this noble Domain of Morality (sīla-kkhandha) he feels in his heart an irreproachable happiness.

Control of the Senses (Sixth Factor)

Now, in perceiving a form with the eye, a sound with the ear, an odour with the nose, a taste with the tongue, an impression with the body, an object with the mind, he cleaves neither to the whole, nor to its details. And he tries to ward off that which should he be unguarded in his senses, might give rise to evil and unwholesome states, to greed and sorrow; he watches over his senses, keeps his senses under control. By practising this noble 'Control of the Senses' (indriya-saṃvara) he feels in his heart an unblemished happiness.

Mindfulness and Clear Comprehension (Seventh Factor)

He is mindful and acts with clear comprehension when going and coming; when looking forward and backward; when bending and stretching his limbs; when wearing his robes and alms-bowl; when eating, drinking, chewing and tasting; when discharging excrement and urine: when walking, standing, sitting, falling asleep and awakening; when speaking and keeping silent.

Now being equipped with this lofty 'Morality' (sīla), equipped with this noble 'Control of the Senses' (indriya-saṃvara), and filled with this noble, 'Mindfulness and Clear Comprehension' (sati-sampajaññā), he chooses a secluded dwelling in the forest, at the foot of a tree, on a mountain, in a cleft, in a rock cave, on a burial ground, on a wooded table-land, in the open air, or on a heap of straw. Having returned from his alms-round, after the meal, he seats himself with legs crossed, body erect, with mindfulness fixed before him.

Absence of the Five Hindrances (nīvaraṇa)

He has cast away 'Lust' (kāmacchanda); he dwells with a heart free from lust; from lust he cleanses his heart.

He has cast away 'Ill-will' (vyāpāda); he dwells with a heart free from ill-will; cherishing love and compassion toward all living beings, he cleanses his heart from ill-will.

He has cast away 'Torpor and Sloth' (thīnamiddha); he dwells free from torpor and sloth; loving the light, with watchful mind, with clear comprehension, he cleanses his mind from torpor and sloth.

He has cast away 'Restlessness and Mental Worry' (uddhacca-kukkucca); dwelling with mind undisturbed, with heart full of peace, he cleanses his mind from restlessness and mental worry.

He has cast away 'Doubt' (vicikicchā); dwelling free from doubt, full of confidence in the good, he cleanses his heart from doubt.

The Absorptions (Eighth Factor)

He has put aside these five 'Hindrances' (nīvaraṇa), the corruptions of the mind which paralyse wisdom. And far from sensual impressions, far from evil things, he enters into the Four Absorptions (jhāna).

Insight (vipassanā) (First Factor)

IX. 36

But whatsoever there is of corporeality, feeling, perception, mental formations, or consciousness: all these phenomena he regards as 'impermanent' (anicca), 'subject to pain' (dukkha). as infirm, as an ulcer, a thorn, a misery, a burden, an enemy, a disturbance, as empty and 'void of an Ego' (anattā); and turning away from these things, he directs his mind towards the Deathless thus; 'This, truly, is Peace, this is the Highest, namely the end of all Karma formations, the forsaking of every substratum of rebirth, the fading away of craving, detachment, extinction, Nibbāna. And in this state he reaches the 'cessation of passions' (āsavakkhaya).

Nibbāna

M. 39

And his heart becomes free from sensual passion (kāmāsava), free from the passion for existence (bhavāsava), free from the passion of ignorance (avijj'āsava), 'Freed am I!' this knowledge arises in the liberated one ; and he knows: 'Exhausted is rebirth, fulfilled the Holy Life; what was to be done, has been done; naught remains more for this world to do'.

M. 26

For ever am I liberated.

This is the last time that I'm born,

No new existence waits for me.

M. 140

This is, indeed, the highest, holiest wisdom: to know that all suffering has passed away.

This is, indeed, the highest, holiest peace: appeasement of greed, hatred and delusion.

The Silent Thinker

'I am' is a vain thought; 'This am I' is a vain thought; 'I shall be' is a vain thought; 'I shall not be' is a vain thought. Vain thoughts are a sickness, an ulcer, a thorn. But after overcoming all vain thoughts, one is called 'a silent thinker'. And the thinker, the Silent One, does no more arise, no more pass away, no more tremble, no more desire. For there is nothing in him whereby he should arise again. And as he arises no more, how should he grow old again? And as he grows old no more how should he die again? And as he dies no more, how should he tremble? And as he trembles no more, how should he have desire'?

The True Goal

M. 29

Hence, the purpose of the Holy Life does not consist in acquiring alms, honour, or fame, nor in gaining morality, concentration, or the eye of knowledge. That unshakable deliverance of the heart: that, indeed, is the object of the Holy Life, that is its essence, that is its goal.

M. 51

And those, who in the past were Holy and Enlightened Ones, those Blessed Ones also have pointed out to their disciples this self-same goal as has been pointed out by me to my disciples. And those who in the future will be Holy and Enlightened Ones, those Blessed Ones also will point out to their disciples this self-same goal as has been pointed out by me to my disciples.

D. 16

However, disciples, it may be that (after my passing away) you might think: 'Gone is the doctrine of our master. We have no Master more'. But thus you should not think; for the 'Law' (dhamma) and the 'Discipline' (vinaya) which I have taught you, will after my death be your master.

> The Law be your isle,
> The Law be your refuge!
> Look for no other refuge!

Therefore, disciples, the doctrines which I taught you after having penetrated them myself, you should well preserve, well guard, so that this Holy life may take its course and continue for ages, for the weal and welfare of the many, as a consolation to the world, for the happiness, weal and welfare of heavenly beings and men.

New Words and Expressions

hindrances / ˈhɪndrənsiz / *n.*		障碍
desirous / dɪˈzaɪərəs / *adj.*		渴望的
unchastity / ʌnˈtʃæstɪti / *n.*		不贞
chaste / tʃeɪst / *adj.*		纯洁的；朴素的

celibate / ˈselɪbət / *adj.*	禁欲的；独身的
aloof from	远离；不参与
deceiver / dɪˈsiːvə(r) / *n.*	骗子
gladden / ˈɡlædn / *vt.*	使高兴；使喜悦
courteous / ˈkɜːtiəs / *adj.*	有礼貌的；谦恭的
argument / ˈɑːɡjumənt / *n.*	依据
forenoon / ˈfɔːnuːn / *n.*	午前
ointment / ˈɔɪntmənt / *n.*	香膏
adornment and embellishment	装饰品
gorgeous / ˈɡɔːdʒəs / *adj.*	华丽的
eschew buying and selling things	离买卖
crooked ways of bribery, deception and fraud	行贿、欺诈、造假等邪曲
plundering and oppressing	掠夺及压迫
alms bowl	僧人用的钵
Domain of Morality	圣戒蕴
irreproachable happiness	无过之乐
ward off	抵御
unblemished / ʌnˈblemɪʃt / *adj.*	无瑕的
alms-round	乞食
ulcer / ˈʌlsə(r) / *n.*	溃疡
forsake / fəˈseɪk / *vt.*	舍弃
substratum of rebirth	转生之依
passing away	灭度
preserve / prɪˈzɜːv / *vt.*	守
guard / ɡɑːd / *vt.*	护
the holy life	梵行；圣洁的生活
weal / *n.*	幸福；福祉
consolation / ˌkɒnsəˈleɪʃn / *n.*	慰藉；安慰
heavenly beings	天人；天众

Grammar

读起来"古色古香",有点类似汉语的"文言文",这是《佛言》语言的另一个特点。具体表现在以下方面。

1. 古英语的词汇

例如:"ere"(before),"unto"(to), whereby(adv. 凭什么;靠那个)、thereby(adv. 从而;因此)、thereupon(adv. 因此;于是;立即;随即)、herein(adv. 此中;于此)、whither(adv. 在哪里;conj. 无论在哪里)、whence(adv. 何处;出于什么原因;conj. 因此;由此;pron. 何处,那里;n. 根源,来处)、whilst(conj. 同时,当……的时候)。

在现代英语中,除了特殊文体,这些词已经很少使用了。

2. 较古老的结构

例如:…I make known unto you.

"Five and forty years"

这是古英语(Middle English)数词的语序。

Attain to:(archaic)

动词"attain + to"是 20 世纪前的用法,现代英语中已经不用介词"to"了。

例如:

All Buddhas of the three periods of time attain Anuttara-samyak-sambodhi through reliance on Prajna Paramita.

三世诸佛,依般若波罗蜜多故。得阿耨多罗三藐三菩提。

再如,不定式和动名词的用法:

…not to get what one desires, is suffering.

求不得是苦。

现代英语中一般要说：Not getting what one desires…

例如：

Not getting what you want can make you stronger.

There are only two tragedies in life: one is not getting what one wants, and the other is getting it.（Oscar Wilde）

再如："Just as … even so…"

Just as one calls 'hut' the circumscribed space which comes to be by means of wood and rushes, reeds, and clay, even so we call 'body' the circumscribed space that comes to be by means of bones and sinews, flesh and skin.

这种表示比喻，类比的结构中，现代英语中已经不用"even"了。

造成以上这种语言现象原因，可能是译者有意要传达巴利语佛经"古雅"的语言风格。也可能是译者刻意追求某一类语言风格（如：模仿英语圣经文体）。

自 20 世纪初（1907）《佛言》英译本问世以来，100 多年已经过去了。而语言是在不断发展的。《佛言》中的词汇和结构，与今天的英语已经有了很大的差异。因此，要提醒学生对《佛言》的"古雅"风格，不宜盲目模仿。

Exercises

1. Can one attain Nibbana without renouncing the world and joining the monastic order?

2. What is the true goal of the Holy Life?

3. How do you know if you have attained Nibbana?

4. How do you define "A silent thinker"?

Appendix

Appendix I

Buddhist Literature

A Selection for Further Study

I. Life of the Buddha

E. H. Brewster. *The Life of Gotama the Buddha*. Compiled from the Pali Canon. London, Kegan Paul.

Narada Thera. *The Life of the Buddha in his own words*. Colombo, Y.M.B.A.

E. J. Thomas. *The Life of Buddha as Legend and History*. London, Kegan Paul.

Bhikkhu Silacara. *A Young People's Life of the Buddha*. Colombo, W. F. Bastian & Company.

Edwin Arnold. *The Light of Asia*. (Poetical). Many editions. Pivadassi Thera. *The Buddha*, *A Short Study of His Life and His Teachings*. Kandy, Buddhist Publication Society.

Kassapa Thera & Siridhamma Thera. *The Life of the Buddha*. Colombo 1958, Dept. of Cultural Affairs.

II. Translations from the Sutta-pitaka

1. Anthologies

H. C. Warren. *Buddhism in Translations*. 496 pp. Harvard Oriental Series.

F. L. Woodward. *Some Sayings of the Buddha*. Oxford Press.

E. J. Thomas. *Early Buddhist Scriptures*. London, Kegan Paul.

Nyanatiloka Thera, *The Path to Deliverance*. Colombo, Lake House Bookshop.

David Maurice. *The Lion's Roar, An Anthology of the Buddha's Teaching*. Rider & Co.

Selected Buddhist Texts from the Pali Canon. (Sutta translations from 'The Wheel' Series) Vol. I-lI) Buddhist Publication Society, Kandy.

2. Complete Texts

Prof. T. W. Rhys Davids, Tr. *Dialogues of the Buddha (Dîgha Nîkāya)*. London, Pali Text Society. 3 vols.

I. B. Horner, Tr. *The Middle Length Sayings (Majjhima Nikāya)*. Pali Text Society. 3 vols.

F. L. Woodward and F. M. Hare, Tr. *Gradual Sayings (Anguttara Nikāya)*. Pali Text Society. 5 vols.

C. A. F. Rhys Davids and F. L. Woodward, Tr. *Kindred Sayings* (Sa.myutta Nikāya). Pali Text Society. 5 vols.

Narada Thera, Tr. *Dhammapada* (Pali text with English prose translation). Wisdom of the East Series, John Murray.

Professor S. Radakrishnan, Tr. *Dhammapada*. London, George Allen & Unwin.

F. M. Hare, Tr. *Woven cadences (Sutta Nipāta)*. (Sacred Books of the Buddhists). Pali Text Society.

FL. Woodward, Tr. *Minor Anthologies. Vol. II: Udāna and Itivuttaka*. (Sacred Books of the Buddhists). Pali Text Society.

C. A. F. Rhys Davids, Tr. *Songs of the Brethren (Theragātha)*. Pali Text Society.

C. A. F. Rhys Davids, Tr. *Songs of the Sisters (Therigātha)*. Pali Text Society.

3. Single Discourses

Soma Thera. *The Way of Mindfulness* (Transl. of the Satipatthāna Sutta and its Commentary, 3rd ed.) Buddhist Publication Society.

Soma Thera. *Right Understanding* (Transl. of the 9th Discourse of Majjhima Nikāya and its Commentary). Colombo, Lake House Bookshop.

The Wheel Series contains annotated translations of many Discourses. Buddhist Publication Society.

III. Abhidhamma

Nyanatiloka Mahathera. *Guide through the Abhidhamma* Pi.taka (Synopsis of all 7 Abhidhamma Books). 3rd ed. Colombo 1971, Lake House Bookshop.

Narada Thera. *A Manual of Abhidhamma (Abhidhammattha Sangaha).* Pali text, translation and explanatory notes. 2nd ed. Buddhist Publication Society.

Shwe Zan Aung & C. A. F. Rhys Davids, Tr. *Compendium of Philosophy (Abhidhammattha Sangaha).* Pali Text Society.

Dr. W. F. Jayasuriya. *The Psychology and Philosophy of Buddhism, An Introduction to the Abbidhamma.* M. D. Gunasena & Co., Colombo.

Anagarika B. *Govinda. Psychological Attitude of Early Buddhist Philosophy and its systematic representation according to Abhidhamma tradition.* Rider & Co.

Nyanaponika Thera. Abhidhamma Studies. Researches in Buddhist Psychology. 2nd enlarged Ed. Kandy, Buddhist Publication Society.

IV. Non-canonical Pali Literature

I. B. Horner, Tr. *Milinda's Questions.* 2 vols. Pali Text Society.

T. W. Rhys Davids, Tr. *The Ouestions of King Milinda.* 2 vols. Dover Books.

Buddhaghosa (Bhikkhu Ñānamoli, Tr.) *The Path of Purification (Visuddhi Magga).* 2nd ed. A. Semage, Colombo. (The most important and comprehensive systematic treatment of the entire Buddhist teachings).

V. Historical Literature

B. C. Law. *History of Pali Literature.* 2 vols. London, Kegan Paul.

S. C. Banerji. *An introduction to Pali Literature.* Punthi Pustak, Calcutta.

M. Wînternitz. *History of Indian Literature, Vol. II: Buddhist and Jain Literature.* Calcutta University.

T. W. Rhys Davids. *Buddhist India.*

F. J. Thomas. *History of Buddhist Thought.* London, Kegan Paul.

G. P. Malalasekera. *Pali Literature of Ceylon.* M. D. Gunasena & Co., Colombo.

E. W. Adikaram. *Early History of Buddhism in Ceylon.* Colombo, 1946, Lake House Bookshop.

H. R. Perera. *Buddhism in Ceylon, Its Past & Present.* Buddhist Publication Society.

Karuna Kusalasaya. *Buddhism in Thailand, Its Past and Present.* Buddhist Publication Society.

VI. General Literature

Nyanatiloka Thera. *Buddhist Dictionary: A Manual of Buddhist Terms & Doctrines.* 3rd enlarged ed., Frewin & Co., Colombo, 1971.

Nyanatiloka Thera. *Fundamentals of Buddhism: Four Lectures.* Lake House Bookshop, Colombo.

Piyadassi Thera. *The Buddha's Ancient Path.* Rider & Co.

Nyanasatta Thera. *Basic Tenets of Buddhism: Aids to the Study and Teaching of the Dhamma.* Ananda Semage, Colombo 11.

Narada Thera. *Buddhism in a Nutshell.* Buddhist Publication Society.

Khantipalo Bhikkhu. *Buddhism Explained: An Introduction to the Teaching of Lord Buddha.* Social Science Association Press, Bangkok.

Dr. Walpola Rahula. *What the Buddha Taught.* Gordon Frazer, Oxford. (also

Grove Press, NY.)

R. G. de S. Wettimuny. *Buddhism and its Relation to Religion and Science.* M. D. Gunasena & Co., Colombo,

Nyanaponika Thera. *The Heart of Buddhist Meditation* (Satipa.t.thana). 3rd enlarged ed., Rider & Co.

P. Vajirañana Mahathera. *Buddhist Meditation in Theory and Practice.* M. D. Gunasena & Co., Colombo.

Nanamoli Thera. *Mindfulness of Breathing: Buddhist Texts from the Pali Canon & Commentaries.* Buddhist Publication Society.

K. N. Jayatilleke. *Early Buddhist Theory of Knowledge.* George Allen & Unwin.

G. P. Malalasekera, Ed. *Encylopaedia of Buddhism: Vol. 1, Vol. II, fasc. 1ff (to be continued).* Published by the Government of Ceylon (Distributors: K. V. G. de Silva & Sons, Colombo).

VII. Periodicals

The Maha Bodhi, A Monthly Journal for International Buddhist Brotherhood. Calcutta, Maha Bodhi Society

The Middle Way. A quarterly; organ of the Buddhist Society, London, W.C.I.

The Buddhist. Monthly organ of the Colombo Y.M.B.A. Colombo.

World Buddhism. Monthly international Buddhist News Magazine. Published at 91/1 Dutugemunu St., Dehiwala, Ceylon.

Appendix II

Index of Pali Terms

Pali 巴利语	English 英　语	Chinese 中文释义	Page 原蓝皮书页码
A			
abhidhamma-piṭaka	Philosophical Collection	论藏	2；9；11
abhidhamma		阿毗达摩	2；9；11
abhiññā	Psychical Powers	神通；神足	63
adosa	kindness	慈悲（无瞋）	32
ājīva			
Lokiya-sammā-ājīva	Mundane Right Livelihood	世间正命	53
sammā-ājīva	Right Livelihood	正命	27；53；54
akusala	Karmically unwholesome	不善	23；30；31
Akusala-kammapatha	Evil Courses of Action	不善业道	31
alobha	unselfishness	无贪	32
amoha	wisdom	智慧	32
anāgāmi	Non-Returner	不还果（阿那含）	36；37；66
ānāpāna-sati	Watching over in-and-out-breathing	入出息念； 数息观	58；59；68
anattā	without a self	无我；无我的	13；14~16；24； 38；44
anattaniya	Not belonging to a self	非我所的	14
anattatā	impersonal nature	无我性	23；74
āneñjābhisaṅkhāra	imperturbable karma-formations	静业；不动业； 没有现行的业	43

续表

Pali 巴利语	English 英　语	Chinese 中文释义	Page 原蓝皮书页码
anicca	transient；impermanent	无常	13；24；38；81
aniccatā	impermanecy	无常性	74
an-upādisesa-nibbāna	nibbāna without the Groups remaining	无余涅槃	25
anurakkhana-ppadhāna	effort to maintain	随护勤；勤守持（已生善令增长）	57
āpo-dhātu	Fluid Element	水大	9；10
appanāsamādhi	attainment concentration	安止定；根本定	73
arahat	Holy One	阿罗汉	25；26；36；37；64；66
ariya			
ariya-puggala	Noble Ones	圣人	36；37
ariya-sacca	Four Noble Truths	四圣谛	68
Ariya-aṭṭhaṅgikamagga	Noble Eightfold Path	圣八支道；八正道	28
arūpa			
arūpa-bhava	Immaterial Existences	无色界	19
arūpa-jjhana	Four Immaterial Absorptions	四无色定（禅）	76
arūpa-rāga	Craving for Immaterial Existence	贪求无色有	36
arūpāvacara	Immaterial Sphere	无色界	43
asaṅkhata	Unconditioned；Unformed	无相；无为的	38；39
āsavakkhaya	Cessation of Passions	无漏（漏尽）	64；81
asubha-bhāvanā	Contemplations of Impurity	不净观	76
avihimsā-saṅkappa	Thought free from cruelty	无害想；离害思维	47
avijj'āsava	Passion of ignorance	无明烦恼；无明漏	81
avijjā	Ignorance	无明	22；36；42；43
avyāpāda-saṅkappa	Thought free from ill-will	无嗔想；离嗔思维	47

续表

Pali 巴利语	English 英　语	Chinese 中文释义	Page 原蓝皮书页码
āyatana	Sense-bases	根处	42；45；67
B			
bhav'āsava	passion for existence	有漏	81
bhava	Process of Becoming； Process of Existence	有	19；20；23；24； 33；42；45
arūpabhava	immaterial Existence	无色有	19
bhava-diṭṭhi	Eternity Belief	常见	19；33
Kamma-bhava	Karma Process；　process of becoming	业有	20；23；42；45
rūpabhava	Fine-material Existence	色有；色界有	19
bhava-taṇhā	Craving for Existence	贪有	19
upapatti-bhava	Rebirth Process	生有	23；45
bhāvanā			
bhāvanā-ppadhāna	Effort to Develop	修勤；勤于修 （未生善令生）	56
vipassana-bhāvanā	development of Insight	修观； 修毗婆舍那	59
bhūta			
mahā-bhūta	(Four) Elements	（四）大	9
bojjhaṅga	Elements of Enlightenment	觉支	56；67；70
Buddha	Enlightened One；　Knower or Awakened One	觉者；佛陀	1
C			
cakkhu-viññāṇa	eye-consciousness	眼识	12
cetanā	volition	意；作意；思	11；12；21；43
kusala-akusala-cetanā	good and evil volitions	善不善意； 善不善心	23
rūpa-cetanā	will directed to forms	色意	11
citt'ekaggatā	concentration	定；一心	73；75；76
citta	mind	心；意	65

Pali 巴利语	English 英　语	Chinese 中文释义	Page 原蓝皮书页码
kusala-citta	wholesome state of consciousness	善心识	73
cittānupassanā	Contemplation of the Mind	观心	65
cittasaṅkhāra	mental functions	心行	69
cittekaggatā	One pointedness of mind; the mind fixed to a single object	一心；定	73
D			
dhamma	law；phenomenon；doctrine；etc.	法	28；36；70；76；83
dhamma（as doctrine）	Teaching of Deliverance	解脱之教义	1
dhamma（as refuge）	dhamma as refuge	皈依法	3
saṅkhata-dhamma	all things that are conditioned or formed	有为法	38；39
dhamma-vicaya	Investigation of the Law	择法	56；67
dhammānupassanā	Contemplation of Mind Objects	法念处	66
dhammavicaya	Investigation of the Law	择法	67
dhammavicaya-sambojjhaṅga	Element of Enlightenment 'Investigation of the Law'	择法觉支	70
dhātu	Four Elements	四大	9~11；61
āpo-dhātu	Fluid Element	水大	9；10
paṭhavī-dhātu	Solid Element	地大	9
tejo-dhātu	Heating Element	火大	9；10
vāyo-dhātu	Vibrating（Windy）Element	风大	9；10
diṭṭhi	Understanding；Belief	见	19；27；30；33；35；37；46
bhava-diṭṭhi	Eternity-Belief；Eternalism	常见	19；33
lokiya-sammā-diṭṭhi	Mundane Right Understanding	世间正见	37
lokuttara-sammā-diṭṭhi	Supermundane Right Understanding	出世间正见	37

Pali 巴利语	English 英 语	Chinese 中文释义	Page 原蓝皮书页码
sakkāya-diṭṭhi	Self-Illusion	身见	33；35
sammā-diṭṭhi	Right Understanding	正见	27；30~46
sassata-diṭṭhi	Eternity-Belief； Eternalism	常见	19；33
uccheda-diṭṭhi	Annihilation-Belief； Annihilationism； Belief in Annihilation	断见	19；33
vibhava- diṭṭhi	Annihilation-Belief； Annihilationism； Belief in Annihilation	断见	19；33
dibba			
dibba-cakkhu	Heavenly Eye	天眼	64
dibba-sota	Heavenly Ear	天耳	63
dosa	Hatred	瞋	31；44
dukkha	Suffering； subject to Pain	苦	5；13；17； 24；38；81
dutiyampi（dutiyaṃ）	for the second time	第二遍	3
G			
gacchāmi	I go for（to）	我去（皈依）	3
ghāna-viññāṇa	Nose-Consciousness	鼻识	13
H			
hadaya-vatthu	Physical Basis of Mind	意根；心基；心 所依靠的色法； 心识所赖以生起 之处	9
I			
iddhi-vidhā	Magical Powers	神通	63
iddhipāda	Bases for obtaining Magical Powers	神足	64
indriya-saṃvara	Control of the Senses	摄诸根	80
J			
jarā-maraṇa	Decay and Death	老死	42；45

Pali 巴利语	English 英　语	Chinese 中文释义	Page 原蓝皮书页码
jāti	Birth	生	20；24；42；45
jhāna	Absorptions	禅那	59；63；64；73；74；75；76；81
arūpa-jjhāna	Immaterial Absorptions	无色定；无色禅	76
jhānaṅga	Factors of Absorption； Constituents of Absorption	禅支	75
jīva	Vital Principle；Soul	命根；生命；灵魂	41
jivhā-viññāṇa	Tongue-consciousness	舌识	13
K			
kāma-taṇhā	Sensual Craving	欲贪；欲爱	19
kām'āsava	Sensual passion	欲漏	81
kāmacchanda	Lust（attachment to sensual pleasure）	贪爱；执着欲爱	66；80
kāma-loka	Sensuous Sphere	欲界	36
kāmarāga	Sensual Lust（sensual passion）	贪爱	35
Kamma	Karma；Action；actions；deeds； life-affirming activities	业	20~23；30~32；42~46
kamma-bhava	Process of Becoming；Karma Process	业有	20；23；42；45
kāya-kamma	Bodily Action	身业	30；31
mano-kamma	Mental Action	意业	31；32
Vacī-kamma	Verbal Action	语业	30；32
Kammantā			35
lokiya-sammā-Kammantā	Mundane Right Action	世间正业	51
lokuttara-sammā-Kammanta	Supermundane Right Action	出世间正业	51
sammā-kammanta	Right Action	正业	27；51~52
karunā	Compassion	悲悯	76

续表

Pali 巴利语	English 英　语	Chinese 中文释义	Page 原蓝皮书页码
kāya			
kāya-kamma	Bodily Action	身业	30；31
kāya-viññāṇa	Body Consciousness	身识	13
kāyānupassanā	Contemplation of the Body	身念住；身念处	58
kāyā-saṅkhāra	Bodily Function	身行：出入息	59
khandha	Group	蕴	8~13；15；16；25；65；67；68；79
khandha-parinibbāna	Extinction of the Five-Khandha-process	五蕴之灭尽	25
rūpa-khandha	Group of Corporeality	色蕴	9
saṅkhāra-khandha	Group of Formations	行蕴	11
saññā-khandha	Group of Perception	想蕴	11
vedanā-khandha	Group of Feeling	受蕴	11
viññāna-khandha	Group of Consciousness	识蕴	12
kilesa-parinibbāna	Extinction of Impurities	不净（烦恼）之灭尽	25
kusala	Wholesome	善	31；73
kusala-citta	Wholesome state of consciousness	善心识	73
kusala-kammapatha	Good Courses of Action	善业道	32
kusala-akusala-cetanā	Good and evil volitions	善思及不善思	23
L			
lobha	Greed	贪	31；44
loka			
kāma-loka	Sensuous Sphere	欲界	36
rūpa-loka	Fine-Material Sphere	色界	36
lokiya			
lokiya-sammā-ājīva	Mundane Right Livelihood	世间正命	53
lokiya-sammā-diṭṭhi	Mundane Right Understanding	世间正见	37

续表

Pali 巴利语	English 英　语	Chinese 中文释义	Page 原蓝皮书页码
lokiya-sammā-kammanta	Mundane Right Action	世间正业	51
lokiya-sammā-saṅkappa	Mundane Right Thought	世间正思维	47
lokiya-sammā-vācā	Mundane Right Speech	世间正语	49
lokuttara			
lokuttara-sammā-ājīva	Supermundane Right Livelihood	出世间正命	53
lokuttara-sammā-diṭṭhi	Supermundane Right Understanding	出世间正见	37
lokuttara-sammā-kammanta	Supermundane Right Action	出世间正业	51
lokuttara-sammā-saṅkappa	Supermundane Right Thought	出世间正思维	47
lokuttara-sammā-vācā	Supermundane Right Speech	出世间正语	49
M			
magga			
sotāpatti-magga	Path of Stream Entry	初果道	36
paṭisambhidā-Magga		无碍解道	46
Visuddhi-magga		清净道（论）	41；42；46；60；61；75；76
mahā-bhūta	Elements	大	9
māna	Conceit	慢；骄慢	36
majja	Intoxicating drinks	酒	4
manasikāra	Attention	作意	12
mano			
mano-kamma	Mental Action	意业	31；32
mano-viññāna	mind-consciousness	意识	13
mettā	Loving-Kindness	慈；慈爱	76
moha	Delusion	痴；愚痴	31；44
muditā	Sympathetic Joy	喜	76
musāvāda	False Speech	妄语	4

续表

Pali 巴利语	English 英　语	Chinese 中文释义	Page 原蓝皮书页码
N			
nāma-rūpa；nāmarūpa	Mental and Physical Existence	名色	42；45
nekkhamma-saṅkappa	Thought free from lust	离欲想；离欲思维；出离心	47
nibbāna			
an-upādisesa-nibbāna	Extinction of the Five-Khandha-process；Nibbana without the Groups remaining	无余涅槃	25
saupādisesa-nibbāna	Extinction of Impurities Nibbana with the Groups of Existence still remaining	有余涅槃	25
nīvarana	Hindrances	盖；障	66；80；81
P			
paṭhavī-dhātu	Solid Element	地大	9
paṭicca			
paṭicca-samuppāda	Dependent Origination	缘起	6；20；41；42；44；
paṭikūla-saññā	Contemplation of loathsomeness	厌恶想（不净观）	60
pahāna-ppadhāna	Effort to Overcome	断勤；勤于断（已生恶令断）	55
pañca-sīla	Five Moral Precepts	五戒	3
paññā	Wisdom	慧；智慧	27；28
paramattha	Absolute sense	胜义；究竟法	65
parassa-cetopariya-ñana	Insight into the Hearts of Other Beings	他心智；他心通	63
parinibbāna			
khandha-parinibbāna	Extinction of the Five-Khandha-process	五蕴之灭尽	25
kilesa-parinibbāna	Extinction of Impurities	不净（烦恼）之灭尽	25

Pali 巴利语	English 英　语	Chinese 中文释义	Page 原蓝皮书页码
passaddhi	Tranquillity	轻安	56；67
passaddhi-sambojjhaṅga	Element of Enlightenment 'Tranquillity'	轻安觉支	71
phala			
sotāpatti-phala	Fruition of Stream Entry	须陀洹果；初果	36
phassa	Sense Impression; Sensorial Impression	触	12；42；45
phoṭṭhabba	Bodily impressions	身触	9
piṭaka			
Abhidhamma-piṭaka	Philosophical Collection	论藏	2
Sutta-piṭaka	Collection of Discourses	经藏	2
Ti-Piṭaka	Three Baskets	三藏	2
vinaya-piṭaka	Collection of Discipline	律藏	2
pīti	Rapture	喜	56；67；69；75
pīti-sambojjhaṅga	Element of Enlightenment 'Rapture'	喜觉支	70
ppadhāna			
anurakkhaṇā-ppadhāna	Effort to maintain	随护勤；勤守持（已生善令增长）	57
bhāvanā-ppadhāna	Effort to develop	修勤；勤于修（未生善令生）	56
pahāna-ppadhāna	Effort to Overcome	断勤；勤于断（已生恶令断）	55
saṃvara-ppadhāna	Effort to avoid	律仪勤；勤于护（未生恶令不生）	55
pubbe-nivāsānussati-ñāṇa	Remembrances of many Previous Births	宿命智；宿命通	64
puthujjana	Worldling	凡夫	37；64
R			
rāga			
rūpa-rāga	Craving for Fine-material Existence	执着于色界；色界爱	36

续表

Pali 巴利语	English 英 语	Chinese 中文释义	Page 原蓝皮书页码
arūpa-rāga	Craving for Immaterial Existence	执着于无色界； 无色界爱	36
rūpa	Corporeality；visible form	色	13；67
rūpa-bhava	Fine-material Existence	色（界）有	19
rūpa-cetanā	Will directed to forms	色思	11
rūpa-khandha	Group of corporality	色蕴	9
rūpa-loka	Fine-material Sphere	色界	36
nāma- rūpa	Mental and Physical Existence	名色	42
rūpa-rāga	Craving for Fine-material Existence	执着于色界；色 界爱	36
rūpakkhandha	Group of corporality	色蕴	9；68
rūpāvacara	Fine-material Sphere	色界	43
rūpāvacarajjhāna	Absorptions belonging to the Fine-material Sphere	色界定	74
S			
saḷ-āyatana			
Six Sense-Organs	六根	42；45	
Saṃsāra	the wheel of existence；lit；the 'Perpetual Wandering'	轮回	16-18
saṃyojana	Fetters	系缚；烦恼；结	33；35
Sakadāgāmi	Once-Returner	一来；斯陀含	36；37
sakkāya			
sakkāya-diṭṭhi	Self-Illusion	身见	33；35
samādhi	Concentration	定；三昧	27；28；56；67
samādhi-sambojjhaṅga	Element of Enlightenment 'concentration'	定觉支	71
sammā-samādhi	Right Concentrtion	正定	27；73~77
samādiyāmi	I undertake to observe	（我）受持； 承诺遵守	4
samatha-bhāvanā	Development of tranquillity	修止； 修舍摩他	59

续表

Pali 巴利语	English 英 语	Chinese 中文释义	Page 原蓝皮书页码
sambojjhaṅga			
dhammavicaya-sambojjhaṅga	Element of Enlightenment Investigation of the law	择法觉支	70
passaddhi-sambojjhaṅga	Element of Enlightenment 'Tranquillity'	轻安觉支	71
pīti-sambojjhaṅga	Element of Enlightenment 'Rapture'	喜觉支	70
samādhi-sambojjhaṅga	Element of Enlightenment 'Concentration'	定觉支	71
sati-sambojjhaṅga	Element of Enlightenment 'Mindfulness'	念觉支	70
upekkhā-sambojjhaṅga	Element of Enlightenment 'Equanimity'	舍觉支	71
viriya-sambojjhaṅga	Element of Enlightenment 'Energy'	精进觉支	70
Sammā			
Sammā-ājīva	Right Livelihood	正命	27；53~54
Sammā-diṭṭhi	Right Understanding	正见	27；30
Sammā-kammanta	Right Action	正业	27；51~52
Sammā-samādhi	Right Concentrtion	正定	27；73~77
Sammā-sambodhi	Perfect Enlightenment	正等正觉	1
Sammā-saṅkappa	Right Thought	正思维	27；47
Sammā-sati	Right Mindfulness	正念	27；58~72
Sammā-vācā	Right Speech	正语	27；48~50
Sammā-vāyāma	Right Effort	正精进；正勤	27；55~57
Sampajañña			
Sati-Sampajañña	Mindfulness and Clear Comprehension	念和清净知（正念正知；正智；正心）	60；80
Samuppāda			
Paṭicca-Samuppāda	Dependent Origination	缘起	6；20；41；42~46

续表

Pali 巴利语	English 英　语	Chinese 中文释义	Page 原蓝皮书页码
Sangha			
Sangha（as community）		僧团	2
Sangha（as refuge）		僧宝	3
Samathayānika	one who has taken tranquility as his vehicle	奢摩他行者； 止行者	74
saṅkappa			
avihimsā-saṅkappa	Thought free from ill-will	无嗔想； 离嗔思维	47
lokiya-sammā-saṅkappa	Mundane Right Thought	世间正思维	47
lokuttara-sammā-saṅkappa	Supermundane Right Thought	出世间正思维	47
nekkhamma-saṅkappa	Thought free from lust	出离心； 离欲想； 离欲思维	47
sammā-saṅkappa	Right Thought	正思维	27；47
saṅkhāra	Formations	行；造作	12；13；38；39；42；43；45；65；67
kāya-saṅkhāra	bodily function	身行	59
saṅkhāra-khandha	Group Of Mental Formations	行蕴	11；65；68
vacī-saṅkhāra	verbal operations	语行	47；75
saṅkhārakkhandha	Group Of Mental Formations	行蕴	11；65；68
saṅkhata			
saṅkhata-dhamma	All possible physical and mental constituents of existence; All things that are conditioned or 'formed'	有为法	38；39
saññā	Perception	想	13；67

续表

Pali 巴利语	English 英　语	Chinese 中文释义	Page 原蓝皮书页码
saññā-khandha	Group of perception	想蕴	11
paṭikūla-saññā	Contemplation of loathsomeness	厌恶想 （不净观）	60
saraṇaṃ	For refuge	为皈依	3
sassata			
sassata-diṭṭhi	Eternity-Belief	常见；相信永恒的存在	19；33
sati	Mindfulness	念	56；67
ānāpāna-sati	Watching over-in and out-breathing	观出入息	58；59；68
sati-sambojjhaṅga	Element of Enlightenment 'Mindfulness'	念觉支	70
Sammā-sati	Right Mindfulness	正念	27；58~72
Sati-Sampajañña	Mindfulness and Clear Comprehension	念和清净知（正念正知；正智；正心）	60；80
satipaṭṭhāna	Foundations of Mindfulness Four Foundations of Mindfulness	念处；四念处	58；59；68；69
saupādisesa-nibbāna	Extinction of Impurities Nibbana with the Groups of Existence still remaining	有余涅槃	25
sikkhāpadaṃ	Precept	学处；戒条；戒	4
sīla	Morality	戒；禁戒	27；80
sīla-kkhandha	Domain of Morality	戒学处；戒蕴	79
pañca-sīla	Five Moral Precepts	五戒	3
sīlabbata-parāmāsa	Attachment to mere Rule and Ritual	戒禁取 （执着于律仪）	35
sotāpanna	Stream Enterer	须陀洹；入流	35；36
sotāpatti			
sotāpatti-magga	path of stream entry	须陀洹道；初果道	36
sotāpatti-phala	fruition of stream entry	须陀洹果；初果	36

续表

Pali 巴利语	English 英　语	Chinese 中文释义	Page 原蓝皮书页码
sota-viññāna	Ear-consciousness	耳识	13
Suddhavipassanā-yānika	He who has realized one or other of the Four Supermundane Paths wihtout ever having attained the Absorption	纯观行者	74
sukha	Joy	喜悦	69；75
upekkhā-sukha	equanimous Happiness	舍的喜悦	76
sukkha-vipassaka	He who has realized one or other of the Four Supermundane Paths without ever having attained the Absorption	干观者 （纯观行者）	74
suñña	void of a permanent self or substance	空	14
sutta-piṭaka	Collection of Discourses	经藏	2
T			
taṇha	Craving	贪爱；贪	22；24；25；41；45
taṇhā			
bhava-taṇhā	Craving for existence; the desire for eternal life	贪有； 执着于有（常见）	19
kāma-taṇhā	Sensual Craving	欲贪；欲爱	19
vibhava-taṇhā	Craving for Self-Annihilation	无有爱；执着于无（断见）	19
tatiyampi	for the third time	第三次	3
tejo-dhātu	Heating Element	火大	9；10
thīna-middha	Torpor and Sloth	昏沉睡眠	66
thīnamiddha	Torpor and Sloth	昏沉睡眠	80
ti-lakkhaṇa	Three Characteristics	三法印	13；32
ti-piṭaka	Three Baskets	三藏	2
ti-ratana	Three Jewels	三宝	3
ti-saraṇa	Threefold Refuge	三皈依	3

Pali 巴利语	English 英　语	Chinese 中文释义	Page 原蓝皮书页码
U			
uccheda-diṭṭhi	Annihilation-Belief；Annihilationism；Belief in Annihilation	断见	19；33
uddhacca	Restlessness	掉举	36
uddhacca-kukkucca	Restlessness and Mental worry	掉举和悔；掉悔盖	66；81
upacāra-samādhi	Neighborhood Concentration	近行定	76
upacārasamādhi	Neighborhood Concentration	近行定	73
upādā rūpa	Corporeality derived from the four primary elements	四大所造色	9
upādāna	Clinging	取	20；24；25；42；45
upādāya rūpa	Corporeality derived from the four primary elements	四大所造色	9
upapatti-bhava	Rebirth Process	生有	23；45
upekkhā	Equanimity	舍	56；67；76
upekkhā-sambojjhaṅga	Element of Enlightenment 'Equanimity'	舍觉支	71
upekkhā-sukha	equanimous Happiness	舍的喜悦	76
V			
vācā			
lokiya-sammā-vācā	Mundane Right Speech	世间正语	49
lokuttara-sammā-vācā	Supermundane Right Speech	出世间正语	49
sammā-vācā	Right-Speech	正语	27；48~50
vacī	Verbal	讲话；口头的；言语的	30；32
Vacī-kamma	Verbal Action	语业	30；32
vacī-saṅkhāra	verbal operations	语行	47；75
vatthu	Physical basis	依处；根	9

Pali 巴利语	English 英 语	Chinese 中文释义	Page 原蓝皮书页码
hadaya-vatthu	Physical basis of mind	意根；心处：心识赖以生起之处	9
vāyāma	Effort	精进	27；55~57
Sammā-vāyāma	Right Effort	正精进；正勤	27；55~57
vāyo-dhātu	Vibrating（Windy）Element	风大	9；10
vedanā	feeling	受	13；20；42；45；67
vedanā-khandha	Group of Feeling	受蕴	11
vedanākkhandha	Group of Feeling	受蕴	68
vedanānupassanā	contemplation of the feelings	受念处；受念住	64
veramaṇī	abstain from	禁止；戒；离	4
vibhava			
vibhavadiṭṭhi	Annihilationism Annihilation-Belief	断见	19；33
vibhava-taṇhā	Craving for Self-Annihilation	无有爱；执着于无（断见）	19
vicāra	Discursive thinking	伺	65；75
vicaya			
dhamma-vicaya	Investigation of the Law	择法	56；67
vicikicchā	Scepticism；Doubts；Doubt	疑	35；66；81
vijjā-vimutti	Wisdom and Deliverance	慧解脱	71
vinaya-piṭaka	Collection of Discipline	律藏	2
viññāṇa	consciousness	识	13；42；45；65；67
cakkhu-viññāṇa	eye- consciousness	眼识	12
ghāna-viññāṇa	nose- consciousness	鼻识	13
jivhā-viññāṇa	tongue- consciousness	舌识	13
kāya-viññāṇa	body- consciousness	身识	13
viññāṇa-khandha	the group of consciousness	识蕴	12
mano-viññāṇa	mind- consciousness	意识	13

续表

Pali 巴利语	English 英　语	Chinese 中文释义	Page 原蓝皮书页码
sota-viññāṇa	ear- consciousness	耳识	13
viññāṇakkhandha	the group of consciousness	识蕴	12
vipāka	result of actions	异熟；业报；果报	22
vipassanā	Insight	观；毗婆舍那	28；74；81
vipassana-bhāvanā	development of Insight	修观；修毗婆舍那	59
viriya	Energy	精进；勤	56；67
viriya-sambojjhaṅga	Element of Enlightenment 'Energy'	精进觉支	70
vitakka	thought-conception	寻：最初的心专注；念头的开端	65；75
vohāravacana	conventional expression	方便说；方便语	65
vyāpāda	Ill-Will	瞋	35；66；80

巴利语字符：a ā b c d ḍ e g h i ī j k l ḷ m ṁ ṃ n ñ ṅ ṇ o p r s t ṭ u ū v y

198

Appendix III.

Chinese Text of the Word of the Buddha

缩略语

每一引文的出处在引文开头以旁注标识, 旁注采用如下缩略语:

缩略语	所指的文献
D.	《长部》（Dihga– Nikaya）, 数字指经号。
M.	《中部》（Majjhima-Nikaya）, 数字指经号。
A.	《增支部》（Aṅguttara- Nikaya）, 罗马数字指主要分部或集号, 第二个数字指经号。
S.	《相应部》（Saṃyutta - Nikaya）, 罗马数字指分部的号（" 相应 "Saṃyutta）, 如诸天相应（Devata Saṃyutta）= I, 等等。第 2 个数字指经号。
Dhp.	《法句经》（Dhammapada）, 数字指偈号。
Ud.	《自说经》（Udana）, 罗马数字指品号, 第二个数字指经号。
Snp.	《经集》（Sutta–Nipāta）, 数字指偈号。
VisM.	《清净道论》（Visuddhi–Magga）
B.Dict	《佛教辞典》, 三界智尊者编纂。
Fund.	《佛教基本教理》, 三界智尊者编纂。

巴利语发音表
源自美国版

在本书中，除少量专有名词外，非英语词汇一律用斜体字。大多数此类词汇是巴利语，也就是原典的书面语言。巴利语发音规则如下：

元 音

字母	发音规则
a	发英语单词 *shut* 中 u 的音，不发 *cat*，或 *take* 中 u 的音。
ā	发 *father* 中 a 的音，不发成 *take* 中 a 的音。
e	长音，发 *stake* 中 a 的音。
i	发 *pin* 中 i 的音。
î	发 *machine* 中 i 的音，不发 *fine* 中 i 的音。
o	长音，发 *hope* 中 o 的音。
u	发 *put* 中 u 的音，或发 *foot* 中 oo 的音。
ū	发 *boot* 中 oo 的音，不发 *refuse* 中 u 的音。

辅 音

字母	发音规则
c	发 *chair* 中 ch 的音，不发 k，s，也不发 *centre*, *city* 中 c 的音。
g	发 *get* 中 g 的音，不发 *general* 中 g 的音。
h	h 总是要发音，在辅音或双辅音后也不例外，例如：bh 发 *cab-horse* 中的 bh 音；ch 发 *ranch-house* 中的 chh 音；dh 发 *handhold* 中的 dh 音；gh 发 *bag-handle* 中的 gh 音；jh 发 *sledge-hammer* 中的 dgh 音，等等。
j	发 *joy* 中的 j 音。
ṃ	如 "Ceylon" 中的鼻化音，ṃ 通常发 *sung*, *sing* 中的 ng 音。
s	通常发 *this* 中的 s 音；不要发成 *these* 中的 s 音。

续表

字母	发音规则
ñ	如 "Canyon"（西班牙语 *cañon*）中的鼻化音 ny，或 *Mignon* 中的 gn 音。
ph	发 *haphazard* 中的 ph 音；不要发 *photograph* 中的 ph 音。
ʈh	发 *hot-housez* 中的 th 音；不要发 *thin* 或 *than* 中的 th 音。
y	发 *yes* 中的 y 音。

t, ʈh, ḍ, ḍh, ḷ 是舌音；发音时，舌头抵上颚。

双辅音：两个音都要发出来，如：*bb* 在 *scrub-board* 中的发音；*tt* 在 *cat-tail* 中的发音。

Chinese
Translation

前 言

佛 陀

佛陀或觉者——字面意为知者或觉悟者——是对印度圣哲乔达摩的尊称。他发现并向世人揭示了解脱之法，在西方被称为佛教。

他于公元前 6 世纪诞生在迦毗罗卫，是释迦国王之子，释迦国位于现今尼泊尔疆界一带。他名叫悉达多，族姓乔达摩。他在 29 岁时放弃了尊贵的太子生活和王族身份，出家苦修，为他早年所认知的苦难世间寻找一条出路。历经 6 年求索，先后依止于多位宗师，经历了一段徒劳的苦修，最终他在迦耶（现今的菩提迦耶，Buddh-Gayā）的菩提树下，证得无上正等正觉（sammā-sambodhi）。这之后 45 年间，他孜孜不倦地弘法讲学，80 岁时，这位"为饶益世间福乐而出世的觉者"在拘尸那罗涅槃。

佛陀既非神，亦非先知或神的化身，而是人中无上士，他凭己力精进用功，证得究竟解脱和圆满智慧，成为举世无双的"天人师"。仅从教导人类如何自救的意义看，他是"救世主"，真正循其足迹和教示前行，终将获得解脱。而从佛陀证得的无上悲智圆融看，他示现了超越时空之理想可由人来圆满。

法

法是佛陀所发现、证悟和宣说的彻底的解脱之教义，以古巴利语留传至今，保存于《三藏》——（1）律藏，包括僧团的戒律；（2）经藏，包括各种教理、对话、偈颂、故事等，可归纳为四圣谛法；和（3）论藏（阿毗达摩），或哲学论集，以严谨系统化和哲学化形式，演说《经藏》之教义。

法不是神示的教义，而是以对现实透彻认识为基础的觉悟之法。法是四圣谛的教义，它揭示了生命最基本的事实，说明了人类凭借己力精进修行，可以证得清净和谛观智，获得解脱。法提供了崇高而切实可行的伦理体系，以及对生命的透彻剖析，深刻的哲学，实用的心灵修持方法，简言之，它是朝向解脱之路的包罗万象的圆满指南。法解答了心和理两方面问题，可使我们避免思想和行为中两种无益且毁灭性的极端，指出了实现解脱的中道。不论何时何地，只要心识足够成熟，领会法义，法总会产生超越时空的强大的感召力。

僧

僧，字面意是"集会"或"团体"，是比丘（托钵僧）团体，由佛陀创立，现今尚以最原始形态存在于缅甸、暹罗、锡兰、柬埔寨、老挝和孟加拉吉大港。佛陀僧团与耆那教僧团是世界上最古老的僧院团体。在佛陀时代最著名弟子有：舍利弗，他对法的透彻理解，仅在佛陀之下；目犍连，神通第一；阿难，佛陀的虔诚弟子和常随侍者；大迦叶，佛陀灭度后王舍城结集的主持者；阿那律，证得天眼通，精通正念；罗睺罗，佛陀亲生子。

僧伽为所有渴望体证究竟解脱而尽形寿修行者提供了良好外缘环境，使其不为世俗所扰。因此，在宗教的发展达到成熟的地方，僧伽是具有超时空的意义。

三皈依

佛法僧，因其无上清净性，被称为"三宝"（*ti-ratana*），是佛教徒在世间最为珍贵之物。"三宝"也构成佛教的"三皈依"（*ti-saraṇa*），佛教徒通过皈依誓词表达或重申将三宝作为生活和思想的指南。

巴利文三皈依誓词与佛陀时期所使用的相同：

我皈依佛。
我皈依法。
我皈依僧。

人们只要三诵此誓词，即可宣布自己为佛教徒。[在诵第二遍、第三遍时，在誓词前加诵"第二遍（Dutiyampi）"和"第三遍（Tatiyampi）"]。

五 戒

在诵三皈依誓词之后，通常还要受持五戒（pañca-sila）。持五戒是最基本的准则，为实现正当生活和进一步走向解脱所必须。

1. 我受持离杀生戒。

2. 我受持离不与取戒。

3. 我受持离邪淫戒。

4. 我受持离妄语戒。

5. 我受持离饮酒放逸戒。

四圣谛

佛陀、觉者如是说：

《长部》第16经

因不觉知、不彻悟四种法，弟子们啊，我曾与汝等如此长久流转于轮回。四者为何也？是为：

苦圣谛（dukkha）

苦之集圣谛（dukkha-samudaya）

苦之灭圣谛（dukkha-nirodha）

苦灭之道圣谛（dukkha-nirodha-gāmini-paṭipadā）

《相应部》第五十六集第11经

若我于此四圣谛之真实智观，尚非十分明达，我于天、魔、梵世、沙门、婆罗门、人、天众生中，不敢言我已证无上正等觉。然，一旦我于此四圣谛之真实智观已彻底明达，我确信我已证得众生无法超越之无上正等觉。

《中部》第26经

我所发觉此甚深法，如此难见、难解、寂静、殊妙，不可以思虑获得，而唯智者所见。

然此世间众生，沉迷于乐、以乐为快、惑于乐。彼类众生实难理解因缘法、诸法之缘起（paṭicca-samuppāda），亦不能理解寂止一切行，舍离一切转生之依，灭贪爱，无著，寂灭，涅槃。

然，世间有眼为微尘所覆众生，彼将悟此真谛。

第一圣谛

苦圣谛

《长部》第22经

何为苦圣谛？

生是苦，老是苦，死是苦；悲、哀、痛、忧、绝望是苦，求不得是苦，简言之：五蕴有是苦。

何为生？属于此类或彼类之有情之生，彼等之入胎、孕育和转为实体、五蕴显现，根业出现，此名为生。

何为老？属于此类或彼类之有情之老，彼等之变老、变弱、发灰白、皮皱，生命力衰减，诸根衰退，此名为老。

何为死？从此类或彼类有情离开与消失，彼等之毁灭、消失、死亡、一期生命之终结、诸蕴的散离、躯体被舍弃：此名为死。

何为悲？因遭遇这样或那样之丧失或不幸而起，担忧、惊惶、内悲、内怆，此名为悲。

何为哀？凡因面临这样或那样之丧失或不幸，悲、哀，哀号和叹息，怆然和悲伤，此名为哀。

何为痛？身之痛苦和不快，由身触所生痛苦和不快的感受，此名为痛。

何为忧？心之痛苦和不快，由意触所生痛苦和不快的感受，此名为忧。

何为绝望？痛苦绝望因遭遇这样或那样之失落或不幸而生，痛苦，绝望，此名为绝望。

何为"求不得苦"？受制于生法之众生，生如是欲求："啊，我等不愿受制于生法！啊，我等不愿有来生！"受制于老、病、死、悲、哀、痛、忧及绝望之众生，生如是欲求："啊，我等不愿经受这些！啊，我等不愿老、病、死、悲、哀、痛、忧、绝望等法而来！"。然，此非以欲求可偿，求而不得，是为苦。

五蕴或五蕴有

《中部》第28经

简言之，何为五蕴有？五蕴有是色、受、想、（心）行、识。

《中部》第109经

一切过去、现在或将来之色、若内若外、若粗若细、若胜若劣、若远若近，皆属色蕴；一切受皆属受蕴；一切想皆属想蕴；一切心行皆属行蕴，一切识皆属识蕴。

五蕴是五种分类，佛陀以此概括了存在的一切物质和精神现象，特别是那些被无明者视为"自我"或"本体"的现象。因此，生、老、死等亦可归入五蕴，五蕴实际上构成了整个世间。

色蕴（rūpa-khandha）

《中部》第28经

何为色蕴？色蕴是指四大及四大所造色。

四大（界）

何为四大？四大是指地大、水大、火大和风大。

通常称作地、水、火、风的四大（dhātu or mahā-bhūta），应被理解为物质的基本属性。它们在巴利语中被命名为：paṭhavī-dhātu、āpo-dhātu、tejo-dhātu、vāyo-dhātu，可译为坚、湿、暖、动（惯性、黏性、辐射性和振动性）。所有的四大都存在于每个物体里，但它们各自所占比重不同，比如说，如果地大占主导，那么这一物体就称为"固体"，等等。

根据《论藏》，"四大所造色"，由以下24种物质现象和特性构成，即：眼净色、耳净色、鼻净色、舌净色、身净色、色、声、香、味、男性根色、女性根色、命根色、心所依处（hadaya-vatthu；见《佛教辞典》）、身表、语表、空界（耳孔、鼻孔等）、色老性、色无常性和食色等。

在上述 24 相中没有专门提及身触（phoṭṭhabba），因为身触等同于地火风诸界，可通过压、冷、热、痛等感觉来感知。

1. 何为"地大（界）"（paṭhavī-dhātu）？地大可以是内地界或外地界。何为内地界？凡依业存于有情身内的坚硬性、坚固性，例如：头发和体毛、指甲、牙齿、皮肤、肉、腱、骨、骨髓、肾、心、肝、隔膜、脾、肺、胃、肠、肠系膜、粪便等等，都称作内地界。无论是内地界还是外地界皆是地界。

应据真实和真实智作如是观："此非我所有，我非此，此非我之自我"。

2. 何为"水大（界）"（āpo-dhātu）？凡依业存于有情身内的液态或流动性，都称作内水界，例如胆汁、痰、脓、血、汗、脂肪、泪、皮脂、唾、涕、关节滑液、尿液等等。无论是内水界还是外水界皆是水界。

应据真实和真实智作如是观："此非我所有，我非此，此非我之自我"。

3. 何为"火大（界）"（tejo-dhātu）？火界可以是内火界或外火界。何为内火界？凡依业存于有情身内的热量或暖性，例如依它而得以加热、消耗、燃烧；依它，所食、所饮、所嚼、所尝而得以完全消化等等，都称作内火界。无论是内火界还是外火界皆是火界。

应据真实和真实智作如是观："此非我所有，我非此，此非我之自我"。

4. 何为"风大（界）"（vāyo-dhātu）？风界可以是内风界或外风界。何为内风界？凡依业存于有情身内的风或风性，例如上行风或下行风、胃肠风、在各肢体间循环、移动的风、入息和出息等等，都称作内风界。无论是内风界还是外风界皆是风界。

应据真实和真实智作如是观："此非我所有，我非此，此非我之自我"。

譬如人们称"小木屋"——由木头、灯心草、芦苇和泥土围成的空间，我们称身体——由骨骼、筋腱、肌肉和皮肤构成的空间。

受蕴（vedanā-khandha）

《相应部》第三十六集第 1 经

受蕴有三种：乐受、苦受、非苦非乐受（舍受）。

想蕴（saññā-khandha）

《相应部》第二十二集第 56 经

何为想蕴？想蕴有六种：色想、声想、香想、味想、身触想以及心法想。

行蕴（saṅkhāra-khandha）

何为行蕴？行蕴有六种思：色思、声思、香思、味思、身触思以及心法思。

行蕴是心理活动众多功能或方面的一个统称，与受和想共存于当下一念的心识。《论藏》划分了五十种行（心所法），其中七种是遍一切心心所。其他心所的数量和构成根据心识类别各自的特点而不同（见《佛教辞典》中表格）。《正见经》（《中部》第 9 经）提到行蕴的三种主要表现形式：思（cetanā）、触（phassa）、作意（manasikāra）。其中，思又是"行"的首要构成元素，是行蕴特别之特性。因此，上文以思为例来讲解。

有关 saṅkhāra 一词的其他用法，参见《佛教辞典》。

识蕴（viññāna-khandha）

《相应部》第二十二集第 56 经

何为识蕴？识有六种：色识、声识、香识、味识、身触识、心法识（字面意：眼识、耳识等）。

识的缘起

《中部》第 28 经

若内眼不坏，然外色未入视野，且无眼根色尘相合，即不现其所对应之识之部分；或，若内眼不坏，外色入视野，然若无眼根色尘相合，亦不现其所对应之识之部分；然，若内眼不坏，外色入视野，且眼根色尘相合，其时现其所对应之识之部分。

《中部》第 38 经

是故我说：识依缘生起；若无外缘，识即不生。识依何缘而生起，即依何缘而得名。

依眼根色尘生起之识，名为眼识（cakkhu-viññāna）

依耳根声尘生起之识，名为耳识（sota-viññāna）。

依鼻根香尘生起之识，名为鼻识（ghāna-viññāna）。

依舌根味尘生起之识，名为舌识（jivhā-viññāna）。

依身根触尘生起之识，名为身识（kāya-viññāna）。

依意根法尘生起之识，名为意识（mano-viññāna）。

《中部》第 28 经

凡有如是状态之色皆属色蕴。

凡有受皆属受蕴。

凡有想皆属想蕴。

凡有行皆属行蕴。

凡有识皆属识蕴。

识依其他四蕴的缘起

《相应部》第二十二集第 53 经

如离于色、受、想、行，而施设（paññatti, Skt Prajbapt）命之死、生，或识之成长、增益、广大者，无有是处。

三法印（ti-lakkhana）

《增支部》第三集第 134 经

诸行无常（anicca）；诸行是苦（dukkha）；诸法无我（anattā）。

《相应部》第二十二集第 59 经

色是无常，受是无常，想是无常，行是无常，识是无常。

凡是无常者，皆为苦；凡是无常、苦且变化者，不能说"此是我所有，此是我，此是我之自我"。

因此，凡色、受、想、行或识，若过去、若现在、若未来，若内若外、若粗若细、若胜若劣、若远若近，如是应以正智慧作如实观："此非我所有，我非此，此非我之自我"。

无 我 说

个体生命乃至整个世间，其实无非是五蕴和合而成之现象不断变化着的过程而已。此过程自无从追忆的无始时来，一直持续，跨越了生命的前生与来世。只要因缘具足，它将继续下去，无有穷尽。如前所述，五蕴—无论是其中单独的某一蕴还是它们的组合——都不构成一个真实的我或存续的个体，同样的，在五蕴之外，也找不到一个作为它们"主宰"的自我、灵魂或实质。换言之，五蕴既非"我"（anatta），也非"我所"（anattaniya）。鉴于一切存在之无常和缘起，相信有任何形式的"自我"存在，都应被视为一种虚妄。

正如我们所谓的"牛车"，除了轮轴、车轮、车辕、车身等，并没有其他存在，或如"房子"这个词，不过是一个方便的称呼，指称不同材料以特定方式组合围成的空间，并没有什么独立房子实体存在。同理，我们称为"生命"、"个体"、"人"或"我"的，无非是不断变化的身心现象组合体而已，本身没有一个真实的存在。

以上，简言之，就是佛陀的无我说，一切存在都没有一个恒常的我或实体的教法。这是佛教的根本教义，是在其他任何宗教或哲学体系里找不到的。完全掌握无我说——不仅用抽象和知性的方式，并以持续的实证体验，这是真正认知佛法和证悟其目标的必备条件。无我说是对事实进行透彻剖析的必然结果，对此，五蕴说中有更详尽的论述。凭借本书前面引用的经文段落我们仅能略见一斑。

有关五蕴说的详细内容，参见《佛教辞典》。

《相应部》第二十二集第95经

譬如此恒河起大聚沫，具眼之士夫，见此观之，则如理于观察。于是如理观察，彼观得：无所有、无实、无坚固。如是色、受、想、行、识，有过去、现在或未来，乃至远近，比丘见此观之，如理于观察，观得：此皆无所有、无实、无我。

《相应部》第二十二集第29经

凡有人因色、受、想、行、识而欢喜，即欢喜苦；欢喜苦者，我说彼无由苦解脱。

《法句经》第146～148颂

> 常在燃烧中，
> 何喜何可乐？
> 幽暗之所蔽，
> 何不求光明？
> 观此粉饰身，
> 疮伤一堆骨，
> 疾病多贪欲，
> 无常不坚固。
> 此衰老形骸，
> 病薮而易坏，
> 朽聚必毁灭，
> 有生终有死。

三 示 诫

《增支部》第三集第35经

汝岂未曾于此世上见男人或女人，或八十，或九十，或百岁，衰如椽曲、驼屈、赖杖、步履蹒跚，衰弱，青春远去，齿列缺欠，发白疏或无，面皱、体有斑痣散在者耶？汝岂未曾作如是思维耶——"己亦必老，不可避免"？

汝岂未曾于此世上见男人或女人，染疾，受苦，重病，辗转于已便溺之中，卧而受他人扶起，并受他人扶至床上耶？汝岂未曾作如是思维，己亦必病，不可避免耶？

汝岂未曾于此世上见男人或女人之尸，死后一日或二日或三日而肿胀、青瘀、溃烂也？汝岂未曾作如是思维，己亦必死，不可避免耶？

轮　回

《相应部》第十五集第 3 经

轮回起点不可思议；生命初始无迹可寻，众生为无明所障，贪欲所缚，流转奔波于轮回。

轮回——存在之轮，字面意："永无休止的游荡"——巴利经文中赋予不停起落之生命海的名称，象征循环无休之生老病死的过程。更确切地讲：轮回是自不可思议的无始以来，时刻变化的五蕴组合体之不断相续。一期生命只是这轮回极小的一部分。因此，为能了知第一圣谛，就必须谛思于轮回，谛思这可怖的无数次重生，而不仅着眼于一期生命，毕竟有情的一生并非总是痛苦不堪。所以，"苦"这个词，在第一圣谛中不仅指由不悦意的触所生起的身心苦受，还包括会带来苦的一切。苦圣谛教示，由于无常的普遍法则，即便是高而胜妙的天道之乐也会变易和毁灭，因此所有的生命状态都是不如意的，无一例外带有苦的种子。

于意云何？汝等长时流转轮回，与怨憎会，与爱别离，悲泣恸哭流注之泪，与四大海之水，二者孰多？

汝等长时流转轮回，于父、母、子、女、兄弟、姐妹之死而受苦痛，流注之泪为更多，非四大海之水所能比也。

《相应部》第十五集第 13 经

于意云何？汝等长时流转轮回，被斩流注之血，与四大海之水，二者孰多？

汝等长时流转轮回，因劫盗淫被斩流注之血为更多，非四大海之水所能比也。

所以者何？

轮回起点不可思议，生命初始无迹可寻，众生为无明所障，贪欲所缚，流转奔波于轮回。

《相应部》第十五集第1经

汝等如是长久受苦、受痛、受失，增大其墓所，足以应厌恶、厌离、解脱诸有。

第二圣谛

苦之集圣谛

《长部》第 22 经

复次，何为苦之集圣谛？此是爱，能引导再生，有俱喜贪，随处不断寻求新的欲乐。

三种贪爱

三种爱是指欲爱（kāma-tanhā）、有爱（bhava-tanhā）和无有爱（vibhava-tanhā）。

欲爱是享受五尘快乐的欲望。有爱是希求持久或永恒生命的欲望，特别是希求更高色界和无色界生命的欲望，与"常见"或有见关系密切，即：相信有一个独立于身体之外的绝对永恒之自我实体。无有爱是断见——即虚妄的唯物论——的产物，断见论者们认为有一个或多或少的真实的我，这个"我"在死亡时就断灭了，它与死亡前及死亡后的时间不存在任何因果关系。

贪爱之集

贪爱于何处生起和生根？凡世间有可喜可爱者，贪爱即于此处生起和住。眼、耳、鼻、舌、身、意，为可喜可爱者，贪爱即于彼处生起和生根。

色、声、香、触、法，为可喜可爱者，贪爱即于彼处生起和生根。

识、触、触生起之受、想、意、爱、寻、伺，为可喜可爱者，贪爱即于彼处生起和生根。

此名为苦之集圣谛。

诸法之缘起

《中部》第38经

彼以所识之色、声、香、味、触，或法，著于乐受，厌于苦受。

彼如是随其所受，或乐，或苦，或不苦不乐之受，彼喜其受，珍爱之、执着之，如是则生爱，对受之爱即取也，取为缘而（现世）有，有为缘而（未来）生，生为缘而老死、悲、哀、痛、忧、绝望。如是彼有苦蕴之生起。

缘起法可作为对第二圣谛的具体解释，上文仅涉及缘起法十二支中的一部分。

现业（果）报

《中部》第13经

如是，以欲为因，以欲为缘，为欲所驱，全然为欲所使，诸王与诸王争，王族与王族争，婆罗门与婆罗门争，民与民争，母与子争，子与母争，父与子争，子与父争，兄弟与兄弟争，兄弟与姊妹争，姊妹与兄弟争，友与友争。由此，彼等不睦，争吵，争斗，或以拳相击，或以杖相击，或以兵械相击。彼等如是受死或受如死之痛。

又更，以欲为因，以欲为缘，为爱所驱，全然为爱所使，而破入他宅、抢劫、掠夺、洗劫、拦路抢劫、诱奸人妻。如是彼等被王捕，处以种种刑罚折磨彼等如是受死或受如死之痛。此是欲之苦，今生之苦蕴也，盖以欲为因，以欲为缘，为欲为引，全然依于欲。

后次受业

复次，彼等以身行恶、以口行恶、以意行恶；彼等由身口意之恶业故，身坏命终，堕于恶生、恶趣、苦途、地狱。此是欲之苦，来生之苦蕴也，盖以欲为因，以欲为缘，为欲所驱，全然为欲所使。

《法句经》第127颂

非在于虚空，

亦非海洞中，

欲避恶果者，

世间无避处。

思 即 业

《增支部》第六集第63经

我说思（cetanā）为"业"（行）。

思已，而以身口意造业。

有业受地狱道……受傍生道……有业受鬼道……受人道……受天道。

业之异熟（vipāka）有三种：于现法现生受业累、于次生受业累、于后次（未来）生受业。

业行的承负

《增支部》第十集第206经

（PTS. 205）

一切有情，为业行之主人、业行之承负者：以业为胎、以业为缘、以业为归趣。彼等承负其所造之善恶业。

《增支部》第三集第33经

一切有情于彼所生处，其业成熟，于其业所熟处，彼感其业之异熟果——或于今生，或于次生，或于其他未来生。

《相应部》第二十二集第99经

大海有枯竭消失，归无之时，大地有为烈火吞噬毁灭、归无之时，然众生为无明所障、贪爱所噬、徘徊流转于轮回，彼等之苦无有穷尽。

然而，贪爱（tanhā）非恶业之唯一之因，故而亦非恶业所致此生和来世一切苦难之唯一之因，凡有贪爱处，即有缘爱而生之妒忌、忿怒、仇恨和诸多其他能生苦难之恶业。所有这些自私的、执着生命的冲动和行为，以及现在和以后生起的种种苦难，乃至五蕴和合之生命一切现象，都最终扎根于无明和愚痴（avijjā）。

业

第二圣谛也用于解释世间的表面上的不公正——通过教示世间没有任何事物可无因缘而存在，不只我们潜在的趋向，还有我们整个命运、所有福祸，均由业（kamma）而生，这些业部分须在此生查找，部分须从前世探寻。这些业是身口意所造作的导致生命轮回的行为（kamma，梵文：karma）。因而，是此三业决定了众生的特性和命运。准确定义，业指的是伴随转生之善的思和不善的思（kusala-akusala-cetanā）。如是，存在——或更准确地讲，"有"（bhava），是由造作的、形成条件的业力过程（kamma-bhava）及其果报——"转生的过程"（upapatti-bhava）构成的。

当考虑业时，我们一定不能忘记生命的无我性（anattatā）。在暴风雨肆虐的大海，不是同一个海浪在海面上涌没，而是无数不同的水体在起伏跌宕。同样，必须要理解在转生海洋中没有一个真正的自我在流转，只不过是生命的朵朵浪花，各缘其本性和善恶业行，在此展现为人、在彼处展现为傍生、或其他的隐形生命。

在此，再次明确"业"这个词只针对前述的业行本身，而不表示为或包括其业报。

有关业的详细内容，参见《佛教基本教理》和《佛教辞典》。

第三圣谛

苦之灭圣谛

《长部》第22经

何为苦之灭圣谛？此是对此贪爱之无余舍离、止灭、弃除、解脱和无著。

然此贪爱于何处舍离，止灭？于世间有可爱、可喜者，此贪爱即于此处舍离、止灭。

《相应部》第十二集第66经

任何过去现在或未来之沙门、婆罗门，对此世间可爱、可喜者，视为无常、苦和无我，视为病和疮，彼则断贪爱。

诸法的缘灭

《相应部》第十二集第43经

依贪爱（tanhā）之无余舍离而"取"（upādāna）灭。依取灭而"有"（bhava）灭，依有灭而"生"（jāti）灭，依生灭而有老、死、愁、悲、哀、痛、恼、绝望灭。如是而苦蕴灭。

《相应部》第二十二集30经

因此，色、受、想、行、识灭、断、止息，即是苦之灭、病之灭、老死之灭。

我们称之浪的波动，在无明者眼中生起这样的错觉——以为它是在湖面移动之同一水体。其实并非如此，波动依风生起、得到能量，并藉所储能量而维持。那么，风止后，若无新风吹拂湖面，所储能量逐渐消耗，整个波动终将止灭。同样，若火焰得不到新的燃料，它将在旧燃料耗尽后熄灭。五蕴和合之过程也是同理，它在愚痴凡夫心中造成了"我"的错觉。实际上，五蕴和合的产物是由造业的贪爱（tanhā）所产生和滋养，并通过储存的生命

221

能量维持下去。当"燃料"（*upādāna*）－对生命的"爱和取"燃尽时，如果没有新的贪爱来推动此五蕴和合之过程，在仍有生命能量在仍有生命能量储备的时候，生命还将持续。但，一旦能量耗尽，死亡来临，五蕴和合之过程即最终完结。

因此，涅槃或寂灭（梵文：nirvāna；由前缀 nir 和词根 vā 构成，意思是"不吹了"，"灭了"。）可从以下两个方面来理解，即：

一、"不净（烦恼）之灭尽"（kilesa-parinibbāna），证得阿罗汉或圣果——通常发生在有生之年，佛经中称之为"有余涅槃"（saupādisesa-nibbāna），即诸蕴余留之涅槃。

二、"五蕴之灭尽"（khandha-parinibbāna），发生在阿罗汉圆寂之时，佛经中称之为"无余涅槃"（an-upādisesa-nibbāna），即诸蕴灭尽之涅槃。

涅 槃

《增支部》第三集第 32 经

此是寂静，此是最胜妙，即一切行之止，一切转生之依之舍离，贪爱之灭尽，出离，灭，涅槃。

《增支部》第三集第 55 经

因染着于贪、因嗔而怒、为痴所蔽，心为之没，为之缚，彼思害己，思害人，思害自己与他人，彼感受心之苦与忧。然于贪、嗔、痴断除时，彼不思害己，不思害人，不思害自己与他人，彼不感受心之苦与忧。如是，涅槃是当下的，于此生可见，涅槃对于智者是招感的，吸引的，可解的，于现法当下可见可证。

《相应部》第三十八集第 1 经

贪之灭尽、嗔之灭尽、痴之灭尽，此称为涅槃。

阿罗汉或圣人

《增支部》第六集第 55 经

彼心如是解脱之弟子，心住于寂，所做已办，无有可做。譬如山石之坚实，风来亦不动。无论所欲所不欲之色、声、香、味、触皆不能使此人动摇。其心坚住而得解脱。

《经集》第 1048 偈

彼思世间一切之分别，不为世间一切所动，寂静者离嗔、离悲、无所求，已超越于生和老。

常

《自说经》第八品第 1 经

确有一处：无地大，亦无水大，无火大，亦无风大，无此世界，亦无他世界，无日，亦无月。

我称之无生，亦无灭，无所住，亦无生、死。无住处，亦无增广，无基础。此是苦之止息。

《自说经》第八品第 3 经

有无生、无源、无创造、无形状。若无此无生、无源、无创造、无形状，则逃离于此有生、有源、有创造、有形状之世间，是为不可能。

因有此无生、无源、无创造、无形状，故逃离此有生、有源、有创造、有形状之世间，是为可能。

第四圣谛

灭苦之道圣谛

两边和中道

《相应部》第五十六集第 11 经

沉溺于欲乐者，乃下劣、粗俗、凡夫之所行、非圣、无益也；执着于苦修者，为苦、非圣、无益也；如来舍此二边，现中道，成眼、成智，导向寂静、证智、正觉、涅槃。

八 正 道

此是八圣道，导向灭尽之道路，即：

1.	正　见	三、慧 （Paññā）
2.	正思维	
3.	正　语	一、戒 （Sīla）
4.	正　业	
5.	正　命	
6.	正精进	二、定 （Samādhi）
7.	正　念	
8.	正　定	

此乃如来发现之中道，成眼、成智，导向寂静、证智、正觉、涅槃。

圣八正道（Ariya-aṭṭhaṅgikamagga）

"道路"或"途径"这种比喻的说法有时让人产生错误的理解——以为

八正道的每一支必须按给的顺序，一支一支地次第修习。按照这种理解，在考虑修习正思维或正语等（道支）之前，正见——即对真谛的完全洞察，必须首先被证悟。然而事实上，构成"戒"（Sīla）的三道支（道支 3 至 5），应当先修习圆满。此后，就要通过三个"定"（samādhi）道支（道支 6 至 8）的修习，系统地训练心。只有经过如此准备之后，行者的"德行与心"才会在修"慧"（paññā，道支 1、2）的过程中达到圆满。

不过，在刚开始（修道）的时候，需要初步的、最低限度的正见。因为在某种程度上理解苦的真相等，对于为勤勉修道提供具有说服力的理由和动机是必要的。而一定程度的正见，对于帮助其他道支明了、有效地践行它们在"解脱"这一共同任务中的各自功能，也是必需的。因此，并为强调其重要性，正见被置于八正道的第一位。

然而法的最初正见须在其他道支帮助下渐进成就，直至最终达到最高的清净观（毗婆舍那：vipassanā），它是证入四种果位（参见 36 页"圣人"一节）和证得涅槃的直接条件。

因此，正见既是八正道之起点，亦是八正道之究竟处。

《中部》第 139 经

此是无苦、无恼害、无烦愁、无热恼之道，是圆满之道。

《法句经》第 274 ～ 276 颂

实唯此一道。

无余知见净。

汝顺此道行，

使汝苦灭尽。

汝当自努力！

如来唯说者。

《中部》第 26 经

汝当谛听，我已得不死之法，我教示之。汝当如所教而行！诸善男子出家，为梵行之无上究竟处，汝当不久于现法中知之、证之、住于之。

第一道支

正见（Sammā-diṭṭhi）

《长部》第24经
复次，何为正见？

见四谛

见苦；见苦之集；见苦之灭；见灭苦之道。此名为正见。

见善与恶

《中部》第9经

复次，若圣弟子见善业、见善业之根者，见不善业、见不善业之根者，彼如是具足正见。

复次，何为不善业（akusala）？

1.	杀生是不善业	身业	
2.	偷盗是不善业	（kāya-kamma）	
3.	邪淫是不善业		
4.	妄语是不善业	语业	
5.	两舌是不善业	（vacī-kamma）	
6.	恶口是不善业		
7.	绮语是不善业		
8.	悭贪是不善业	意业	
9.	嗔恚是不善业	（mano-kamma）	
10.	邪见是不善业		

此十名为不善业道。（akusala-kammapatha）。

何为不善业之根？贪（lobha）是不善业之根；嗔（dosa）是不善业之根；痴（moha）是不善业之根。

是故我说不善业有三种：或由贪生，或由嗔生，或由痴生。

因贪、嗔、痴生起的一切有意识的身口意业被视为是不善业。其被视作不善业—即有害的或愚笨的，是因为其会给此生或未来生带来恶果和苦果。意或思的状态才真正被视为业（kamma）。业可表现为身业或语业，若未显于外，则被视为意业。

贪（lobha）和嗔（dosa）一样，总是为痴（moha）所随，后者（痴）是万恶之源。然而，贪和嗔不会在心识的当下一刻同时现起。

复次，何为"善业"（kusala）？

1.	戒杀生是善业；	身业
2.	戒偷盗是善业；	（kāya-kamma）
3.	戒邪淫是善业；	
4.	戒妄语是善业；	语业
5.	戒两舌是善业；	（vacī-kamma）
6.	戒恶口是善业；	
7.	戒绮语是善业；	
8.	无悭贪是善业；	意业
9.	无嗔恚是善业；	（mano-kamma）
10.	正见是善业；	

此十名为"善业道"（kusala-kamma-patha）

何为善业之根？无贪（a-lobha= 无私）是善业之根；无嗔（a-dosa= 仁慈）是善业之根；无痴（a-moha= 慧）是善业之根。

正见三法印（Ti-lakkhaṇa）

《相应部》第二十二集第51经

复次，若见色、受、想、行、识之无常（苦、无我）者，则得正见。

无益的问题

《中部》第63经

若有人如是说，世尊当先为彼说世界为常恒，抑或非常恒；世界为有边，抑或无边；命即身，抑或命与身异；如来死后继续存在否……若世尊对彼不说此等，彼不于世尊处修梵行。于如来可尽言前，彼人或已命终矣。

犹若有人被涂毒之箭所射，彼之亲友、同事、亲族为彼遣请箭医疗治。然彼言：尚未知射予之人是刹帝利耶？婆罗门耶？吠舍或首陀罗耶之前，此箭不得取出。又彼言：于未知射予之人是何名、何姓之前，此箭不得取出。彼又如是言：于未知射予之人为高、为中、为矮之前，此箭不得取出。如是，彼人尚未彻知此等前，或已命终矣。

《经集》第592经

是故，为求自乐者，当拔除此箭—哀、痛、悲之箭。

《中部》第63经

是故，无论此说是否存在，世界为常恒抑或无常，为有边抑或无边，然皆定有生、老、死、悲、哀、痛、忧、绝望，彼等之灭甚至今生可得，我授汝彼等灭之法。

五结（Saṃyojana）

《中部》第64经

若有如是无闻凡夫，不敬圣贤，不知诸圣之教法，于圣人教理无所学者，其心被身见、疑、戒禁取、贪、嗔所缚所困，如何解脱于此等，彼不能如实知。

身见（sakkāya-diṭṭhi）可表现为：

一、常（见）：bhava-or sassata-diṭṭhi，字面意思——"常恒的见解"，即有一个我、自我或灵魂独立于肉体存在，甚至在肉体消亡后继续存在的观点。

二、断（见）：或无有见（vibhava-or uccheda-diṭṭhi），字面意思——"断

灭的见解"，就是唯物论的观点，认为当下之生命个体（身）即为自我，所以，当肉体消亡时，自我亦即断灭。

有关十结（Saṃyojana），参见本单元"十结"一节。

非理作意

《中部》第2经

不知何为应作意之法，何为不应作意之法，于不应作意之法而作意，于应作意之法而不作意。

彼如是非理作意："我于过去世存在否？抑或，我于过去世不存在？我于过去世为何？我于过去世如何？我于过去世由何态转为何态？

"我于未来世存在否？抑或，我于未来世不存在？我于未来世为何？我于未来世如何？我于未来世由何态转为何态？"

彼于现在世又自疑："我存在否？我不存在？我为何？我如何存在？此有情从何处来？将往何处去？"

六种我见

对于如是不如理作意，彼于六邪见中则生起任何一见，笃信："我之有自我"之见，或"我之无自我"之见，或："我由有自我而以自我想"之见，或："我由无生我而以自我想"之见，或"我由有自我而以无自我想"。复次，彼生如是之邪见："此我之自我者，可想可受，于此处、彼处受善及不善业之果报。此我之自我常住、坚固、常恒、不变，如是永存。"

《中部》第22经

若实有自我存在者，则亦有我所之物存在。然，于实际中，无我，亦无我所可得。故，若言"此是世界，此是我，我于死后常住、常恒、久远"，岂非极愚者之理？

《中部》第2经

此名为纯乎戏论，见之丛林，见之机巧，见之混浊、见之罗网。无明凡夫被见结所缚，不得从生、老、死、悲、痛、忧、绝望而解脱。我言彼不能解脱于苦。

如理作意

然，诸闻法之圣弟子，尊敬诸圣贤，知诸圣之教法，精通于圣人教理者，彼知何为应作意之法，何为不应作意之法。知此，彼作意应作意之法，不作意不应作意之法。彼如理作意，何为苦；彼如理作意，何为苦之集；彼如理作意，何为苦之灭；彼如理作意，何为灭苦之道。

须陀洹或预流果

由如是思维，则三结消解，三结即身见、疑、戒禁取。

《中部》第22经

如是已断三结之诸弟子，皆已证入预流果（sotāpanna）。

《法句经》第178颂

> 一统大地者，
>
> 得生天上者，
>
> 一切世界主，
>
> 不及预流胜。

十结（Saṃyojana）

有十结——Saṃyojana，众生出之而缚于轮回。它们是：

一、身（我）见（sakkāya-diṭṭhi）

二、疑（vicikicchā）

三、戒禁取（sīlabbata-parāmāsa）

四、欲贪（kāma-rāga）

五、嗔（vyāpāda）

六、色贪（rūpa-rāga）

七、无色贪（arūpa-rāga）

八、慢（māna）

九、掉举（uddhacca）

十、无明（avijjā）

圣者（Ariya-puggala）

断最初三结的行者名预流（巴利语：Sotāpanna 须陀洹）——已入趣向涅槃之流者。他对佛法僧有坚定信心，不可能犯五戒。他最多再受生七次，且不堕于劣于人道之恶道。

在其粗重相上断第四、五结的行者名斯陀含，字面意思"一来"——他只再受生欲界（kāma-loka）一次，之后将达到圣果。

阿那含，字面意思"不还"，完全解脱于使有情在欲界转生的最初五结（注：即五下分结）。死后，在居于色界期间，他将证果。

阿罗汉，即完美圆满的"圣人"，解脱于所有的十结。

上述圣人四次第的每一次第皆由"道"（magga）和"果"构成，例如"预流道"（sotāpatti-magga）和"预流果"（sotāpatti-phala）。相应地，有八种或四双"圣人"（ariya-puggala）。

"道"由证入各果位的当下一刻构成。"果"是作为"道"的结果，紧随"道"后生起的识之当下一念，在特定情况下，可于一生中重复无数次。

世间正见和出世间正见

《中部》第 117 经

是故，我说，正见有二种：

1. 布施与供养，非为无益；诸善行恶行各有果报；有今生和来世；有父有母，亦有生（于诸天界）之有情，此非空言；此世间有沙门、婆罗门，彼等无漏且圆满，堪以解说彼已证之今生来世。此见名为"世间正见"（lokiya-sammā-diṭṭhi），生世间果和善报。

2. 然，凡与"道"（须陀洹，斯陀含、阿那含、或阿罗汉）相合之智慧、洞见、正见——其心出离世间，与道相合，行于圣道，此名"出世间正见"（lokuttara-sammā-diṭṭhi），彼非世间，而为出世间并与道相合。

因此，八正道有二种：

（1）世间（lokiya）八正道——为尚未证圣初果之凡夫（puthujjana）

所修行。

（2）出世间（lokuttara）八正道—为圣人（ariya-puggala）所修行。

与其他道支俱行

若能知邪见为邪，正见为正，其人则行"正见"（第 1 道支）；若能努力断邪见，生正见，其人则行"正精进"（第 6 道支）。若能专注而断邪见，且住于正见，其人则行"正念"（第 7 道支）。因此，有三法相伴、相随于正见，即：正见、正精进、正念。

解脱于一切见

《中部》第 72 经

若有人问，我究竟有所见否，应如是答：如来解脱于一切知见。因为，如来已悉知何为色，知其如何生起，知其如何灭去。如来已悉知何为受，知其如何生起，知其如何灭去。如来已悉知何为想，知其如何生起，知其如何灭去。如来已悉知何为行，知其如何生起，知其如何灭去。如来已悉知何为识，知其如何生起，知其如何灭去。是故我说，如来于一切见解和猜想，一切"我""我所"之虚妄倾向，尽皆灭之，离之、舍之、弃之、除之，已得究竟解脱。

三 法 印

《增支部》第三集第 134 经

无论如来（佛陀）住世，抑或不住世，它依然常住，是不变的事实和决定的法：诸行无常、诸行皆苦、诸法无我。

巴利语：Sabbe saṅkhārā aniccā, sabbe saṅkhārā dukkhā, sabbe dhammā anattā.

"行"一词在此包括一切因缘和合而成之有为法（saṅkhata-dhamma），亦即所有可能的物质和精神的存在要素。然而"法"一词应用更广，包罗万象，因为它也包括了所谓的"无为法"（asaṅkhata）——即涅槃。

因此，说一切法皆无常变易是错误的，因为涅槃法是常恒不变的。同理，说不仅一切行（= saṅkhata-dhamma：有为法）无我，一切法（包括无为法 asaṅkhata-dhamma）也无我，是正确的。

《相应部》第二十二集第94经

常恒、稳固、永久、不变之色、受、想、行、识，世间智者不认为有如是之法，我亦言世间无有如是之法。

《增支部》第一集第15经

具足正见之有情，不视任何法为我。

我 见 论

《长部》第15经

若有人言受是彼之自我，当如是对之："有三种受：乐受、苦受、不苦不乐受。此三种受中，汝认为何为汝之自我也？"。因为，在体验某一种受的同时，不体验其他两种受。此三种受是无常的，缘起的，必会衰退和消亡、消失和断灭。无论何人领纳此三种受之一种，认为此是彼之自我者，则必于此受灭后承认彼之自我已灭。是故，其人会认为已在此生之彼之自我是无常的，苦乐混合的，生灭的。

若有人言受非彼之自我，彼之自我是不可感受者，当如是诘之："既无一切受，还可能说'此是我'吗？"

或言："受的确不是我之自我。然，我之自我不可感受，也是不真实的。因为，是我之自我去感受，是我之自我有感受的能力"。于此人，应如是答之："假设受完全灭了，那么，如果在受灭后，没有任何受存在，还可能说'此是我'吗？"

《中部》第148经

说"意，或法尘，或意识构成自我"，无有根据。因于彼处见生灭；见彼诸法之生灭，则得"自我有生灭"之结论。

《相应部》第12集第62经

于无智凡夫，与其视彼之心为"我"，莫如视四大所造身为"我"。显然，其身可住一年、二年、三年、四年、五年、十年乃至百年或更久，而称为"意"，或"心"，或"识"者，则生、灭、变异，昼夜不断。

《相应部》第22集第59经

是故，无论是色，还是受，或想，或行，或识，若过去、若现在、若未来，若内若外，若粗若细，若胜若劣，若远若近，于之皆应以正智慧作如实观："此非我所有，此非我，此非我之自我"。

《清净道论》第16品引用以下偈子，说明存在之无我及彻底之空性：

> 有苦而无苦受者，
>
> 有行而无造作者，
>
> 有涅槃而无入灭者，
>
> 有道而无行道者。

过去、现在和未来

《长部》第9经

若有人问:"你过去存在过吗,'你没有存在过'是不正确的吗?你未来将存在吗,'你将不存在'是不正确的吗?你现在存在吗,'你不存在'是不正确的吗?"你可回答,你过去存在过,'你没有存在过'是不正确的;你未来将存在,'你将不存在'是不正确的;你现在存在,'你不存在'是不正确的。

在过去,只有过去的存在是真实的,而未来和现在的存在是不真实的。在未来,只有未来的存在将是真实的,而过去和现在的存在是不真实的。在现在,只有现在的存在是真实的,而过去和未来的存在是不真实的。

《中部》第28经

见缘起(paṭicca-samuppāda)者见真相,见真相者见缘起。

《长部》第8经

譬如从牛出乳,从乳出酪,从酪出生酥,从生酥出熟酥,从熟酥出醍醐,当它为乳时,它不被视为酪、生酥、熟酥,或醍醐,只被视为乳,当它为酪时,它只被视为酪。同理,我之过去的存在,在彼时是真实的,而未来和现在的存在是不真实的;我之未来的存在,在彼时将是真实的,而过去和现在的存在是不真实的;我之现在的存在,在现在是真实的,而过去和未来的存在是不真实的。所有这些不过是世间立言,不过是方便说,不过是世俗义。如来用此,而不执着。

《相应部》第四十四集第4经

如是,若人不如实(即不以"无我")见色、受、想、行、识,不如实见彼之生、彼之灭、彼灭之道,斯人将信,如来灭后相续,或灭后不相续,如此等等。

两边（断见和常见）与中道

《相应部》第十二集第 25/35？经

若有人持命（jiva，"灵魂"）与身同之见，则梵行不立；若有人持命与身异之见，梵行亦不立。如来已离此等两边，而说中道法，此法云：

缘起（paṭicca-samuppāda）

《相应部》第十二集第 1 经

　　缘无明有行。

　　缘行有识（viññāṇa：始于母胎中的转生识）

　　缘识有名色。

　　缘名色有六根。

　　缘六根有触。

　　缘触有受。

　　缘受有爱。

　　缘爱有取。

　　缘取有有。

缘有（此处"有"指的是：业有或业的过程 kamma-bhava, or karma-process）有生。

缘生有老死、悲、哀、痛、忧、绝望。

如是而苦蕴生。此名苦之集圣谛。

　　诸天和梵神，

　　尽非轮回主。

　　诸法皆空性，

　　依缘而转起。

　　　　　　（引自《清净道论》第十九品）

《相应部》第十二集第51经

弟子舍无明而生明，如是弟子既不积善业，亦不积恶业，亦不积静业。

sankhārā 这个词此处被译为"业行"，因为，在"缘起法"的语境下，它指的是业方面的善意和不善意（cetanā），或意行，简言之，"业"。

前文所述的三种业，囊括了一切界或精神层次的业行。善业亦存于色界（rūpāvacara）。无色界（arūpāvacara）唯有静业。

《相应部》第十二集第1经

如是无明灭尽则行灭。行灭则识灭。识灭则名色灭。名色灭则六根灭。六根灭则触灭。触灭则受灭。受灭则爱灭。爱灭则取灭。取灭则有灭。有灭则生灭。生灭则老死、悲、哀、痛、忧、绝望灭。如是而苦蕴灭。此名苦之灭圣谛。

受生之业

《中部》第43经

因众生为无明（avijjā）所障，为贪爱（taṇhā）所缚，随处寻求新的欲乐。因此，不断有新的受生。

《增支部》第三集第33经

由贪嗔痴所造之业，从贪嗔痴而生，以贪嗔痴为源，以贪嗔痴而起，此业于有情受生处异熟，有情于业成熟处受此业之果，或于此生，或于次生，或于未来若干生。

业 之 灭

《中部》第43经

以无明灭，以智慧生，以贪爱尽，则无再生。

《增支部》第三集第33经

非由贪嗔痴所造之业，非从贪嗔痴而生，非以贪嗔痴为源，非以贪嗔痴而起：此业因离贪嗔痴而被舍弃、根除，犹如棕榈树其根被拔，被毁，不能再生。

《增支部》第八集第 12 经

依于此，彼如是说我亦不为错：我教授断灭法，我为断灭而说法，我如是教弟子。的确，我教断灭，贪嗔痴之断灭，诸恶及不善法之断灭。

缘起（Paṭicca samuppāda），即一切物质和精神现象的因缘论，它与无我（anattā）法一起构成了真实证悟佛陀教法不可或缺的必要条件。它揭示了习惯上被称为我、人、傍生等的种种身心生命过程不是偶然的，而是诸多因缘和合的结果。首先，缘起解释了转生和苦如何依缘而生。在因缘论的第二部分，它揭示了如何以诸缘灭而一切苦必然灭。因此，因缘论用于阐明第二、三圣谛，从其根源开始说明，并给予它们一个确定的哲学模式。下表简要说明了缘起法则十二环节是怎样贯穿于相续三世—过去现在和未来的。

前世	1. 无明	业有 5 个因：1, 2, 8, 9, 10
	2. 行	
今生	3. 识	生有 5 个果：3-7
	4. 名色	
	5. 六处	
	6. 触	
	7. 受	
	8. 爱	业有 5 个因：1, 2, 8, 9, -10
	9. 取	
	10. 有	
来生	11. 生	生有 5 个果：3-7

1 ~ 2 支和 8 ~ 10 支表示造业之过程，包括 5 个转生之业因。

3 ~ 7 支和 11 ~ 12 支表示转生过程，包括 5 个业果。

依《无碍解道》：

　　　　过去有五因，
　　　　今世见五果。
　　　　今世造五因，
　　　　来生受五果。
　　　　　　（见《清净道论》第十七品）

　　详细的解释，参见《佛教基本教理》和《佛教辞典》。

第二道支

正思维（Sammā-saṅkappa）

《长部》第22经

何为正思维？

1. 离欲思维；

2. 离嗔思维；

3. 离害思维。

此名正思维。

世间思维和出世思维

《中部》第117经

正思维，我说有两种：

1. 离欲思维、离嗔思维、离害思维，此名"世间正思维"，产生世间果和善报。

2. 凡是思，寻，伺，想，推理，思量，若此心圣洁，出离世间，与道相合，追寻圣道，此等心之"语行"（vacī-saṅkhārā）名为"出世正思维"（lokuttara-sammā-saṅkappa）。此非为世间所有，而是出世间的，并与道相合。

与其他道支俱行

若能知邪思维为邪，正思维为正，其人则行"正见"（第1道支）；若能努力断邪思维，生正思维，其人则行"正精进"（第6道支）；若能专注而断邪思维，且住于正思维，其人则行"正念"（第7道支）。因此，有三法相伴、相随于正思维，即：正见、正精进、正念。

第三道支

正语（Sammā-vācā）

何为正语？

离 妄 语

《增支部》第十集第176经

1. 于此，有人不说妄语，断妄语。彼说实语，忠于真实，可靠，可信，非欺诳者。彼于集会处，或大众中，或亲族内，或团体里，或王殿上，被传唤作证，言其所知。彼不知则言："我不知"；彼知则言："我知"；彼未见则言："我未见"；彼见则言"我见"。如是，彼从不为一己之利，或为他人之利，或为任何之利，而故说虚诳。

离 两 舌

2. 是人不两舌，离两舌。彼闻于此处，为不引起彼处不和，而不言于彼处。彼闻于彼处，为不引起此处不和，而不言于此处。如是，彼令分者合，励和合。彼乐和合，喜和合，悦和合，并以其言传播和合。

离 恶 口

3. 是人不说恶语，断恶语。彼说柔和、悦耳、可爱之语，此语入心、谦恭、友善、令人愉悦。

《中部》第 21 经中，佛陀说：诸比丘！即令有众强盗凶犯断汝等肢节，凡于此起嗔恚者，非为顺我教法。尔等当如是训练自己：

"我心不扰乱，口不发恶语。我以俱慈之心持悲悯，而不怀丝毫嗔恚。我以广、深、无量、无嗔之慈心，而感化之。"

离绮语

《增支部》第十集第 176 经

4. 是人不说绮语，断绮语。彼适时而言，合于真实，言辞有益，说法说戒：彼言如珍，适时，有据，适度且富有道理。

此名为正语。

世间正语和出世正语

《中部》第 117 经

正语，我说有两种：

1. 离妄语、两舌、恶口、绮语，此名世间正语（lokiya-sammā-vācā），产生世间果和善报。

2. 不说四种恶语，断除、止息、戒绝四种恶语，若此心圣洁、出离世间、与道相合、追寻圣道，此名"出世正语"，此非为世间所有，而是出世间的，并与道相合。

与其他道支俱行

若能知邪语为邪，正语为正，其人则行"正见"（第 1 道支）；若能努力断邪语，生正语，其人则行"正精进"（第 6 道支）；若能专注而断邪语，且住于正语，其人则行"正念"（第 7 道支）。因此，有三法相伴、相随于正语，即：正见、正精进、正念。

第四道支

正业（Sammā-kammanta）

《增支部》第十集第176经
何为正业？

离杀生

1. 于此，有人不杀生，断杀生。舍棍棒或刀剑，知耻而尽责，悲悯，渴望饶益一切有情。

离偷盗

2. 是人不偷盗、断偷盗。他人在村落或林野之财物、财产，彼不以盗心而取。

离邪淫

3. 是人不邪淫，断邪淫。彼不与受父、母、兄弟、姊妹，或亲眷监护之人行淫，亦不与已婚之妇、受刑女犯，乃至订婚之女子行淫。
此名正业。

世间正业和出世正业

《中部》第117经
正业，我说有二种：

1.戒杀生、戒不与取、戒欲邪行，此名世间正业（lokiya-sammā-kammanta），产生世间果和善报。

2.不犯三种邪行，断除、止息、戒绝三种邪行，若此心圣洁、出离世间、与道相合、追寻圣道，此名"出世正业"（lokuttara-sammā-kammanta），此非为世间所有，而是出世间的，并与道相合。

与其他道支俱行

若能知邪行为邪，正行为正，其人则行"正见"（第1道支）；若能努力断邪行，生正行，其人则行"正精进"（第6道支）；若能专注而断邪行，且住于正行，其人则行"正念"（第7道支）。因此，有三法相伴、相随于正业，即：正见、正精进、正念。

第五道支

正命（Sammā-ājīva）

何为正命?

《长部》第22经

1. 圣弟子离邪命，以正命谋生，此名正命。

《中部》第117经言："欺骗、背信，占卜，诈骗、放高利贷，此等为邪命。"

《增支部》第五集第177经言：弟子不可作此等五种交易：武器、有情、肉、酒、毒药。

邪命还包括军人、渔夫、猎户等职业。

正命，我说有二种：

世间正命和出世正命

《中部》第117经

1. 圣弟子断邪命，以正命谋生，此名世间正命（lokiya-sammā-ājīva），于此，产生世间果和善报。

2. 不事邪命，因断除、止息、戒绝邪命，成就梵心、出世而与道相合、求圣道之心者，此名为"出世正命"，非为此世间所有、乃为出世而与道相合。

与其他道支俱行

若能知邪命为邪，正命为正，其人则行"正见"（第1道支）；若能努力断邪命，立正命，其人则行"正精进"（第6道支）；若能专注而断邪命，且专注而住于正命，其人则行"正念"（第7道支）。因此，有三法相伴、相随于正命，即：正见、正精进、正念。

第六道支

正精进（Sammā-vāyāma）

《增支部》第四集第 13、14 经

何为正精进？

正精进有四：律仪勤、断勤、修勤、随护勤。

律仪勤（Saṃvara-ppadhāna）

何为律仪勤？于此，有弟子对未生之恶、不善法，起志令不生，为此精进、发奋、策心、努力。

如是，当其以眼见色、以耳闻声、以鼻嗅香、以舌尝味、以身感触、以意识法，彼不执于全部，亦不执于部分。彼竭力防止因六根失护而至恶不善法及贪、忧生起。彼守护六根，收摄六根。

都摄诸根故，彼成就内在喜乐，无有恶法可以侵入。

此名律仪勤。

断勤（Pahāna-ppadhāna）

何为断勤？于此，有弟子对已生之恶、不善法，起志令断除，为此精进、发奋、策心、努力。

彼不保留任何已生之贪、嗔、忧或任何其他恶不善念，弃舍之，消除之，毁灭之，使之消失。

除恶念之五法

《中部》第 20 经

弟子缘境而观时，若因境生起与贪、嗔、痴关联之恶、不善想，彼应（1）依此境而取另外之善境。（2）或，思维此等想之过患：此等想乃不善者！此等想应受责备！此等想必生苦果！（3）或，不注意（忆念）此等想。（4）或，思维此等想之缘生性。（5）或，咬紧牙关，舌抵上颚。彼应用心抑制、压伏、根除此等想。如是，此等贪、嗔、痴之不善想将散灭、消失；彼心向内而住、平静、专一、入定。

此名断勤。

修勤（Bhāvanā-ppadhāna）

《增支部》第四集第 13、14 经

何为令生勤？于此，有弟子对未生之善法，起志令生起，为此精进、发奋、策心、努力。

如是，彼依独处、舍离、灭尽，修行"七觉支"（bhojjhaṅga），终至解脱。七觉支是：念（sati）觉支、择法（dhamma-vicaya）觉支、精进（viriya）觉支、喜（pīti）觉支、轻安（passaddhi）觉支、定（samādhi）觉支、舍（upekkhā）觉支。

此名修勤。

随护勤（Anurakkhaṇa-ppadhāna）

何为随护勤？有弟子对已生之善法，起志不令灭失，使增长、成熟、修习（bhāvanā）圆满，为此精进、发奋，策心、努力。

譬如彼于心随护已生适宜之所缘境：骨想、虫啖想、青瘀想、脓烂想、穿孔想、肿胀想。

此名随护勤。

《中部》第 70 经

于师所教已深解之具信弟子，如是思维是如法的：纵使皮囊筋骨枯萎，纵使血肉干竭，若以丈夫之刚毅、精进、勇猛所能得者尚未得时，当无精进之止息。

此名正精进。

《增支部》第四集第 14 经

律仪、断、修与随护，
太阳子说四正勤，
励力修此正勤者，
彼能得获苦灭尽。

第七道支

正念（Sammā-sati）

何为正念？

四念处（Satipaṭṭhāna）

《长部》第22经

趣向获清净、断悲、哀，灭痛、忧、入正道、证涅槃的一行道，是四念处。此四者为何耶？

于此有弟子，住于观身，住于观受，住于观心，住于观法，调伏世间之贪、忧，热诚，于身、受、心、法清楚觉知，正念专注。

身念处（kāyanupassanā）

弟子如何住于观身？

入出息念（ānāpāna-sati）

于此，有弟子隐至林间、树下或僻静处，结跏趺坐，身正直，正念现前，正念而入息，正念而出息。

长入息时，彼知："我长入息"。长出息时，知："我长出息"。短入息时，知："我短入息"。短出息时，知："我短出息"。"我清楚觉知整个呼吸身而入息"，彼如是训练自己。"我清楚觉知整个呼吸身而出息"，彼如是训练自己。"我止身行（kāya-saṅkhāra，呼吸本身）而入息"，彼如是训练自己。"我止身行而出息"，彼如是训练自己。

彼如是住于观身，或于己身，或于他人身，或于己他之身。观身如何生起，观身如何灭，观身之生灭。有一个身存在——

有身存在，然无生命、无个体、无女人、无男人、无自我、无我所有，既无人，亦无属于人之任何物。（注释）

彼有此正觉知现前，足以获得智与念，彼无所依而住，不执着于世间之任何法。佛弟子如是住于观身。

"入出息念"（*ānāpāna-sati*）是最重要的禅修之一。它可用于修止（奢摩他 samatha-bhāvanā），即用于获得四禅那（jhāna；参见第 67 页"四禅那"），用于修观（毗婆舍那 vipassanā-bhāvanā），或用于止观双修。在修习四念处（*satipaṭṭhāna*）中，"入出息念"主要为了获得静和定——它们是为修观做准备的。以下是修观的一种方法：

通过经常练习"入出息念"，获得一定程度静和定，或一种禅那后，佛弟子进而观察呼吸的起源。

他观到，入息和出息依于身，身由四大，以及源于四大之各种物质现象，如五根等构成。依于五种触生起识，其他三种蕴亦随之生起，即：受蕴、想蕴和行蕴。

如是，禅修者清晰地观到："在这个所谓的'个体'的里面，没有实我或自我，它只不过是一个依于诸多因素的身心过程而已"。

因此，他以"三法印"观这些现象，彻底了知它们是无常的，苦的，和无我的。关于入出息念（*ānāpāna-sati*）的详细内容，参见《中部》第 118 经第 62 节，《清净道论》第 8 品第 3 节。

四 威 仪

复次，于行、住、坐、卧之时，佛弟子如实了知这些表述——"我行""我立""我坐""我卧"。彼明了身体之任何姿势。

佛弟子明悉，无有情，无行走、站立……之"实我"。人们说"我行走""我站立"等等，不过是借由一种比喻罢了（注释）。

正念正知（sati-sampajañña）

复次，佛弟子于去、来时，以正知而行；彼于前瞻、后视时，以正知而行；于屈、伸（肢体任何部位）时，以正知而行；于持钵、着衣时，以正知而行；于啖、饮、嚼、味时，以正知而行；于大小便时，以正知而行，于行、住、坐、寐、寤时，以正知而行；于语、默时，以正知而行。

佛弟子于做一切行为时，于彼之意图、益处、责任以及真相皆有清楚觉知（注释）。

厌恶想（paṭikkūla-saññā）

复次，佛弟子从足底往上，于头顶向下，观此皮肤所覆、充斥秽物之身体：此身有头发、身毛，有指甲、牙齿、皮肤、肉、肌腱、骨骼、骨髓、肾、心、肝、横隔膜、脾、肺、胃、肠、肠系膜、粪、胆汁、痰、脓、血、汗、淋巴液、泪、皮脂、唾液、鼻涕、关节液，以及尿液。

犹若有一两端开口之袋，装满种种谷物——稻谷、豆子、胡麻和糙米（去了壳的米）。眼明者开解之，检视内中物："那是稻谷，此系豆子，此为芝麻，此乃糙米"。佛弟子如是审视此身。

四大（界）分别观（dhātu）

复次，佛弟子从四界观此身——不论它立或行，"此身由地界、水界、火界和风界构成。"犹如一熟练屠牛者或其学徒，宰杀一牛，分割成块，将坐于四衢交汇处。彼佛弟子如是从四界观此身。

《清净道论》第十三品第2节对此喻解释如下：

屠夫饲牛，带至屠场，缚于柱，使站立，杀并看被杀之牛，于此过程，彼一直有"牛"之想。然，彼将被杀之牛切割成块，坐其侧而售卖时，"牛"想于彼心中消失，"肉"想生起。彼不认为其在卖牛或人们买牛，而认为卖与买的是"肉"。

同样，对于无明凡夫—无论僧俗，"生命""人""我"……之想不会消失，直至彼于心中解剖此身—不论它立和行，并据其构成元素（大）观察它。彼如是做后，则"我"……之想消失，彼心依于观照四界而稳固建立。

冢 间 观

1.复次，恰若佛弟子观视弃于冢间之尸，死后一日、二日抑或三日，肿胀、青瘀、腐烂，彼亦观视其身："我身亦有如是性质，如是结局，难逃于此！"

2. 复次，恰若佛弟子观视弃于冢间之尸，为乌鸦、鹰、鹫所啄，或犬、豺所啖，或各种虫类所噬，彼亦观视其身："我身亦有如是性质，如是结局，难逃于此！"

3. 复次，恰若佛弟子观视弃于冢间之尸，有骨相连，肉悬骨上，血痕尚存，由筋所系；

4. 骨虽相连，已无肉，血痕尚存，由筋所系；

5. 骨虽相连，血肉已无，尚由筋所系；

6. 尸骨四下离散，此处手骨，彼处足骨，彼处胫骨，一处股骨，一处骨盆，另一处脊柱，又一处颅骨。

—彼亦如是观视其身："我身亦有如是性质，如是结局，难逃于此！"

7. 住于观身，或于已身，或于他人身，复次，恰若佛弟子观骨横于冢间，颜色变白如螺之骸骨；

8. 经年累月，尸骸堆积；

9. 骸骨风化碎成尘。

——彼亦如是观视其身："我身亦有如是性质，如是结局，难逃于此！"

彼如是或于已他之身。彼观身如何生起，观身如何灭，观身之生灭。"有一个身存在"，彼有此正觉知现前，足以获得智与念，彼无所依而住，不执着于世间之任何法。佛弟子如是住于观身。

获十种功德

《中部》第119经

若佛弟子修习观身，发展之、常习之、使之成为习惯、基础，稳固建立、强化和完善，彼可期待十种功德：

1. 彼调伏乐与不乐，不为不乐所制，一旦不乐生起即克制之。

2. 彼征服怖、畏，不为怖、畏所制，一旦怖、畏生起即克制之。

3. 彼忍耐冷、热、饥、渴，风吹、日晒，虻、蚊、爬虫之侵袭；堪忍恶毒语，忍受身受之诸苦——不管它们何等激烈、猛烈、辛辣、不愉快、不可意乃至危及生命。

4.使其净心及乐住此生之四禅（jhāna），彼任运获得，没有困难、无需费力。

六神通（智）（Abhiññā）

5.彼得享种种之神足通（iddhi-vidhā）。

6.彼以清净、超人之天耳（dibba-sota）听闻或远、或近之天界与人界二种声音。

7.以此心，彼获得他心通（parassa-cetopariya-ñāṇa），了知他人心。

8.彼获得宿命通（pubbe-nivāsānussati-ñāṇa）。

9.彼以清净、超人之天眼，见诸众生之逝灭与重现，见诸卑、尊、美、丑、乐、苦之众生；彼觉知诸众生如何随业转生。

10.彼以漏尽通（āsavakkhaya），于此生自证无漏之心解脱、依慧之解脱。

后6种功德（5～10）是神通。其中，前5种是世间（lokiya）神通，因此即使凡夫（puthujjana）也可获得。最后一种神通是出世间（lokuttara）神通，唯阿罗汉（圣者）所独有。只有在获得全部四禅（jhāna）之后，才能完全获得五种世间神通。另有四神足（获得神通的基础），即：欲神足、勤神足、心神足和观神足。

受念处（vedanānupassanā）

《长部》第22经

然佛弟子如何住于观受？

弟子于感受时，知："我有乐受"，或："我有苦受"，或："我有不苦不乐受"，或："我有感世间之乐受"，或："我有出世间之乐受"，或："我有世间之苦受"，或"我有出世间之苦受"，或"我有世间之不苦不乐受"，或："我有出世间之不苦不乐受"。

彼如是住于观受，或于己之受，或于他人之受，或于己他之受。观受如何生起，观受如何灭，观受之生灭。"有受存在"，彼有此正觉知现前，足以获得智与念，彼无所依而住，不执着于世间之任何法。佛弟子如是住于观受。

佛弟子深知"我感受"这一表述本身并无真实意义，只不过是"方便说"（vohāra-vacana），从究竟法（paramattha）来看，唯有"受"，无"自我"，亦无感受者。

心念处（Cittānupassanā）

然佛弟子如何住于观心？

于此有弟子知贪心为贪，不贪心为不贪；知嗔心为嗔，不嗔心为不嗔；知痴心为痴，不痴心为不痴。彼知收摄心

为收摄，散乱心为散乱；知广大心为广大，不广大心为不广大；知有上心为有上，无上心为无上；知有定心为有定，无定心为无定；知解脱心为解脱，未解脱心为未解脱。

在此处，Citta（心）用作各种心或识的瞬间的总称。Citta（心）与viññāṇa（识）是同一的，不应当用"思维"这个词来翻译它。"思维"和

"思考"其实相当于"心之语行"：寻（vitakka：thought-conception）和伺（vicāra： discursive thinking），属于行蕴（saṅkhāra-kkhandha）。

彼如是住于观心，或于己之心，或于他人之心，或于己他之心。彼观识如何生起，观识如何灭，观识之生灭。"有心存在"，彼有此正觉知现前，足以获得智与念，彼无所依而住，不执着于世间之任何法。佛弟子如是住于观心。

法念处（dhammānupassanā）

然佛弟子如何住于观心法？

于此有弟子住于观此心法：五盖。

五盖（nīvaraṇa）

彼于己贪（kāmacchanda）存在者，知："我于己贪欲存在"；或于己嗔（vyāpāda）存在者，知："我于己嗔恚存在"；或于己昏沉睡眠（Thīna-middha）存在者，知"我于己昏沉睡眠存在"；或于己掉悔（uddhacca-kukkucca）存在者，知："我于己掉悔存在"；或于己疑存在者，知："我于己疑（vicikicchā）存在"。彼于己五盖不存在者，知："我于己五盖不存在"。彼知五盖如何生起，知五盖一旦生起，如何断除，知其未来如何不再生起。

譬如："贪欲"缘于可悦意处无明思维而生起，可用如下六法降服之：使心专注于引人厌恶的想法；身不净想；收摄六根；节制饮食；与智者善士为友；学于正教。证得阿那含果，可永断贪与嗔；证得阿罗汉果，可断除掉举；证得须陀洹果，可断除懊悔。

五取蕴（khandha）

复次，佛弟子住于观此心法——五蕴。彼知何为色（rūpa），知其如何生起，如何灭；知何为受（vedanā），知其如何生起，如何灭；知何为想（saññā），知其如何生起，如何灭；知何为心行（saṅkhāra），知其如何生起，如何灭；知何为识（viññāṇa），知其如何生起，如何灭。

六处（āyatana）

复次，佛弟子住于观此心法——六内外处。彼知眼和色、耳和声、鼻和香、舌和味、身和触、心和心法；亦知缘彼等（眼和色……）生起之结缚。彼知结缚如何生起，知结缚如何断除，知已舍之结缚未来如何不再生起。

七觉支（bojjhanga）

复次，佛弟子住于观此心法——七觉支。彼知于己有"念"（sati）、"择法"（dhammavicaya）、"精进"（viriya）、"喜"（pīti）、"轻安"（passaddhi）、"定"（samādhi）、"舍"（upekkhā）存在。彼知于己七觉支不存在，知其如何生起，知其如何修习圆满。

四圣谛（ariya-sacca）

复次，佛弟子住于观此心法—四圣谛。彼如实知何为苦；如实知何为苦之集；如实知何为苦之灭；如实知何为苦灭之道。

彼如是住于观心法，或于己之心法，或于他人之心法，或于己他之心法。彼观心法如何生起，观其如何灭，观心法之生灭。"有心法存在"，彼有此正觉知现前，足以获得智与念，彼无所依而住，不执着于世间之任何法。佛弟子如是住于观心法。

趣向获清净、断悲、哀，灭痛、恼、入正道、证涅槃的一行道，是四念处。

四念处与五取蕴相关，即：1.身念处与色蕴相关；2.受念处与受蕴相关；3.心念处与识蕴相关；4.法念处与想蕴和行蕴相关。

有关四念处的更多内容，参见《念住之道》（斯里兰卡康提，佛教出版社，1967 年出版）中，苏摩比丘所译的对于念处经的注。

依观入出息证涅槃

《中部》第118经

于观入出息（ānāpāna-sati），修习、多修，可圆满"四念处"；于四念处，修习、多修，可圆满"七觉支"；于七觉支，修习、多修，可圆满"智慧和解脱"。

修习、多修观入出息，如何使"四念处"（Satipaṭhāna）圆满？

一、凡弟子（1）依正念而长入息或长出息，或（2）依正念而短入息或短出息，或（3）训练自己，觉知整个呼吸身而入息或出息，或（4）止身行（即呼吸）。此时，佛弟子住于观身，舍离世间之贪、忧，热诚，正知（身），具念。因为，我称入息和出息是色法之一。

二、凡弟子训练自己入息或出息时（1）感受喜（pīti），或（2）感受乐（sukha），或（3）感受心行（cittasaṅkhāra），或（4）止心行。此时，佛弟子住于观受，舍离世间之贪、忧，热诚，正知（受），具念。因为，我称完全觉知入出息是受法之一。

三、凡弟子训练自己入息或出息时（1）感受心，或（2）使心喜悦，或（3）使心定，或（4）使心解脱。此时，彼住于观心，舍离世间之贪、忧，热诚，正知（心），具念。因为，我说，若无正念正知，则无观入出息。

四、凡弟子训练自己入息或出息时，观（1）无常，或（2）离贪，或（3）灭，或（4）出离，此时，佛弟子住于观心法，舍离世间之贪、忧，热诚，正知（心法），具念。此时，彼以慧观见贪忧之舍断，以完全之舍心观察之。

于观入出息（ānāpāna-sati），如是修习、多修，可圆满"四念处"。

然，于四念处，修习、多修，如何使七"觉支"（bojjhaṅga）圆满？

1. 凡佛弟子观身、受、心、心法时，舍离世间之贪、忧，热诚，正知（身、受、心、心法），具念；此时，彼念安住不失；若彼念现前不失，此时，彼获得并修习"念"觉支（sati-sambojjhaṅga）。如是，此觉支达到圆满。

2. 凡彼以念安住时，以慧观察、审查、慎虑此"法"（dhamma）。此时，彼获得并修习"择法"觉支（dhammavicaya-sambojjhaṅga）。如是，此觉支达到圆满。

3. 凡彼以慧观察、审查、慎虑此"法"（dhamma）时，彼之精进坚定不移。此时，彼获得并修习"精进"觉支（viriya-sambojjhaṅga）。如是，此觉支达到圆满。

4. 凡于彼精进坚定时，超感官之喜生起。此时，彼获得并修习"喜"觉支（pīti-sambojjhaṅga）。如是，此觉支达到圆满。

5. 凡心喜时，彼神寂，心亦寂。此时，彼获得并修习"轻安"觉支（passaddhi-sambojjhaṅga）。如是，此觉支达到圆满。

6. 凡神轻安及喜悦时，彼心得定。此时，彼获得并修习"定"觉支（samādhi-sambojjhaṅga）。如是，此觉支达到圆满。

7. 凡以完全之无分别，观彼如是得定之心。此时，彼获得并修习"舍"觉支（upekkhā-sambojjhaṅga）。如是，此觉支达到圆满。

于四念处修习、多修，可圆满"七觉支"（bojjhaṅga）？

然，于七觉支修习、多修，如何使"慧解脱"（vijjā-vimutti）圆满？

于此有佛弟子依出离，依离贪，依灭及舍弃，修习七觉支：念、择法、精进、喜、轻安、定、舍。如是修习、多修七觉支，可圆满智慧和解脱。

《中部》第125经

譬如调象师，掘地以立大柱，系野象之颈，以去其林野之习气与忆念，及桀骜，执拗，暴烈之性，使习惯于村镇，以与人相处所需之行为调训之；圣弟子亦当以如是方式，紧系其心于四念处，以去其世间之习气与忆念，及桀骜，执拗，暴烈之性，洞见真谛，证悟涅槃。

第八道支

正定（Sammā-samādhi）

《中部》第 44 经
何为正定？

正定的定义

心专注于一处（cittekaggatā，即心一境性）：这是定。

正定，最广义地讲，是存在于一切善心识（kusala-citta）中的精神专注状态。因此，它至少伴随有正思维（第 2 道支），正精进（第 6 道支）和正念（第 7 道支）。邪定存在于不善心识中，因此，它只存在于欲界，在更高界中不存在。定（Samādhi）在佛经中单独使用时，总是指正定（三摩地：Sammā-samādhi）。

正定的所缘境

四念处（第 7 道支）：此是定之所缘境。

正定的资粮

四正勤（第 6 道支）：此是定之资粮。

正定的修习

以下诸法之练习、修习、多所作，是定之修习（bhāvanā）：

正定（Sammā-samādhi）有两个修习次第：1.近行定（*upacāra-samādhi*），是接近尚未证得初禅的定；2.安止定（*appanāsamādhi*），是（the concentration present）存在于四禅（jhāna）中的定。禅定是超脱于五根造作之外的心理状态，只有在寂止和精勤不懈的定的修习中才可证得。在禅定状态五根一切活动都止息了。无眼触或耳触生起，也没有身触可感知。虽然外感之触止息了，意识还保持活跃、警醒、完全的觉知。

但是，证得禅定不是成就出世四圣道的必要条件；近行定和安止定，就其本身而言，都不具备证入出世四圣道的能力：所以二者均不具备使行者永久解脱于恶法之能力。出世四圣道只有在深入谛观（vipassanā）到诸行的无常（aniccatā）、苦（dukkhatā）和诸法的无我（anattatā）的时刻才可实现。这种谛观只有在近行定时可证得，在安止定则不可。

证得出世四圣道之一道或几道，而未证得禅定者，称之为干观者（Sukkha-vipassaka），或纯观行者（Suddhavipassanā-yānika），即："以谛观（vipassanā）为舟车的修行者"。但是，如果行者修得禅定后，证入一种出世圣道，则被称为止行者（Samathayānika），或"以止（samatha）为舟车（yāna）的修行者"。

有关止和观，参见《佛教基本教理》第四篇和《佛教辞典》。

四禅定（jhāna）

《长部》第22经

佛弟子舍弃感官享乐、舍弃不善法，进入初禅。初禅伴有寻伺，由远离而生起，具足喜乐。

初禅是色界禅。通过定力，五根的活动暂时中止，五盖也暂时消除，此时，获得初禅。参见《佛教辞典》：（修禅的取相）遍、禅相、三摩地词条。

《中部》第43经

初禅舍弃五盖，具足五禅支。佛弟子入初禅时，舍弃五盖：贪欲、嗔恚、昏沉睡眠、掉悔、疑；五禅支现前：寻（vitakka）、伺（vicāra）、喜（pīti）、乐（sukha）、及心一境之定（citt'ekaggatā = samādhi）。

初禅里的五种心之要素称为禅支（jhānaṅga）。寻（抽象思维之最初形成）和伺（推论思维，沉思）称为心之语行（vacī-saṅkhāra）；因此，较之于意识，它们是次一级的。

在《清净道论》中，寻被喻为手执壶，伺被喻为擦壶。初禅中，寻和伺都存在，但只专注于冥想的对象，此处，"伺"不是推论，而是具有观察的性质。寻和伺在更高的禅境中是不存在的。

《长部》第22经

寻和伺止息后，获得内心的轻安和心一境性，彼进入无寻无伺的状态——由定（samādhi）而生、具足喜（pīti）乐（sukha）之二禅。

二禅有三禅支：喜、乐、心一境之定。

喜舍离后，彼住于舍，正念、正知。彼于自身体验圣者所述之感受："具舍与正念者，住于快乐"，如是彼进入第三禅。

三禅有二禅支：舍之乐（upekkhā-sukha）和心一境之定（citt'ekaggatā）

断乐与苦后，由灭先前之喜、忧，彼进入不苦不乐之状态，进入依舍与正念而清净之四禅。

四禅有二禅支：心一境之定和舍（upekkhā）。《清净道论》详细讲述了禅修的四十种业处（kammaṭṭhāna）。成功修习这些业处，可证得以下禅境：

可证得所有四禅的业处包括：出入息念（见《清净道论第八品第3节》），修习十遍（《清净道论》第四、五品和《佛教辞典》），舍心想（upekkhā）——即修习第四梵住（见《清净道论第9品第4节》）。

可证得前三种禅的业处包括：修习慈、悲、喜，即前三个梵住的修习（《清净道论》第九品第1-3节）。

可证得前初禅的业处包括：修习十种不净观（即冢间观，据《清净道论》第六品中的列举，有十种）；身念处（即身体32个业处，《清净道论》第八品第2节）；可证得近行定的业处包括：通过随念佛、法、僧、戒、施舍、天、寂静（涅槃）和死（《清净道论》第六、七品）；食厌想（《清净道论》第十一品第1节）；四界分别（《清净道论》第九品第2节）。

四无色定（arūpa-jjhāna or āruppa）基于第四禅，由观想它们各自的对象而证得，并由此得名：空无边处定、识无边处定、无所有处定、非想非非想处定。

《清净道论》第三至十三品讲述了定与禅修（观）的一切业处。（也可参考佛学基础四）

《相应部》第22集第5经

汝当修定。有定者，如实了知诸法。何为诸法？色、受、想、行、识之生灭。

《中部》第149经

如是，于五蕴，应智慧地观察；于无明与贪爱，应智慧地断除；于止（samatha）与观（vipassanā），应智慧地修习。

《相应部》第56集第2/11？经

此为如来所见之中道。使人见，使人知，可证入寂静、证智、正觉和涅槃。

《法句经》第275颂

汝顺此道行，可使苦灭尽。

弟子依八正道次第的修习

信与正思维（第二道支）

《中部》第38经

若有家主或家主之子，或生于其他善人家者闻此法，彼听此法，得信世尊，彼得信作是念："居家多障碍尘劳，出家如处旷野。在家者不易圆满一切梵行。若我剃除须发，着黄袈裟，由在家为出家行者何如？"。彼遂舍其财物，无论多少，舍其亲族，无论众寡，彼剃除须发，着黄袈裟，由在家而为出家行者。

戒（第三、四、五道支）

如是彼出家而持比丘之律仪。彼不杀生，断杀生，舍棍棒或刀剑，知耻而尽责，悲悯，渴望饶益一切有情。彼舍偷盗而离不与取，唯待予彼时而取之，以诚实清净心而住。彼舍非梵行为梵行，禁欲而离淫欲之行。彼舍妄语而离之。彼说实语，忠于真实，可靠，可信，非欺诳者。彼舍两舌而离之。彼闻于此处，为不引起彼处不和，而不言于彼处。彼闻于彼处，为不引起此处不和，而不言于此处。如是，彼令分者合，励和合。彼乐和合，喜和合，悦和合，并以其言传播和合。

彼不说恶语，断恶语。彼说柔和、悦耳、可爱之语，此语入心、谦恭、友善、令人愉悦。彼不说绮语，断绮语。彼适时而言，合于真实，言辞有益，说法说戒：彼言如珍，适时，有据，适度且富有道理。

佛言

彼于日中（午前）一食，夜不食而不非时食。离观听歌、舞、乐、剧等。离华鬘、涂香、香膏、装饰、庄严而住。不用高广大床。

离受金、银。离受生谷、生肉，离领受女子少女、男女仆人、山羊、绵羊、家禽、猪、象、牛、马、农田、财物。离为杂役信使。离买卖。离诈秤称、假货币、诈度量。离贿赂、欺骗、造假等邪曲。离刺、打、缚、攻击、掠夺、压迫。

彼以衣可覆身为足，以托钵乞食而自活为足。彼行处唯此二物俱行，恰如鸟之飞翔，其翼如影随形。彼以持圣戒蕴（sīla-kkhandha），内受无过之乐。

根律仪（第六道支）

彼以眼见色、以耳闻声、以鼻嗅香、以舌尝味、以身感触、以意知法，彼不执于总相，亦不执于细相。彼竭力避免因不防护六根而至恶不善之法，贪、忧生起。彼守护六根，收摄六根。由修习此圣根律仪（indriya-saṃvara），受内无秽之乐。

正念正知（第七道支）

彼具正念，于去、来时，以正知而行；彼于前瞻、后视时，以正知而行；于屈、伸肢体时，以正知而行；于持钵、着衣时，以正知而行；于啖、饮、嚼、味时，以正知而行；于大小便时，以正知而行，于行、住、坐、寐、寤时，以正知而行；于语、默时，以正知而行。彼具足此圣"戒"（sīla），具足此圣"摄诸根（根律仪）"（indriya-saṃvara），具足此圣"正念正知"，隐居于森林、树下、山上、山隙、岩洞，或于冢间、林丛、露天处及稻草堆。彼乞已归来，饭食讫，跏趺端身坐，正念现前。

离五盖（nīvaraṇa）

彼弃除贪欲（kāmacchanda），心离贪而住；离贪而心清净。

彼弃除嗔恚（vyāpāda），心离嗔而住，具慈悲饶益一切有情，离嗔而心

266

清净。

彼弃除昏沉睡眠（thīnamiddha），心离昏沉睡眠而住；以正念正知作光明想；离昏沉睡眠而心清净。

彼弃除掉悔（uddhacca-kukkucca），心寂定而住，离掉悔而心清净。

彼弃除疑（vicikicchā），心无疑碍而住，于善法具足正信，离疑而心清净。

诸禅定（第八道支）

彼舍离五盖（nīvaraṇa）——此等心之杂染，令智慧障蔽。彼离诸欲，离恶法，进入四禅（jhāna）。

谛观（vipassanā）（第一道支）

《增支部》第九集第 36 经

彼观色、受、想、行、识诸法为"无常"（anicca）、"苦"（dukkha），是弱，是疮、刺、痛、累、敌、烦恼，是空和无我（anattā）；舍此诸法，引心于不死界："此乃寂静，此乃至高，即一切行之寂灭，一切再生之断弃，贪爱之消除，舍离，灭尽，涅槃。"彼乃于此境界而成就诸漏尽（āsavakkhaya）。

涅　槃

《中部》第 39 经

彼心由欲漏解脱，由有漏解脱，由无明漏解脱，解脱者知"我解脱"。彼知"再生已尽，梵行已立，所作已办，不受后有"。

《中部》第 26 经

我恒已解脱，

此乃最后生，

我无有再生。

《中部》第 140 经

此乃无上至圣之智，尽一切苦之智。

此乃无上至圣之寂静，贪、嗔、痴之止息。

默照者

"我是"是无益想；"此是我"是无益想；"我将是"是无益想；"我将不是"是无益想。无益想是病、是疮、是刺。离诸无益想，名为"默照者"。观者，寂默者，不生，不灭，无忧，亦无求。彼无有再生所依者。生已尽，何有老？老已尽，何有死？死已尽，何有忧？忧已尽，何有求？

真实趣处

《中部》第 29 经

如是，此梵行不以获取利养、恭敬、名声为目的，不以成就戒、定、慧为目的。此心之坚定不动之解脱，为此梵行之目的，之实质，之究竟。

《中部》第 51 经

于过去世有圣者、觉者，彼等世尊亦为其弟子指出目标，尽如我今为弟子所示者。

于未来世亦有应供者、等正觉者，彼等世尊实有为如是之殊胜比丘众示行正道，亦如今我为依我之众弟子示行正道。

《长部》第 16 经

（我入灭后，）汝等或作如是思惟："大师之教法灭，我等无复有大师"。汝等勿作如是见，依我为汝等所教之法（dhamma）和律（vinaya），于我灭后，作为汝等之大师。

以法为洲，

以法为皈依！

勿皈依他人！

诸弟子，我所教法是我亲证得之，汝等当善加护持，使此梵行长驻世间，饶益有情，慰藉世间，利乐人天。

Glossary

A

abandoning of greed and grief	断除贪忧
abandonment / ə'bændənmənt / *n.*	抛弃；放纵
absence of ...	无……
absolute sense	胜义；究竟法义
absolutely / 'æbsəluːtli / *adv.*	绝对地；完全地
Absorptions / əb'sɔːpʃnz / *n.*	禅；禅那
abstain (from) / əb'steɪn / *vi.*	戒绝；戒除
abysses of the hells	地狱深渊
activities / æk'tivitiz / *n.*	业
actuality / ˌæktʃu'æləti / *n.*	现实；事实
adornment and embellishment	装饰品
advantage / əd'vaːntɪdʒ / *n.*	益处
agreeable feeling	乐受
all states of existence	一切有；一切存在；一切境有
alms bowl	僧人用的钵
alms-round	乞食
aloof from	远离；不参与
Analysis of the Four Elements	四界分别观
Ananda / *n.*	阿难陀
Anatta Doctrine	无我说
animal kingdom	畜生道；傍生趣
annihilation / əˌnaɪə'leɪʃn / *n.*	断灭、灭绝；消灭
Annihilationism / əˌnaɪə'leɪʃənɪzəm / *n.*	断见；断灭论
Anuruddha / *n.*	阿那律
anxiety / æŋ'zaɪəti / *n.*	焦虑
application / ˌæplɪ'keɪʃn / *n.*	用（心）；专注；思量
argument / 'aːgjumənt / *n.*	依据
arise / ə'raɪz / *vi.*	生起；出现
arouse / ə'raʊz / *vt.*	生；引起
ascetic / ə'setɪk / *n.*	苦行者；禁欲者
adj.	苦行的；禁欲主义的

assembly / əˈsemblɪ / *n.*	集会；集合
Attachment to Mere Rule and Ritual	戒禁取；对戒和仪轨的执着
attain (to) / əˈteɪn / *vt. / vi.*	证得
attainable / əˈteɪnəbl / *adj.*	可证的；可得的
attainment / əˈteɪnmənt / *n.*	证得；达到；获得
Attainment Concentration	安止定
attainment of purity	获清净
attention / əˈtenʃn / *n.*	作意；注意力
attentive mind	专注的心念
Awakened One	觉者；佛陀
awareness / əˈweənəs / *n.*	觉察；觉知

B

base / beɪs / *adj.*	卑鄙的；低劣的
Bases for Obtaining Magical Powers (Four Iddhipada)	四神足；四如意足
be dependent on	以……为缘；依赖于
be ensnared by	为……所缚
behead / biˈhed / *vt.*	斩首
behold / bɪˈhəʊld / *vt.*	注视；看；观照
being / ˈbiːɪŋ / *n.*	有情；存在；生命
Bengal / benˈgɔːl, beŋ–,ˈbeŋəl, ˈbeŋ– / *n.*	孟加拉
Bhikkhu / *n.*	比丘
Birth / bɜːθ / *n.*	生
bodhi tree / *n.*	菩提树
bodily action	身业
bodily function	身行（入出息）
bodily impression	身触
body / ˈbɒdɪ / *n.*	身净色；身体
body, speech, and mind	身口意
body-consciousness	身识
Buddha / ˈbʊdə / *n.*	佛陀；佛像
Buddha-Dhamma	佛法

Buddhism / 'bʊdɪzəm / *n.*		佛教
Buddhist / 'bʊdɪst / *n.*		佛弟子；佛教徒
adj.		佛教的；佛陀的
Burma / 'bɜːmə / *n.*		缅甸

C

calm / kɑːm / *adj.*	平静的
calming (down) this bodily function	安定身行；安定出入息
calming down the mental functions	安定心行
Cambodia / kæm'bəʊdɪə / *n.*	柬埔寨
causal relation	因果关系
cause / kɔːz / *n.*	因；原因；事业
causes / 'kɔːzəz / *n.*	业
celibate / 'selɪbət / *adj.*	禁欲的；独身的
cemetery meditations	冢间观
cessation / se'seɪʃn / *n.*	灭；停止；中止；中断
Cessation of Passions	漏尽通
Ceylon / si'lɔn / *n.*	锡兰（斯里兰卡 Srilanka）
chaste / tʃeɪst / *adj.*	纯洁的；朴素的
Chittagong / 'tʃitəgɔŋ / *n.*	吉大港
clan / klæn / *n.*	宗族；部落；集团
clearly comprehending	正知；清楚地觉照
cling (to) / klɪŋ / *vi.*	执取；执着；附着；坚持
Clinging / 'klɪŋɪŋ / *n.*	取
Collection of Discipline	律藏
Collection of Discourses	经藏
community / kə'mjuːnətɪ / *n.*	团体
companion / kəm'pænɪən / *n.*	侍者；同伴
compassion / kəm'pæʃn / *n.*	悲；悯；四无量心之一
composed / kəm'pəʊzd / *adj.*	镇定的
compound nature	因缘和合性；复合性
comprehend / ˌkɒmprɪ'hend / *vt.*	理解；领悟
comprise / kəm'praɪz / *vt.*	包含；构成

conceit / kən'si:t / *n.*	慢；骄慢
concentrated / 'kɒnsntreɪtɪd / *adj.*	入定的；专一的
concentrated mind	专注心；定心
concentration / ˌkɒnsn'treɪʃn / *n.*	定
Concentration / ˌkɒnsn'treɪʃn / *n.*	心一境之定
Concentration of Energy	勤神足；精进如意足
Concentration of Investigation	观神足；思维如意足
Concentration of Mind	心神足；念如意足
Concentration of Will	欲神足；欲如意足
concord / 'kɒŋkɔːd / *n.*	和合；和谐
condition / kən'dɪʃn / *n.*	缘；条件；
vt.	决定；以……为条件
Conditionality / kən'dɪʃə'næləti / *n.*	缘起性
conditionality / kəndiʃən'æliti / *n.*	缘起；缘；条件
conditions / kən'dɪʃnz / *n.*	诸缘
Conjoined with Other Factors	与其他道支俱行
Conjoined with the Path	与道相合
conscientious / ˌkɒnʃi'enʃəs / *adj.*	认真负责的；本着良心的；谨慎的
Consciousness / 'kɒnʃəsnəs / *n.*	识
considering / kən'sɪdərɪŋ / *n.*	寻
consolation / ˌkɒnsə'leɪʃn / *n.*	慰藉；安慰
Constant factors of mind	遍一切心心所
Contemplation of Equanimity	舍心想；舍：四无量心之一
Contemplation of Loathsomeness	厌恶想；不净观
Contemplation of the Body	观身；身念处
Contemplation of the body (32 parts)	观 32 身分
Contemplation of the Elements	四界分别观
Contemplation of the Feelings	观受；受念处
Contemplation of the Mind	观心；心念处
Contemplation of the Mind-Objects	观法；法念处
Contemplation on the Loathsomeness of Food	食厌想
Contemplations of Impurity	不净观
Control over the Senses	摄诸根

conviction and firm belief	定解
corporeal and mental process	物质及精神过程
corporeal phenomena	色法；物质现象
corporeality / kɔːˌpɔːrɪˈælɪtɪ / *n.*	色；物质性；肉体的存在
corporeality derived from the four primary elements	四大所造色
corporeality, feeling, perception, (mental) formations, and consciousness / *n.*	色，受，想，（心）行，识
corpse blue-black in colour	青淤（相）
corpse infested by worms	虫聚（相）
corpse riddled with holes	穿孔（相）
corpse swollen up	膨胀（相）
courteous / ˈkɜːtɪəs / *adj.*	有礼貌的；谦恭的
covetousness / ˈkʌvɪtəsnɪs / *n.*	悭贪
craving / ˈkreɪvɪŋ / *n.*	贪
Craving for (Eternal) Existence	有爱；贪有
Craving for Fine-material Existence	色界爱
Craving for Immaterial Existence	无色界爱
Craving for Self-Annihilation	无有爱；断灭贪
crooked ways of bribery, deception and fraud	行贿、欺诈、造假等邪曲
cultivate / ˈkʌltɪveɪt / *vt.*	培养

D

death / deθ / *n.*	死；死亡
decay / dɪˈkeɪ / *n.*	老
Decay and Death / *n.*	老死
deceiver / dɪˈsiːvə(r) / *n.*	骗子
deeds / diːdz / *n.*	业；行为；行动
delight (in) / dɪˈlaɪt / *vi.*	对……很喜欢；喜于……
deliverance / dɪˈlɪvərəns / *n.*	解脱
delusion / dɪˈluːʒn / *n.*	痴
delusive / dɪˈluːsɪv / *adj.*	迷惑的
demeritorious / diˌmerɪˈtɔːrɪəs / *adj.*	不善的

demeritorious actions	不善业
depend on…	以……为缘；依赖于
dependent / dɪ'pendənt / *adj.* *n.*	依靠的；从属的；取决于……的；依赖他人者；受赡养者
Dependent Extinction	缘灭
Dependent Origination	缘起
desirous / dɪ'zaɪərəs / *adj.*	渴望的
destiny / 'destənɪ / *n.*	命运
detachment / dɪ'tætʃmənt / *n.*	无著；无住；分离；出离；舍弃；不执着
development / dɪ'veləpmənt / *n.*	修行
development of concentration	定之修习
development of Insight	修观；修毗婆舍那
Development of Tranquility	修止；修定；修奢摩他
devour / di'vauə / *vt.*	吞噬；毁灭
diaphragm / 'daɪəfræm / *n.*	隔膜
diligent / 'dɪlɪdʒənt / *adj.*	勤奋的；精进的
disagreeable feeling	苦受
discernment / dɪ's3ːnmənt / *n.*	有智；识别；洞察力；敏锐；洞察力
disciple / dɪ'saɪpl / *n.*	弟子；佛弟子
discipline / 'dɪsəplɪn / *n.*	戒律；律仪
discourses, dialogues, verses, stories / *n.*	论述，对话，偈颂，故事
discursive / dɪ'sk3ːsɪv / *adj.*	推论的；论证的
Discursive Thinking	伺；伺察：一种心行，即专注在所缘上
discursive thinking / *adj.*	伺：心的随属，即专注在所缘上
disease / di'ziːz / *n.*	病；疾病
dispel / dɪ'spel / *vt.*	打消；祛除
dissect / dɪ'sekt / *vt.*	剖析；仔细分析
dissension / dɪ'senʃn / *n.*	纠纷；意见不合
dissolution / ˌdɪsə'luːʃn / *n.*	衰败；死亡；消亡
dissolve / dɪ'zɒlv / *vt.*	消散；消失

distinguish / dɪ'stɪŋgwɪʃ / *vt.*	辨别；区别
distress / dɪ'stres / *n.*	焦虑
doctrine / 'dɒktrɪn / *n.*	教义
domain of ghosts	鬼道；鬼趣
Domain of Morality	圣戒蕴
Doubt / daʊt / *n.*	疑盖
dwell in	住于
dwell with…in…	以……住于……

E

ear / ɪə(r) / *n.*	耳净色；耳
ear-consciousness	耳识
Effort to Avoid	律仪勤；勤防护；未生恶令不生
Effort to Develop	修勤；勤增长；未生善令生
Effort to Maintain	随护勤；已生善令增长
Effort to Overcome	断勤；生恶令断
Ego / 'iːgəʊ / *n.*	我；自我
Ego-entity	实我；我
Eightfold Path	八正道
eliminate / ɪ'lɪmɪneɪt / *vt.*	消除；息灭
emptiness / 'emptinis / *n.*	空性
empty, void / *adj.*	空的
encounter / ɪn'kaʊntə(r) / *vi.*	遇到（困难或不利的事）
endeavour / ɪn'devə(r) / *vt.*	努力；奋进
Energy / 'enədʒɪ / *n.*	精进（觉支）
Enlightened One	觉者
Enlightenment	七觉支；七菩提分
enlightenment / ɪn'laɪtnmənt / *n.*	觉；悟
enrage / ɪn'reɪdʒ / *vt.*	使暴怒
enrapture / ɪn'ræptʃə(r) / *vt.*	使狂喜
ensnare / ɪn'sneə(r) / *vt.*	进入；落网
entering upon the right path	进入正道

Enthusiasm / ɪn'θjuːziæzəm / *n.*		喜（觉支）；禅悦
enumerate / ɪ'njuːməreɪt / *vt.*		枚举
Equanimity / ˌekwə'nɪməti / *n.*		舍（觉支）；平静
Equanimous Happiness		舍乐（禅支）
escape / ɪ'skeɪp / *vt.*		逃避
eschew buying and selling things		离买卖
eternal / ɪ't3ːnl / *adj.*		永恒的
Eternalism / ɪ't3ːnəlɪzəm / *n.*		常见
Eternity-Belief		常见
evil spirits		魔
examine / ɪg'zæmɪn / *vt.*		审视；检查
excrement / 'ekskrɪmənt / *n.*		排泄物；粪便
experience the fruit of good and evil deeds		受善恶业的果报
expression / ɪk'spreʃn / *n.*		言说
extinction / ɪk'stɪŋkʃn / *n.*		寂灭；灭；消亡；消失
Extinction of Impurities		不净（烦恼）之灭尽
Extinction of the Five-Khandha-process		五蕴之灭尽
extinguish / ɪk'stɪŋgwɪʃ / *vt.*		使熄灭；扑灭；使不复存在
extreme / ɪk'striːm / *n.*		边；极端
eye / aɪ / *n.*		眼净色；眼
eye-consciousness		眼识

F

factor / 'fæktə(r) / *n.*		道支；因素；要素
Factors (Constituents) of Absorption		禅支
fading away		逐渐消失
fading away of passion		离贪
faith / feɪθ / *n.*		信；信心
false speech		妄语
Feeling / 'fiːlɪŋ / *n.*		受
femininity / ˌfemə'nɪnəti / *n.*		女性根色

fetter / ˈfetə(r) / *n.*	结；系缚；桎梏
figure of speech	比喻；修辞格
Final Deliverance	最终的解脱
Fine-material Existence	色界
Fine-material Sphere	色界
First Absorption	初禅
First Factor	第一道支
Five Fetters	五下分结
Five Groups of Existence	五蕴；五蕴有；五取蕴
Five Hindrances	五盖：覆盖心性的五种烦恼；即：贪欲盖、嗔恚盖、惛沉睡眠盖、掉举恶作盖和疑盖
five sense organs	五根；五种感官
fivefold / ˈfaɪvfəʊld / *adj.*	五重的
Fivefold Khandha-combinations	五蕴和合
fivefold sense activity	五根的活动
fivefold sense-impression	五尘触
Fluid Element	水大
foothold / ˈfʊthəʊld / *n.*	立足处；据点
forenoon / ˈfɔːnuːn / *n.*	午前
form with the eye	眼根对色尘
Formations / fɔːˈmeɪʃnz / *n. (pl.)*	行；造作
formed / fɔːmd / *n.*	有为法
forsake / fəˈseɪk / *vt.*	舍弃
forsaking / fəˈseikɪŋ /	放弃；断念；forsake 的动名词
forty subjects of meditation	四十业处
Foundations of Mindfulness	念处；念住：念的住立或现起处
Four Absorptions	四禅；四禅那
Four Elements	四界；四大
Four Foundations of Mindness	四念处
Four Great Efforts	四正勤
Four Immaterial Absorptions	四无色定（禅）
Four Noble Truths	四圣谛

Four Postures	四威仪
four Stages of Holiness / *n.*	四种果位
free from	离；摆脱；除去
free...from...	使……从……解脱
frivolous talk	绮语
from time immemorial	从无始时来
Fruition of Stream Entry	须陀洹果；初果
fruits / fruːts / *n.*	果
Future Karma-Results	未来的业果（业报）
future life	未来世；来世；来生

G

gesture / 'dʒestʃə(r) / *n.*	身表；姿态
gladden / 'glædn / *vt.*	使高兴；使喜悦
gods / 'gɒdz / *n. (pl.)*	梵天；神
good and evil volitions	善不善思
Good Courses of Action	善业道
good results	好的果报
gorgeous / 'gɔːdʒəs / *adj.*	华丽的
Gotama / *n.*	乔达摩（释迦牟尼的俗姓）
grease / griːs / *n.*	油膏；油脂
greed / griːd / *n.*	贪
greediness / griːdinis / *n.*	贪欲
grief / griːf / *n.*	忧；忧伤
groan / grəʊn / *vi.*	呻吟；受折磨
Group of Consciousness	识蕴
Group of Corporeality	色蕴
Group of Feeling	受蕴
Group of Formations	行蕴
Group of Perception	想蕴
Groups of Existence	诸蕴
guard / gɑːd / *vt.*	护

H

Happiness / 'hæpɪnəs / *n.*	乐（禅支）
harmony / 'hɑːmənɪ / *n.*	圆融；和谐
harsh Language	恶口；粗恶语
hatred / 'heɪtrɪd / *n.*	嗔
Heating Element	火大
heavenly beings	天；天人；天众
heavenly ear	天耳（通）
heavenly eye	天眼（通）
heavenly worlds	天道；天趣
heedlessness / hiːdlisnis / *n.*	放逸
hell / hel / *n.*	地狱
hindrances / 'hɪndrənsiz / *n.*	障碍
Holiness / 'həʊlɪnəs / *n.*	圣
Holy One	圣者：佛陀、阿罗汉

I

ignorance / 'ɪgnərəns / *n.*	无明；痴；愚痴
ignorant / 'ɪgnərənt / *adj.*	无知的
illusion / ɪ'luːʒn / *n.*	虚妄；幻觉；错觉
ill-will	嗔；嗔恚；恶意
Immaterial Existence	无色界
immutable / ɪ'mjuːtəbl / *adj.*	常；不变的
impermanence / im'pəːmənəns / *n.*	无常；暂时性
impermanency / 'ɪmpɜːmənənsɪ / *n.*	无常性
impermanent / ɪm'pɜːmənənt / *adj.*	无常的
impersonality / ɪm'pɜːsə'nælətɪ / *n.*	无我
imperturbable karma-formations	静业
impression with the body	身根对触尘
impurities / ɪm'pjʊərɪtɪs / *n.*	不净；秽物
in-and-out-breathing	观（念）出入息；数息观
incarnation / ˌɪnkɑː'neɪʃn / *n.*	化身

incentive / ɪn'sentɪv / *n.*   动机

inconceivable / ˌɪnkən'siːvəbl / *adj.*   不可思议的；不能想象的

indifferent feeling   不苦不乐受；舍受

indulgence / ɪn'dʌldʒəns / *n.*   沉湎；放纵

Inheritance of Deeds (Karma)   业行之承负

initial formation of an abstract thought   寻：一种心行，即把心安置在所缘上

Insight / 'ɪnsaɪt / *n.*   观；毗婆舍那

Insight into the Hearts of Other Beings   他心通

intellectual / inti'lektʃuəl / *adj.*   智慧的；理性的；知识的

intention / ɪn'tenʃn / *n.*   念头；动机；意图

intoxicating / ɪn'tɒksɪkeɪtɪŋ / *adj.*   醉人的

inwardly / 'ɪnwədliː / *adv.*   向内；内心地

irreproachable happiness   无过之乐

K

Kapilavatthu / *n.*   迦毗罗卫城

Karma / 'kaːmə / *n.*   业

Karma Process   业有

Karma-Formations   业行

Karma-Result   业果；业报

karmically / *adv.*   依业地

karmically unwholesome   不善业

karmically wholesome   善业

killing / 'kɪlɪŋ / *n.*   杀生

killing living beings   杀生

Kusinara / *n.*   拘尸那罗

L

Laos / laʊs / *n.*   老挝

Law of Conditionality   缘起法

Law of Deliverance   解脱道（法）

layman   在家众；居士

lead to   趣向；导归

liberation / ˌlɪbəˈreɪʃn / *n.*		解脱
life-affirming		执着生命的
life-period		一期生命
life-principle		命
Loving-Kindness		慈：四无量心之一
lust / lʌst / *n.*		贪；强烈的欲望
lying / ˈlaɪŋ / *n.*		妄语

M

magical powers		神变；神通
Mahā-Kassapa / *n.*		大迦叶
malice / ˈmælɪs / *n.*		怨恨；恶意
manifest / ˈmænɪfest / *vt.*		显现；现行
manifestation (of) / ˌmænɪfeˈsteɪʃn / *n.*		……的显现；表现形式
masculinity / ˌmæskjuˈlɪnəti / *n.*		男性根色
mass of suffering		苦蕴
material body		肉身；肉体
maturity / məˈtʃʊərəti / *n.*		成熟
meditative exercises		禅修训练
meditator / ˈmedɪteɪtə / *n.*		禅修者
men / men / *n.*		人；人道（man 的复数形式）
mendicant / ˈmendɪkənt / *adj.*		乞讨的；托钵僧的
n.		托钵者；出家人
Mental Action		意业
mental activity		心理活动
Mental and Physical Existence		名色
mental formations		行；行蕴；心行
mental functions		心行
mental image / *adj.*		心相：心随诸缘而生种种对境之相
mental impression		意触
mental objects		心法
mere views		戏论
meritorious / ˌmerɪˈtɔːriəs / *adj.*		善的

meritorious Karma-formations	善业
mesentery / 'mesəntərɪ / *n.*	肠系膜
Middle Doctrine	中道法
Middle Path / *n.*	中道
mind / maɪnd / *n.*	心；意
mind-consciousness	意识；心识
Mindfulness	四念处；四念住
mindfulness / 'maɪndfulnɪs / *n.*	念；留心；专注
Mindfulness and Clear Comprehension	正念正知
mindfulness of breathing	观（念）入出息；数息观
mind-object	心法
mirth / mɜːθ / *n.*	欢笑；欢乐；高兴
misconduct / ˌmɪs'kɒndʌkt / *n.*	不善行；不当行为
miserable / 'mɪzrəbl / *adj.*	苦；痛苦的；悲惨的
miserable nature	苦
misery / 'mɪzərɪ / *n.*	痛苦；不幸
misfortune / mis'fɔːtʃən / *n.*	不幸；灾祸
moderation in eating	节制饮食
Moggallana / *n.*	目犍连
monastic / mə'næstɪk / *adj.*	寺院的；修道院的
Monastic Order	僧伽；僧团
Morality / mə'rælətɪ / *n.*	戒
mortification / ˌmɔːtɪfɪ'keɪʃn / *n.*	苦行
mundane / mʌn'deɪn / *adj.*	世间的
Mundane Right Livelihood	世间正命

N

nasal mucus	鼻涕
naught / nɔːt / *n.*	无；零
neighborhood Concentration	近行定
neither pleasant nor unpleasant	非苦非乐
Nepal / nə'pɔːl / *n.*	尼泊尔

Nibbāna with the Groups of Existence Still Remaining	有余涅槃
Nibbāna without the Groups (of Existence) Remaining	无余涅槃
Noble Eightfold Path	八正道
noble man	刹帝利
Noble Truth of the Extinction of Suffering	灭谛
Non-Returner	不还；阿那含
nose / nəʊz / *n.*	鼻净色；鼻
nose-consciousness	鼻识
not to get what one desires	求不得
not-self	无我；无我的
nutriment / ˈnjuːtrɪmənt / *n.*	食色；营养物

O

object of concentration	所观境
object with the mind	意根对法尘
objects of concentration	所观法（境）
observe the precept	守戒
obstinacy / ˈɒbstɪnəsɪ / *n.*	顽固；执拗
obstruct / əbˈstrʌkt / *vt.*	阻碍；障碍
odor with the nose	鼻根对香尘
odour / ˈəʊdə(r) / *n.*	香；气味
ointment / ˈɔɪntmənt / *n.*	香膏
Once-Returner	一来；斯陀含
one who has taken tranquility as his vehicle	止行者；定乘者
oneness of mind	一心；心一境性
One-pointedness of Mind	心一境性
origin / ˈɒrɪdʒɪn / *n.*	起源
Origin of Craving	贪爱之集
overcome / ˌəʊvəˈkʌm / *vt.*	舍离；克服；胜过

P

painful result	苦果
passing away	灭度
past existence	前生；过去世
Path of Stream Entry	预流果道；须陀洹果道
peace / piːs / *n.*	寂静
penetrate / 'penətreɪt / *vt.*	洞察
penetration / ˌpenɪ'treɪʃn / *n.*	彻底洞悉；完全洞察
perceive / pə'siːv / *vt.*	觉知；观察到
perception / pə'sepʃn / *n.*	想
Perfect Enlightenment	正觉
Perfect Wisdom	无上智；圆满的智慧
perpetual wandering	轮回
personality / ˌpɜːsə'næləti / *n.*	个人；个体
personality, self, soul or substance / *n.*	个体，自我，灵魂或实质
phenomena / fə'nɒmɪnə / *n.*	现象（phenomenon 的复数）
Philosophical Collection	论藏
phlegm / flem / *n.*	痰
physical basis of mind	心所依处
pleasant, unpleasant or indifferent	苦、乐或不苦不乐
plundering and oppressing	掠夺及压迫
popular designations and expressions	世间立言
popular notions	世俗义
practice / 'præktɪs / *n.* / *v.*	修习；实践；练习
practice and develop	修习及多修
predominate / prɪ'dɒmɪneɪt / *vi.*	统治；支配
Present Karma-Results	现生业果（业报）
present life	现世；今生
preserve / prɪ'zɜːv / *vt.*	守
priest / priːst / *n.*	婆罗门
Process of Becoming	有；形成的过程

psychical powers	神通；神通力
puppet / 'pʌpit / *n.*	傀儡；木偶；被操纵的人
purification / ˌpjʊərɪfɪ'keɪʃn / *n.*	清净；止
purity / 'pjʊərətɪ / *n.*	清净；寂静
pus / pʌs / *n.*	脓
putrid / 'pjuːtrid / *adj.*	腐烂的；令人厌恶的

R

radiation / reɪdɪ'eɪʃ(ə)n / *n.*	辐射；暖；发光
rage / reɪdʒ / *n.*	嗔；愤怒
Rahula / *n.*	罗睺罗
Rajagaha / *n.*	王舍城
Rapture / 'ræptʃə(r) / *n.*	喜（禅支）
ratiocination / ˌræti̩ɒsɪ'neɪʃn / *n.*	推理
reality / rɪ'ælɪtɪ / *n.*	实相；真实；事实；现实；实际
realization / ˌriːəlaɪ'zeɪʃn / *n.*	证悟；悟道
realization of Nibbana	证得涅槃
realm / relm / *n.*	界；领域；范围
reason / 'riːzn / *n.*	因；理由；动机
Rebirth / ˌriː'bɜːθ / *n.*	生；再生；轮回
Rebirth Process	转生的过程；生有
Reborn according to one's deeds	随业转生（轮回 / 流转）
refrain from	抑制；避免
Remembrances of Many Previous Births	宿命通
renounce / rɪ'naʊns / *vt.*	出离；放弃
renunciation / rɪˌnʌnsi'eɪʃn / *n.*	舍弃
requisite / 'rekwɪzɪt / *n.*	必要条件
requisites for concentration	定的资粮；定的条件
restlessly / 'restəsli / *adv.*	不安地
Restlessness / 'restləsnəs / *n.*	掉举
restlessness and mental worry	掉举恶作盖
restrain / rɪ'streɪn / *vt.*	抑制；阻止

result / rɪˈzʌlt / *n.*	果；结果
reveal / rɪˈviːl / *vt.*	展现；揭示
rigged / rigd / *pp.*	被操纵的；被控制的
Right Action	正业
Right Concentration	正定
Right Effort	正精进
Right Livelihood	正命
Right Mindfulness	正念
Right Speech	正语
Right Thought	正思维
Right Understanding	正见
ripen / ˈraɪpən / *vi.*	成熟；异熟
root out	根除；拔除
round of rebirths	轮回
rouse / raʊz / *vt.*	激发；唤醒；引起
ruin / ˈruːɪn / *n. / vt.*	毁灭；毁坏
rumination / ˌruːmɪˈneɪʃn / *n.*	思路；沉思

S

sage / seɪdʒ / *n.*	圣者
Sakya / ˈsaːkjə / *n.*	释迦族
saliva / səˈlaɪvə / *n.*	唾液
Samsara / səmˈsaːrə /	轮回
Sangha / ˈsæŋgə / *n.*	僧伽
Sanskrit / ˈsænskrɪt / *n.*	梵文
adj.	梵文的
saviour / ˈseɪvjə(r) / *n.*	救世主
scattered mind	散乱心
Scepticism / ˈskeptɪsɪzəm / *n.*	疑
scripture / ˈskriptʃə / *n.*	经；经文；经典
Self / self / *n.*	我
Self-illusion	身见
self-mortification	自我苦修

sensation / senˈseɪʃən / *n.*	感受；感觉
sense / sens / *n.*	根；感觉；官能
sense impression	触；
sense objects	尘；境；感官对象
sense-bases	根；处
Sense-Bases	六根对六尘（境）
Sense-Impression	触
sensorial impression	触
Sensual Craving	爱欲；欲贪
Sensual Lust	欲贪
sensual lust	情欲
sensual objects	所缘境（尘）；感官对象
sensual passion	贪爱
Sensual Pleasure	欲乐
sensuous / ˈsenʃuəs / *adj.*	感觉（上）的；感官的
Sensuous Sphere	欲界
separated from the desired	爱别离
servant / *n.*	首陀罗
setting the mind free	令心解脱
settled / ˈsetld / *adj.*	安稳的
Seven Elements of Enlightenment	七觉支；七菩提分
sexual misconduct	邪淫
Siam / ˈsaiæm,saiˈæm / *n.*	暹罗（泰国）
Siddhattha / *n.*	悉达多
simile / ˈsɪməlɪ / *n.*	喻；比喻
Six Sense-Organs	六根
Six Subjective-Objective Sense-Bases	六根对六尘（境）
Six Views about the Self	六种我见
skeleton / ˈskelɪtn / *n.*	骸骨（相）
Solid Element	地大
solitude / ˈsɒlɪtjuːd / *n.*	隐居；独处
Sorrow, Lamentation, Pain, Grief, Despair / *n.*	悲，哀，痛，恼，绝望
sound / saʊnd / *n.*	声；声音

sound with the ear	耳根对声尘
space / speɪs / *n.*	空界；空间
spectator / spek'teitə / *n.*	观众；旁观者
speech / spiːtʃ / *n.*	语表；讲话
sphere / sfɪə / *n.*	界
Sphere of Neither-Perception-Nor-Non Perception	非想非非想处
Sphere of Nothingness	无所有处
Sphere of Unbounded Consciousness	识无边处
Sphere of Unbounded Space	空无边处
spleen / spliːn / *n.*	脾
spring / sprɪŋ / *vi.*	生长；涌出
steadfast / 'stedfaːst / *adj.*	坚定的；不动摇的
stealing / 'stiːlɪŋ / *n.*	偷盗
stir up	激起；唤起
Stream Enterer	须陀洹
strive / straɪv / *vi.*	努力；进取
Subduing worldly greed and grief	调伏世间的贪与忧
subject to suffering	苦的；受制于苦
sublime / sə'blaɪm / *adj.*	殊妙的；庄严的
subside / səb'saɪd / *vi.*	平息；止息
subsisting / səb'sɪstɪŋ / *pr. / p.*	存在的；实在的
substratum / 'sʌbˌstreɪtəm / *n.*	基础；根据；底层
substratum of rebirth	转生之依
subtle / 'sʌtl / *adj.*	微妙的；微细的
suffering / 'sʌfərɪŋ / *n.*	苦
suffering of not getting what one desires	求不得苦
superhuman / ˌsuːpə'hjuːmən / *adj.*	超人的
supermundane / ˌsuːpə'mʌndeɪn / *adj.*	出世间的
Supermundane Right Livelihood	出世间正命
Supermundane Right Understanding	出世间的正见
supernatural powers	神通

suppress / sə'pres / *vt.*	压制；压服
supreme / suː 'priːm / *adj.*	至高的；极度的
suspend / sə'spend / *vt.*	中止
Sutta / *n.*	经；契经；修多罗
Sympathetic Joy	喜：四无量心之一
sympathy / 'sɪmpəθɪ / *n.*	同情；怜悯

T

take root	住；生根
taking things not given	不与取
tale-bearing / *n.*	两舌
taste / teɪst / *n.*	味；味道
taste with the tongue	舌根对味尘
Ten Blessings	十种功德
the Belief in Annihilation	断见
the Blessed One	世尊
the Dhamma / *n.*	佛法
the First Noble Truth	第一圣谛
the Five (Moral) Precepts	五戒
the Four Truths / *n.*	四谛
the Ganges / *n.*	恒河
the heavenly and the earthly	天道与人道
the holy life	梵行；圣洁的生活
the Knower	觉者
the noble doctrine	圣人教法；圣人教理
The Noble Ones	圣者
the Noble Truth of Suffering	苦圣谛
the Noble Truth of The Origin of Suffering	集圣谛
The Perfect One / *n.*	如来
the ten Kasina-Excercises	十遍
the Third Truth	第三圣谛
the Three Characteristics Of Existence	三法印

the Three Warnings	三示戒
the Truth of Suffering	苦谛
the Unconditioned / ˌʌnkən'dɪʃnd / *n.*	无为法
the wheel of existence	轮回
thinking / 'θɪŋkɪŋ / *n.*	思
thought / θɔːt / *n.*	想
thought-conception	寻：最初的心专注；念头的开端
Three Baskets	三藏
Three Characteristics	三法印
Three Jewels	三宝
Threefold Refuge	三皈依
tongue / tʌŋ / *n.*	舌净色；舌
tongue-consciousness	舌识
torment / 'tɔːment / *n.*	折磨
Torpor and Sloth	惛沉睡眠盖
tradesman / 'treɪdzmən / *n.*	吠舍
Tranquility / træŋ'kwɪlɪtɪ / *n.*	轻安（觉支）；止；奢摩他
tranquilizing / 'træŋkwɪlaɪzɪŋ / *pr. /p.*	寂静；使……安静
transient / 'trænzɪənt / *adj.*	无常；短暂的
true wisdom	真实智
twelve links	十二支
Two Extremes	两边

U

ulcer / 'ʌlsə(r) / *n.*	溃疡
unattached to	不执着于
unblemished / ʌn'blemɪʃt / *adj.*	无瑕的
unchastity / 'ʌn'tʃæstɪtɪ / *n.*	不贞
undisturbed / ˌʌndɪ'stɜːbd / *adj.*	不受干扰的
undulatory / 'ʌndjʊlətərɪ / *adj.*	波动的；起伏的
united with the undesired	怨憎会
unlawful sexual intercourse	邪淫
unlearned / ʌn'lɜːnid / *adj.*	无学问的

unlearned worldling	无知的凡夫
unpleasant impressions	非乐触
unprofitable / ʌn'prɒfɪtəbl / adj.	无利益的；无用的
Unprofitable Questions	不记说；无益的问题
unreal / ʌn'rɪəl / adj.	非真；假的
unstable / ʌn'steɪb(ə)l / adj.	不稳定的；易变的
unsubstantial / ʌnsəb'stænʃ(ə)l / adj.	非实；无实质的；不坚固的
Unwholesome / ˌʌn'həʊlsəm / adj.	不善的
Unwholesome States of Consciousness	不善心识
unwise considerations	非理作意

V

vain talk	绮语
vanish / 'vænɪʃ / vi.	消失
vehicle / 'viːəkl / n.	乘；交通工具
Verbal Action	语业
verbal functions of the mind	心之语行
Vibrating (Windy) Element	风大
visible form	色
visual objects	色尘；色
visual or audible impressions	眼触或耳触
vital force	命；命的根；生命力
vitality / vaɪ'tæləti / n.	命根色；生命力；活力
volition / və'lɪʃ(ə)n / n.	思；意
vulgar / 'vʌlgə(r) / adj.	低俗的

W

wail / weɪl / n. / vi.	痛哭；哀号
ward off	抵御
watch / wɒtʃ / vt.	观察；注视
watching over	
weak / wiːk / adj.	虚弱的
weal / n.	幸福；福祉

welfare / ˈwelfeə(r) / *n.*	福利；福祉
Wholesome / ˈhəʊlsəm / *adj.*	善的
wholesome state of consciousness	善心识
will / wɪl / *n.*	意；意志；意图
will directed to forms	色思
wisdom / ˈwɪzdəm / *n.*	智慧；慧
Wisdom and Deliverance	慧解脱
wise considerations	如理作意
without a Self	无我
woe / wəʊ / *n.*	悲哀；悲苦；苦恼
womb / wuːm / *n.*	子宫；发源地
	执着于无（断见）
worldly fruits	世间的果报
Wrong Concentration	邪定
wrong livelihood	邪命
wrong speech	邪语

图书在版编目(CIP)数据

佛言：汉、英 / 园慈主编. —北京：社会科学文献出版
社，2014.12（2019.3重印）
（法源译丛）
ISBN 978-7-5097-7036-8

Ⅰ.①佛… Ⅱ.①园… Ⅲ.①佛教－高等学校－教材
－汉、英 Ⅳ.①B94

中国版本图书馆CIP数据核字（2014）第312107号

·法源译丛·

佛　言

主　　编 / 园　慈

出 版 人 / 谢寿光
项目统筹 / 袁清湘
责任编辑 / 袁清湘　李建廷

出　　版 / 社会科学文献出版社·人文分社（010）59367215
　　　　　　地址：北京市北三环中路甲29号院华龙大厦　邮编：100029
　　　　　　网址：www.ssap.com.cn
发　　行 / 市场营销中心（010）59367081　59367083
印　　装 / 北京虎彩文化传播有限公司

规　　格 / 开　本：787mm×1092mm 1/16
　　　　　　印　张：19.25　字　数：297千字
版　　次 / 2014年12月第1版　2019年3月第2次印刷
书　　号 / ISBN 978-7-5097-7036-8
定　　价 / 69.00元